Watching Fath

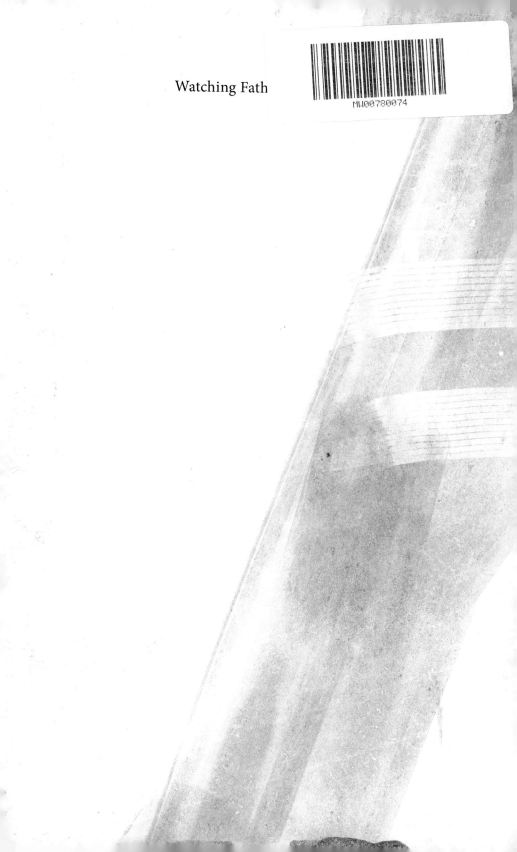

Watching Father Brown

G.K. Chesterton's Mysteries on Film and Television

SANDRA K. SAGALA

McFarland & Company, Inc., Publishers
Jefferson, North Carolina

LIBRARY OF CONGRESS CATALOGUING-IN-PUBLICATION DATA

Names: Sagala, Sandra K., author.
Title: Watching Father Brown : G.K. Chesterton's mysteries
on film and television / Sandra K. Sagala.
Description: Jefferson, North Carolina : McFarland & Company, Inc.,
Publishers, 2023 | Includes bibliographical references and index.
Identifiers: LCCN 2023028521 | ISBN 9781476692661 (paperback: acid free paper) ∞
ISBN 9781476650104 (ebook)
Subjects: LCSH: Brown, Father (Fictitious character) | Chesterton, G. K. (Gilbert Keith),
1874-1936—Characters. | Chesterton, G. K. (Gilbert Keith), 1874-1936. Short stories.
Selections—Adaptations. | Father Brown (Television program : 2013)
Classification: LCC PR4453.C4 Z75745 2023 | DDC 823/.912—dc23/eng/20230711
LC record available at https://lccn.loc.gov/2023028521

BRITISH LIBRARY CATALOGUING DATA ARE AVAILABLE

ISBN (print) 978-1-4766-9266-1
ISBN (ebook) 978-1-4766-5010-4

Front cover: Priest image (Adobe Stock/Shutterstock);
background illustration from a photograph of the Church
of St Peter and St Paul, Blockley, England (DeFacto)

Printed in the United States of America

McFarland & Company, Inc., Publishers
Box 611, Jefferson, North Carolina 28640
www.mcfarlandpub.com

To *Father Brown* researchers Claire Burgess,
Amy Jacks, Naomi Walmsley,
Robert Panners, David Winfield, Lee Saczak,
Harriet Duddy, and Jake Francis. Your efforts made
Father Brown informative and historically accurate.
Thank you for that.

Acknowledgments

In his book *A Short History of England*, G.K. Chesterton maintained that "thanks are the highest form of thought; and that gratitude is happiness doubled by wonder."

In accord with Chesterton's comment, I express my deep appreciation to the following people without whom this book would not exist: Ruth R. Connell, MLS, MA, Grasselli Library & Breen Learning Center, John Carroll University, Cleveland, Ohio, for graciously retrieving copies of the *Chesterton Review* for my perusal and for a personal tour of Chesterton ephemera at the Grasselli Library; the Erie County Library's Interlibrary Loan department, particularly Janet Wolf, who always managed to find and obtain many obscure sources that make all my projects complete; Jen and Adam Moriarty for the *Father Brown* DVD collections and for interesting and informative discussions on the BBC, religion in the UK, and quirky detectives; Suzanne Mahoney for the fun trips to John Carroll University; Jeremy Sagala and Angelika Gressman for the correct German translations of episodes in the Ottfried Fischer *Pfarrer Braun* series; JoAnne Bagwell and Doreen Chaky for beta-reading the many revisions; Susan Schwartz for insightful comments; Linda Jofery and Cheryl Dubuque for the contact info; and Joan Duke for the Kenneth More DVD search and for reading the manuscript and suggesting edits. Special thanks to the editors at McFarland whose continued interest kept me going: Sophia Lyons and Susan Kilby.

I am grateful for the YouTube option that allowed the use of English subtitles of foreign versions of *Father Brown*. The translations were not always perfect or complete, but they made the understanding of many old versions much easier. For basic audience ratings, I found the Internet Movie Database (IMDb) interesting though definitely subjective.

Table of Contents

Preface

It has come to light that in the decades since 1950, thousands of Catholic priests worldwide have been found guilty of sexual abuse of the children they were charged to instruct. Hundreds more bishops turned a blind eye to the situation or neglected to remove the shameful priests from parish service. While I do not doubt the numbers or the torment of the accusers, the news does not reflect the Catholic Church I was baptized into, and grew up in, during the 1950s and 1960s. As students in Catholic grade school and high school, we were taught to respect our parish priests as representatives of Christ. If Father visited our classroom, we stood and asked for his blessing. Given a new rosary, prayer book, or statue of the Virgin, we knocked on the rectory door to ask the priest to bless it. Thus, it is with horror of, and perhaps gratitude for, my ignorance of what went on behind some rectory doors, and my steadfast conviction that 99 percent of priests are holy men doing their best in a difficult vocation.

Now, however, while clerical criminals go unpunished, it is refreshing to return to the halcyon days portrayed in the BBC's *Father Brown* mystery series simply for its similarity to the Church I knew as a child before becoming aware of complex issues—racism, economic disparity, homophobia, mental illness, and clerical and police vice—that are sadly inherent in real life and that are likewise reflected in the series. Mark Williams as Father Brown is supportive and empathetic; I'm sure he would be approachable for the blessing of a child's prayer book; he understands man's inclination to sin, but his unwavering faith rests in a merciful and forgiving God. Murder is the most heinous evil, of course, but television audiences realize that the deaths are staged and that the perpetrator will be hauled off to jail by the end of the episode after having confessed his crime to the authorities. Whatever the sin, Father Brown's purpose is to bring the guilty party back to God through repenting and seeking His mercy.

As for the purpose of this book ... by 1915, with the publication of the earliest Father Brown stories, the *New York Times* noted the "fascinating foreign touches" that could be found in Chesterton's offerings.[1] A few years later when Chesterton visited America, he remarked,

> Suppose an interviewer had said that I had the reputation of being a nut. I should be flattered but faintly surprised at such a tribute to my dress and dashing exterior. I should afterwards be sobered and enlightened by discovering that in America a nut does not mean a dandy but a defective or imbecile person. And as I have here to translate their American phrase into English, it may be very defensible that they should translate my English phrases into American.[2]

More than a decade later, when he published "The Crime of the Communist," Chesterton has Father Brown admit, "I have to do with England, ... I come from there. And the funniest thing of all is that even if you love it and belong to it, you still can't make head or tail of it."[3]

Since my education did not include readings or discussions of any G.K. Chesterton writings, I suspect many others, too, have just now been introduced to him through the television series. It's been great fun to search out and view how other actors have previously interpreted the Father Brown character, both in English-speaking and foreign-made films. But, watching the latest British *Father Brown*, as an American I was occasionally confused by references to such mundane things as the "humbugs" candy that Father Brown prefers or how the game of cricket is played or various exclamations by the frustrated Inspector Mallory. "Sweet Fanny Arkwright!" So it is the differences in our times and cultures that this book attempts to explain. Though both countries speak English, for Americans some British colloquialisms may be unfamiliar. Remember the flower seller Eliza Doolittle in *My Fair Lady* learning to speak like a proper lady. Professor Higgins taunts her, "Why can't the English learn to set a good example to people whose English is painful to your ears? ... There even are places where English completely disappears. In America, they haven't used it for years!" Also, for those unfamiliar with it, some references to relevant British history that can be gleaned through a lot of research are included. Non–Catholics might welcome the explanations of Catholic doctrine or practices.

As for its religiosity, the editor of a Catholic journal sadly referred to the Father Brown of the BBC series as "a pretense."[4] I would argue that, if more priests were like him, perhaps the Catholic Church would not have the many problems it does today. After several years into the series, Mark Williams claimed not to have heard if any priests had been inspired to emulate Father Brown. But it is something to be hoped for.

PART ONE

Father Brown in Literature and Dramatic Media

1

G.K. Chesterton
and His Detective Priest

The "criminologist clergyman" granted, "I'm rather fond of
people who are fools and failures on their own confession."[1]

During the first decade of the 21st century, economic hardship was a
fact of life in Great Britain. The British Broadcasting Corporation (BBC),
along with other political entities, was mandated to comply with universal belt-tightening in order to cope with diminished funding. At the same
time, because many viewers were staying home and watching television
during the recession, its trustees deemed it unwise to diminish the quality
of the programming. After months of strategizing, they developed a plan
which involved not significantly altering the peak time programming in
the evening but a reorganization of the daytime scheduling and the promotion of new programs to replace those that would be eliminated as less
valuable or as having run their course. Surveys had proved that audience
perception of quality was heavily shaped by drama more than any other
kind of program. Therefore, it was imperative that the BBC support drama
and comedy, not only for its British audience but also to increase the success of exporting the programs abroad—to "sell" the UK—as British television broadcasting became even more driven by the worldwide economic
market.[2]

In addition, the development of a "diversity strategy" was to be initi-
ated after the public and BBC staff responded to a survey conducted from
November 2010 to January 2011. Besides some respondents' reactions crit-
icizing the BBC for its stereotyping of lesbian, gay, bisexual people and
black or minority ethnic groups, many commented on the biased treatment of Christians, given that Christianity was the "most widely observed
religion within Britain."[3] Some even considered the BBC to be "anti–
Christian" in its portrayal of "inaccurate ... incorrect, often derogatory
stereotypes."

With those decrees in mind—to produce quality programming economically and to increase its sensitivity to those practicing the Christian faith—in previous years BBC producers usually played it safe by adapting stories familiar to a nation nostalgic for its glorious past. The recent and incredible popularity of historical period dramas like *Downton Abbey* did not escape their notice. But armed with the knowledge that detective fiction was one of the most read of all fiction genres, when a new program was needed for the afternoon schedule, producers generally turned to tried-and-true fictional—some might say quirky—detectives to fit the bill. Performances featuring Arthur Conan Doyle's pipe-smoking, deerstalker-cap-wearing consulting detective Sherlock Holmes or Agatha Christie's Belgian investigator Hercule Poirot with his egg-shaped head and "little gray cells," as well as Dorothy L. Sayers' high society character Lord Peter Wimsey, were established, familiar, and favorite classic characters. And, as the *New York Times* recently noted, "It's hard to go broke giving people more of what they once liked…. When viewers are paralyzed by choice among hundreds of series, it's easier to stand out with a brand people already know."[4] Christie's observant knitting busybody Miss Jane Marple, Colin Dexter's prejudicial Inspector Morse, and Alan Hunter's Inspector George Gently series also ranked high with viewers. Adrian Monk's torment with OCD (Obsessive Compulsive Disorder), the medieval Benedictine monk Brother Cadfael, and even America's disheveled Columbo with his characteristically rumpled raincoat had similarly found success with British audiences. Unlike the "international obsession" with forensics as a crime-solving method wherein "infallible science" solves the mystery, British crime television favored a more traditional mystery fiction format with its often-loner, clearly defined detective.[5]

Despite the BBC having done their research into types of detective shows that worked for daytime television, G.K. Chesterton's *Father Brown* mysteries appear to have been overlooked, even though the character had appeared in a BBC series with other famous fictional detectives more than 40 years previously. By fortuitous chance about this time, though, producer John Yorke happened to hear a radio documentary presented by former British politician Ann Widdecombe about Chesterton and his detective series featuring a Father Brown.[6] The seed was planted, and Yorke nurtured the idea of televising the Chesterton stories that had been originally set in the early 1900s. Any potentially controversial material involving a Catholic priest in a country that was largely split between Anglicans and atheists was overridden by the probability of profit.

In addition, if dramatic conflict was desired (read: required), there was little more conflict at the time than the confrontations raging in worldwide news reports over the scandalous actions of numerous priests in the Catholic Church.[7] Given the situation, perhaps program developers were skittish about dubious non–Catholic (and even Catholic) viewers taking to a series in which a priest is presented as a main character. Such fears were allayed with the consideration that other British series involving clergy had proven to be extremely popular: the comedies of *The Vicar of Dibley*, about a female vicar in a rural parish, and *Father Ted*, an adult satire about one of three exiled priests living on a remote island. Other examples include *Rev.*, featuring an Anglican vicar who moved from the country to a big city parish, and the more serious *Brother Cadfael*, the historical mysteries set in the 12th century. None required any special knowledge or practice of religious doctrine or ritual to be enjoyed.

Yorke consulted with others at the BBC Studios Writers' Academy he had helped to found in 2005 to train students to write for television.[8] Together they finalized details until, a year later, a new Father Brown series starring actor Mark Williams, formerly of *Harry Potter* and *The Fast Show* (a British comedy sketch program) fame, aired on BBC One. It wasn't long before the sleuthing priest series became a well-loved and long-running program for the broadcasting company.

The prospect of a return of Father Brown to television very much pleased Dale Ahlquist, president of the American Chesterton Society. Four years after the series began, he said, "The fact that they went to this character shows a respect for Chesterton among the detective fiction community. And in this case, Catholics should be happy that a priest is at least being portrayed in a very positive, even heroic light. On a larger scale, Catholics should rejoice that Chesterton is being rediscovered."[9]

But just who was G.K. Chesterton and who is this Father Brown?

The beginning, as Chesterton contemporary and fellow mystery writer Reverend Ronald Knox remembered, came about around 1909 when the already prolific 35-year-old author Gilbert Keith Chesterton, having nothing literary at hand, walked into his agent's office and inquired if there was something in particular in which publishers might be interested.

Chesterton, born in London in May 1874, had an exuberant personality and sizable intellectual ability equal to his rotund body or, as remarked upon by the Chesterton society, he possessed a "massive mind in a massive body."[10] His circle of friends included George Bernard Shaw, H.G. Wells, and Hilaire Belloc, all celebrated contemporary writers. He was a creative journalist, artist, philosopher, and biographer of Charles Dickens and Robert Browning with 21 books to his credit including four volumes of essays, two novels, two theology books, and some poetry. His subjects ranged from criticisms of Victorian literature to essays on St. Francis of Assisi to political and social commentaries.

When his agent lamented that there was nothing in his line, only that

Philadelphia's *The Saturday Evening Post* was looking for detective pieces, Chesterton was delighted.[11] A life-long fan of detective fiction, he had once declared that "my taste is for the sensational novel, the detective story, the story about death, robbery and secret societies.... If there was a murdered man under the sofa in the first chapter, I read the story. If there was no murdered man under the sofa in the first chapter, I dismissed the story as tea-table twaddle, which it often really was."[12] He realized the opportunity was at hand to develop an idea that had percolated in his mind for about five years wherein he planned to construct "a comedy in which a priest should appear to know nothing and in fact know more about crime than the criminals."[13] In his capable hands, the dichotomy of a serious professional author and a writer of detective fiction would meet in producing a series of mystery stories that would make Chesterton renowned for more than a century.

Recent Catholic convert Kathleen Mawhinney first wondered in her blog why Chesterton made his hero a "boring little priest," then she decided it had to do with the "human need for repentance." Creating Father Brown as ordinary and rather unremarkable in looks and mannerisms allowed Chesterton, himself a convert to Catholicism, to show the mysterious ways God works.[14] Another advantage of having a Catholic priest as protagonist is his being bound by the Seal of the Confessional, a mandate of extreme confidentiality. If a penitent were to admit that he committed a crime, the priest, under the precepts of the sacrament, cannot report it to authorities directly but can only urge the sinner to admit his deed and face the inevitable consequences. The sin is, in effect, transferred from the doer to the priest who is only contracted for two things: to absolve the penitent or to withhold absolution until the penitent confesses his crime to the police. In mystery stories or television programs, the lone priest, celibate and without family interference and only a bishop to answer to, can then take on the challenge of circuitously seeking clues and bringing the sinner to justice whether he likes it or not, a dictum that the BBC writers of *Father Brown* used to good advantage.

So Chesterton promptly sat down and hastily wrote the first of the Father Brown stories, "Valentin Follows a Curious Trail."

The plot goes like this: Famous Parisian investigator Aristide Valentin had tracked the international thief Flambeau to London. Also in London at the time was "a very short Roman Catholic priest" from a small Essex village in southeast England. Valentin had no love for any priest, let alone this bumbler who hardly managed to hold onto his ticket or his many packages on the train they shared. The priest—Father Brown on his way to a Eucharistic Congress—confided to everyone in the carriage, including another traveling priest, that he was transporting something valuable.

Stopping for lunch, Valentin thought about Flambeau as he added sugar to his coffee, only to discover that it tasted of salt. He complained to a waiter who thought the switch might have something to do with the priest who had, curiously, thrown soup at the wall. He also learned that after the priests had had their lunch, one paid for the meal and, as the other was leaving, the manager realized his customer had paid three times too much. The owner was astonished when the priest said, "Sorry to confuse your accounts, but it'll pay for the window," whereupon he took his umbrella and smashed it. Determined to find the destructive priest and his companion, when Valentin passed a fruit seller, he spied a piece of cardboard advertising oranges that was lying on a pile of nuts. Conversely, on the oranges was a sign indicating the price of Brazil nuts. Confused, Valentin ordered his constables to keep their eyes "skinned for a queer thing."

Valentin, aware that Father Brown carried a valuable blue sapphire-studded cross, finally caught up with the two clerics. "While the detective pitied [Father Brown] for his helplessness, he almost despised Flambeau for condescending to so gullible a victim" in his guise as a fellow priest. But Father Brown was smarter than he looked. Instead of being a naive cleric, Father Brown knew the man only posed as a priest because he had ordered a meat sandwich on Friday, a day when Catholics were forbidden to eat meat. Valentin eavesdropped on their conversation and overheard Flambeau tell Father Brown he had swapped their packages, so *he* now had the treasure, but Father Brown, suspecting the duplicity, swapped them back. Flambeau, incredulous that a simple priest could trick him, tore open the parcel only to find paper and sticks of lead. The thief threatened violence if the priest did not hand over the cross.

When Valentin stepped forward to make an arrest, Father Brown explained how he had orchestrated the various clues. "I changed the salt and sugar, and [Flambeau] kept quiet." That, and his not objecting to the triple-priced bill proved he had a motive for not wanting attention. Father Brown splashed soup on the wall, changed the fruit signs, and broke the window, leaving clues for the pursuing detective. Father Brown also revealed how he had ascertained Flambeau's scheme. He questioned the thief, "Has it never struck you that a man who does next to nothing but hear men's real sins is not likely to be wholly unaware of human evil?"[15]

The Saturday Evening Post published the story in its July 23, 1910, issue. It was later retitled and is universally known as "The Blue Cross." When the editor of *The Storyteller* magazine later re-published the Father Brown stories, he introduced them as "undoubtedly the most extraordinary work Mr Chesterton has yet penned, and show this clever writer in quite a new vein." Presciently, he predicted, "Father Brown is a character destined to be long remembered in fiction."[16]

Even though Chesterton would continue to write the adventures of his clerical detective mostly to finance other, more preferred projects of his such as *G.K.'s Weekly*, a periodical that embodied his views on current cultural, political, and socio-economic issues, his accounts of the priest's sleuthing became some of his best-known, best-loved works. The unique character of Father Brown would ultimately be included in the Golden Age of fictional detectives, along with Sherlock Holmes and Hercule Poirot. Unlike Holmes, however, Father Brown was not tall or lean nor an expert in obscure poisons, clever disguises, or cigarette ash.[17] More like Poirot, Father Brown was short and round and used his brain, applying rationality to solve mysteries. He was able to foresee and occasionally thwart criminals because of his inductive, rather than deductive, reasoning and awareness of the foibles of human nature. Lawbreakers never saw the end of their careers coming from an insignificant and indistinguishable priest. One scholar pointed out that Chesterton created the perfect paradoxical detective story: "the innocent proving worldly-wise, and the sophisticated exposed as gullible."[18] It was a kind of puzzle Chesterton delighted in, the idea of paradox being "truth standing on its head to gain attention."[19] He used the technique frequently and to good advantage in all his writings to the extent that he was occasionally referred to as "the prince of paradox."[20]

In conjunction with his literary career, it was Chesterton's inclination and fortune to travel around England delivering lectures as there was widespread interest in such "bleak entertainments," as he referred to them.[21] Perhaps he realized they were "bleak" to his audiences for, in his obituary, one newspaperman noted that Chesterton, when speaking, seemed to fumble or hesitate as he chuckled to himself at his own jokes.[22] About this same time, which Chesterton referred to as "a landmark in my life," he was debating religious issues with Robert Blatchford, editor of *The Clarion*, a Socialist newspaper promoting materialism, determinism, and atheism. The arguments served, in effect, to concretize Chesterton's Christian faith after a period when, as he acknowledged, "I believed in nothing, I believed in what some have called 'the wish to believe.'"[23]

The concept of a sleuthing cleric solidified after Chesterton met Irish-born John O'Connor, a Roman Catholic priest, at the home of a mutual acquaintance in Keighley, West Yorkshire, in spring 1904 after giving a talk in that area. Their introduction was the beginning of a 30-year friendship, with O'Connor eventually guiding Chesterton through his conversion from Anglicanism to Catholicism 18 years later.[24] As they walked over the moors, they often conversed on thought-provoking topics, such as whether mathematics or literature was the more valued education. O'Connor believed that a "mathematician would put two and two together and the result would be four," but a writer might put them together ingeniously to make 22.[25] Turning the conversation, Chesterton revealed that he was working on an essay concerning "some rather sordid social questions of vice and crime." After his expanding on the topic, Father O'Connor pointed out that several of Chesterton's opinions were "in error, or rather in ignorance."[26] In this instance, after Chesterton had put forth his views on the persecution of tramps and beggars, Father O'Connor shocked his new friend by informing him of the brutal practices of some professional beggars of which he was aware. Expecting a priest to be naive in the ways of the world and the evil in it, Chesterton was surprised to learn that much of O'Connor's perspicacity and knowledge of crimes and criminals derived from his clerical duties, his time spent on the streets of his parish, and specifically from his hours in the confessional hearing from his parishioners a "monstrous monotony of the catalogue of crime."[27] (As Mark Williams' characterization of Father Brown would years later concede, "The things I've heard in confession would make a sailor blush."[28]) Chesterton found it easy to believe that the Catholic Church knew more about good than he did, he pondered in his autobiography, but "that she knew more about evil than I did seemed incredible."[29] With increasing insight, Chesterton understood that his assumption of a priest's naiveté was flawed; instead Father O'Connor was quite cognizant of the depravity in men's hearts and the dark deeds they were capable of committing. Chesterton had assumed, as perhaps many had, that celibate priests are somehow shielded from life and from evil.

He used this new appreciation as a plot device, giving Father Brown more understanding of sin and sinners than any guilty man might suspect and would probably underestimate if he did. Chesterton's biographer Maisie Ward noticed, "O'Connor had startled, indeed almost shattered, [Chesterton] with certain rather lurid knowledge of human depravity which he had acquired in the course of his priestly experience." Of course, O'Connor would have spoken in generalities, as the Seal of Confession prohibited him ascribing a specific sin to an identifiable penitent. So, conjectured Chesterton, "why not a whole comedy of cross purposes based on the notion of a priest with a knowledge of evil deeper than that of the criminal he is converting?"[30]

Ward claimed that once Chesterton was visiting boyhood friend Lucian Oldershaw and searched his house for a detective story he had not yet read. Not finding any, Chesterton decided he would write one.[31] His previous attempts at writing detective fiction featured unlikely amateurs like "retired judges, civil servants, escaped lunatics, and accused felons" who, like Father Brown, managed to be "insightful observers and diviners of paradoxical truths."[32] His novels *The Club of Queer Trades* (1905) and *The Man Who Was Thursday* (1908) predate Father Brown but feature a similar character who doesn't so much examine physical clues to solve crimes à la Sherlock but instead indulges in a psychological discernment of human nature.[33] In *The Club of Queer Trades*, he describes Judge Basil Grant as "a mystic ... who scarcely stirred out of his attic" who had learned that sometimes "mere facts obscure the truth." Basil's younger brother, Rupert, was a professional private detective whose pursuit of clues and logical deductions was eclipsed by Basil's insight. In the end, Rupert invariably got the solution wrong.

In fashioning Father Brown as an original but unlikely protagonist, Chesterton acknowledged that he took the liberty of reshaping and camouflaging his friend Father O'Connor. Simultaneously he made the priest distinguishable from Chesterton himself who often strode about town in a broad-brimmed hat and wearing a flapping cloak that hid his broad bulk. For the purpose of unobtrusiveness, Chesterton made Father Brown's appearance "shabby and shapeless, his face round and expressionless, his manners clumsy.... That, and the rest of his description, was a deliberate disguise for the purpose of detective fiction."[34] The priest's "chief feature [was] to be featureless. The point of him was to appear pointless.... His commonplace exterior was meant to contrast with his unsuspected vigilance and intelligence." In the story of "The Blue Cross," he depicted Father Brown as a "very short Roman Catholic priest ... face as round and dull as a Norfolk dumpling; he had eyes as empty as the North Sea; he had several brown paper parcels, which he was quite incapable of collecting."[35] He wore a black cassock, a clerical hat with a shallow crown and circular brim and was never without a shabby black umbrella that usually ended up on the floor. Father Knox decreed that success of a mystery story often depended on the detective's personality. "He must have idiosyncrasies, eccentricities and ... he must appeal to us through weakness; ... when he appears on the scene of the tragedy, the general reaction must be 'A man like that will never be able to get at the truth.'"[36] Not that Chesterton needed to be reminded of the tenets of how to write a good mystery. As first president of the Detection Club of London (whose members included Agatha Christie, Dorothy L. Sayers, Baroness Orczy, among others), he was well aware of the components of a good mystery and also how to challenge them. However, this was the hook that would separate Father Brown from other literary detectives. In the story of "The Green Man," Inspector Burns acknowledges Father Brown's uniqueness. Burns told Mr. Harker, "I don't take stock in priests or parsons; but I take a lot of stock in Father Brown.... He ought to have been a policeman instead of a parson."[37]

Father O'Connor admitted that his own "talent for detection was of the slenderest, but it appealed to Chesterton's faculty for wonder"; nevertheless, he seemed pleased to discover himself somewhat replicated in the fictional cleric. In turn, he conceded in an essay on Chesterton, "The flat hat is true to life, but it perished in its prime, for it was wrong as wrong for my style of architecture. The large and cheap umbrella was my defence against wearing an overcoat.... Brown paper parcels! I carried them whenever I could, having no sense of style in deportment." He later added to the account, noting that he told Chesterton about once buying five sapphires for five shillings, thus unintentionally supplying the blue jewels in "The Blue Cross."[38]

Chesterton not only borrowed O'Connor's vocation, but his ideas and commentary on their conversations and subsequently tailored them to the Father Brown stories. O'Connor didn't mind. He remembered that "[Chesterton's] wife laughingly warned me not to let him pick my brains," but "to such brain as I had he was always welcome, even to the pick of it. But I cannot, in my inmost consciousness, discover the beginnings of any Father Brown stories."[39] In reality, Father O'Connor might have suspected the influence he had on Chesterton. "He was always working out something in his mind, and when he drifted from his study to the garden and was seen making deadly passes with his sword-stick at the dahlias, we knew that he had got to a dead end in his composition and was getting his thoughts into order," O'Connor wrote.[40] However much as he was appropriated from O'Connor, Father Brown could not deny his creator. Believing Chesterton also to be a man of faith, historian Dermot Quinn observed that Chesterton and Father Brown were very much alike in their "wisdom, innocence, simplicity, a love of the ordinary, insight into the nature of things."[41]

While O'Connor shepherded his flock of parishioners in Bradford, West Yorkshire, Chesterton allowed Father Brown to travel the world: in the United States, which Chesterton himself visited several years after he began to write the Father Brown stories, the priest was chaplain in a Chicago prison in "The Man in the Machine"; a parish priest in Boston ("The Miracle of Moon Crescent"), and, like his creator, saw New York City ("The Arrow of Heaven"). He had served as a curate in Hartlepool ("The Blue Cross"); a parish priest in the fictional Essex village of Cobhole ("The Head of Caesar"). He had resided at St. Francis Xavier Church in Camberwell presumably also as parish priest ("The Eye of Apollo"). He was a kind of missionary to Latin America ("The Arrow of Heaven") and turned up in Scotland ("The Honour of Israel Gow"), Italy ("The Paradise of Thieves"), Paris ("The Secret Garden"), Spain ("The Secret of the Father Brown"), and Belgravia ("The Queer Feet"). The world, ripe with iniquity, was his parish but instead of scouring international cities for clues to solving the mystery, Father Brown simply observed human nature wherever he was. Perhaps, as theology professor William David Spencer suspects, "he is all priests in all places."[42]

1. G.K. Chesterton and His Detective Priest

For all his service in myriad locations, details of his daily clerical life in the stories of Father Brown were not divulged. Readers are not told that he celebrated daily mass, preached sermons, visited the sick, took communion, or read his prayerbook. Instead, his main priestly function was to hear confessions and advise penitents. Had Father Brown not worn a cassock, whispered prayers for the dead, or made the occasional sign of the cross, readers might not distinguish him as a Catholic priest. When King Henry VIII separated England from Rome over the Vatican's refusal to grant him a divorce from Catherine of Aragon, it became a matter of nationalism; therefore "to be Catholic was to be unpatriotic and un–English."[43] Though he had not yet converted to Catholicism, Chesterton, like other novelists, made the faith "appear mysterious and romantic," writes Horton Davies in his book on English theology. Perhaps by not detailing Father Brown's ritualistic Mass celebration or itemizing his daily prayers allowed readers to imagine the priest's prayer life.[44]

Mystery author P.D. James, in her introduction to a reprint of the Father Brown stories, also pointed out that we "never learn where exactly he lives, who housekeeps for him, what kind of church he has or his relationship with his bishop. We are not told his age."[45] On the other hand, Father Knox appreciated the fact that "Father Brown's powers of neglecting his parish always seemed ... even more admirable than Dr Watson's powers of neglecting his practice [in the Sherlock Holmes stories]."[46] As engaged as he appeared to be, the flaw, as Chesterton himself pointed out, was that "Father Brown had nothing in particular to do, except to hang about in any household where there was likely to be a murder." In this respect, he resembled Hercule Poirot who just happened to be in the vicinity when a crime was committed. In the story of "The Green Man," readers are told that Father Brown has "a hearty and enduring appetite for doing nothing."[47] At this, one of Chesterton's friends, Helen Parry Eden, teasingly called Father Brown an "officious little loafer."[48] Perhaps Chesterton borrowed this attribute for Father Brown from Father O'Connor as well. Interviewed by *The Leeds Mercury* in 1931 and already accepted as the inspiration for the sleuthing priest, O'Connor admitted he tended more toward "being" than "doing." He owned, he said, "the art of being idle."[49] And yet, in "The Queer Feet," Chesterton describes Father Brown as a "mild, hard-working little priest," an incompatible phrase given the paucity of any other accounts of his responsibilities.[50]

Readers never learn his first name except that it begins with J, and the very ordinariness of the frumpy little priest holds true even to his surname.[51] Why did Chesterton not call him the equally innocuous Smith or Jones? It may simply be that Chesterton liked the color brown. In his essay "A Piece of Chalk," he remembered one summer holiday when he put six pieces of chalk in his pocket, then asked the cook for brown paper. She naturally assumed he would tie up parcels with it, but he explained that he wanted to draw pictures on it. He admitted, "I not only liked brown paper, but liked the quality of brownness in paper, just as I like the quality of brownness in October woods, or in beer."[52] Can readers assume then that in the story "The Arrow of Heaven," Chesterton grinned to himself when he wrote that Father Brown "was blinking at the carpet in a brown study"?[53] In an essay on his favorite hue, he found that, by using brightly colored chalk on brown paper, "you could pick out points of fire in it, sparks of gold, and blood-red, and sea-green, like the first fierce stars that sprang out of divine darkness."[54]

Color pervades our lives and, as Chesterton once observed, "we all know that our childhood found talismanic gems in the very paints in the paint-box."[55] As an artist-in-training at the Slade School of Art, he was exposed to instruction which may be credited for the intense details in his texts. Myriad images of everyday things, the landscape, and the weather convey a scenic panorama throughout the tales. He describes how "the thousand arms of the forest were grey, and its million fingers silver," "rivers so small that the boat looked like a magic boat, sailing on land through meadows and cornfields," or chocolates "wrapped in those red and gold and green metallic colours which are almost better than chocolate itself." To enter some British homes, one must walk "the very steps up to the dark front doors [which] seem as steep as the side of pyramids." On one day, "the daylight [was] silver rather than gold and pewter." On another, "the sky was as Prussian a blue." Characters populating the stories received their own descriptive portrayals. In "The Flying Stars," a young girl "wrapped in brown furs ... might have been a small toddling bear"; in another story, the hostess's eyes had "that bright and rather prominent appearance which belongs to the eyes of ladies who ask questions at political meetings."[56]

Besides his paints, as a child Chesterton had been fond of playing with a toy theater, and as an adult he attempted to complete a play for characters in a small toy theater, drawing and coloring the figures himself.[57] It's no surprise, then, that theaters provide the *mise en scène* for many of the stories with their numerous and confusing entrances and exits, labyrinths, and galleries. As a plot device in some of the tales, wealthy families dramatize plays for the enjoyment of the community. Other incidents he recounts simply evoke the sense of someone performing a role. He wrote in his essay "On Detective Novels" that the mystery story is "a masquerade ball in which everybody is disguised as somebody else."[58] In that case, flamboyant characters assume false identities and wear disguises, mirrors reflect one's true personality versus that exposed to the world, and dramas are sometimes performed for the express purpose of exposing a criminal.

Props and scenic backdrops feature prominently in the Father Brown stories. The priest sees through the costumes, the makeup, and the staged mannerisms, and they reveal the criminality he suspects, or they become metaphors for all manner of human behavior. In "The Eye of Apollo," when the malevolence of the prophet Kalon is revealed, Father Brown remarks, "There was something shocking about the dropping of his mask; it was like a man's real face falling off."[59] Professor Gertrude White affirms that

> Father Brown's role is that of the spectator at the play who sees beneath the disguise to the hidden truths of identity, motive and conduct. Because he alone has a clear sense of reality and true values, he can penetrate the world of false appearances and assumptions to the truth beneath.[60]

If not in cardboard and plaster, Chesterton nevertheless recreated in the tales his toy theater after all, populating it with characters who play their roles under the priest's watchful eye. Explaining in theatrical terms how he deduced the solution to one particular murder, Father Brown says, "It is true ... that somebody else had played the part of the murderer before me and done me out of the actual experience. I was a sort of understudy; always in a state of being ready to act the assassin. I always made it my business, at least, to know the part thoroughly."[61]

For all the spirituality that a priest as protagonist might suggest, scarce Roman Catholic proselytizing or theology can be found in the stories. Of the earlier stories, this is not surprising. He had admitted in the Preface to his essay "Orthodoxy," written a year or so before the Father Brown stories, that "all I had hitherto heard of Christian theology had alienated me from it. I was a pagan at the age of twelve, and a complete agnostic by the age of sixteen." But by the age of 34, he had accepted the faith of the Church of England and then tried to explain how he had finally come to believe, calling it the answer to a riddle. His doubts were "suddenly satisfied by the Christian Theology."[62] Thus, he began writing the Father Brown stories as an Anglican and ended writing them as a Catholic. From agnostic to a fervent Catholic writing more than 50 stories about a Catholic priest is surely a paradox that Chesterton could appreciate.

When "The Blue Cross" was first published in July 1910, nearly 20 percent of the United States population was Catholic. Catholics in England and Wales numbered fewer than one percent, but that changed when, from 1912 to 1919, a half million people converted to the faith, perhaps because of the desolation of World War I.[63] After all, former scorned Catholic soldiers had served and died along with their Anglican colleagues, proving their allegiance to the nation. Catholic practices and teachings were palliative, particularly the Church's belief in an afterlife and the efficacy of prayers.[64] With so many soldiers having been killed in the war, Anglican families too needed hope that their deceased loved ones could enter heaven if the living offered prayers to that effect.

Throughout the 20th century, the Catholic English middle class increased, in part due to the proliferation of Catholic schools. The predominant Church of England began to transform until it even more strongly resembled Catholicism in its practices, rituals, architecture, and music after an influx of immigrants to England from Catholic countries. Challenging the pervasion of materialism and moral turmoil in British society, Catholicism's conservative emphasis on traditional values was increasingly appealing. One Anglican clergyman even admitted, that "our services are as incomprehensible as if still performed in the Latin tongue. The central service of the Roman church, indeed, with its dramatic and appealing character, is far more intelligible even to the humblest worshipper."[65]

Despite his determination to root out the criminal, no matter his religion or lack thereof and to bring closure to the crime, Father Brown tended to avoid secular authorities also intent on that end. Once he exposed the perpetrator, he was off to other duties. His attitude was "private lives are more important than public reputations. I am going to save the living, and let the dead bury their dead." At the conclusion of "The Three Tools of Death," an acquaintance announces that the coroner had arrived and was ready to begin the inquiry, but the priest picks up his hat. "I've got to get back to the Deaf School," he announces. His apology at leaving also reveals Chesterton's opinion that the solution is at the heart of the mystery. In his essay "The Divine Detective," Chesterton professed that the Church's purpose in discovering the perpetrator of a crime is not to seek vengeance, but to forgive the wrongdoer.[66] Justice was served in this case with the appearance of the police; the priest's involvement was complete with his success at discovering the truth. When his acumen at invariably unveiling the criminal led to accusations of him being a devil himself and so more easily able to spot the villain as a brother-in-crime, as it were, he admitted, "I am a man. Therefore, I have all devils in my heart."[67]

In "The Secret of Father Brown," the priest—and perhaps Chesterton himself—explains his method of detection:

I had planned out each of the crimes very carefully.... I had thought out exactly how a thing like that could be done, and in what style or state of mind a man could really do it. And when I felt quite sure that I felt exactly like the murderer myself, of course I knew who he was.... I really did see myself, and my real self, committing the murders. I didn't actually kill the men by material means.... I thought and thought about how a man might come to be like that, until I realized that I really *was* like that, in everything except final consent to the action.[68]

By matching a pattern in the crimes to an already familiar *modus operandi*, Father Brown finds a solution that occasionally perplexes trained police officers. However, it also follows that, unless the fiction is a police procedural or specifically devoted to criminal investigation, in order to allow the amateur to provide the solution and hand over the criminal to justice, it is necessary that the police be inept, incorrigible, and occasionally even corrupt, somewhat like Inspector Lestrade in the Sherlock stories.[69]

Despite it being the most grievous crime, only about two thirds of the Father Brown stories deal with the fifth commandment—murder or attempted murder—which is puzzling, given Chesterton's claim that he preferred to find a murdered man under the sofa in the first chapter of a mystery story or he wouldn't read it. In what might have been a startling confession had it not been immediately followed by an explanation, Chesterton recalled that he had committed at least 53 murders and thereby gained a reputation as a writer of "murderous short stories," so that publishers and magazines would write to him "ordering a new batch of corpses."[70] Mystery writer H.R.F. Keating claims that "told his bank balance had shrunk to a mere 100 pounds, [Chesterton] would say, 'That means Father Brown again.'"[71] It is unknown if he said those words or in what tone of voice—enthusiastically or glumly—but over the years, he completed 51 stories which were organized into five collections: *The Innocence of Father Brown* (1911), *The Wisdom of Father Brown* (1914), *The Incredulity of Father Brown* (1926), *The Secret of Father Brown* (1927), and *The Scandal of Father Brown* (1935). After Chesterton's death in 1936, writers Ellery Queen named the first volume one of the "four all-time finest collections of detective short stories."[72]

Over the 25 years that he wrote the Father Brown stories, if Chesterton ever tired of his priest who resembled a "big, black mushroom,"[73] he never told, unlike Agatha Christie who admitted regret at creating Poirot. "Why did I invent this detestable, bombastic, tiresome little creature?" she allegedly said. Arthur Conan Doyle once wrote to his mother, "I think of slaying Holmes ... and winding him up for good and all." Doyle finally did grow to detest Sherlock Holmes so much so that he threw him over the Reichenbach Falls in an effort to be done with him.[74] John Dickson Carr who based his French detective Henri Bencolin on Chesterton's Valentin eventually tired of Bencolin and abandoned him after five novels and four short stories.[75]

Perhaps Chesterton subconsciously retired his priest from 1914 to 1923, during which years no new Father Brown stories were published, leading one reviewer of the final compilation to wonder why any author would "kill off their clever geese which have years of golden egg-laying before them."[76] This is not to say that Chesterton was idle during those nine years. In the interval, the *Illustrated London News* published his

"Errors about Detective Stories." Novelists should create real and interesting people, not "sticks, or stock characters," he advised in that essay. "And then, when the hero in question is at last alive and ready to be murdered, when he is ... crying aloud to be murdered, the novelist does not murder him after all. This is a serious waste of a fine opportunity, and I hope in future to see the error rectified."[77]

Chesterton scholars have argued whether he really saw value in ending his character's life. Professor Dermot Quinn believed that "Chesterton never thought of killing off Father Brown who, if not an *alter ego*, was at least a close friend.... Had he dispatched the priest, Chesterton could never have looked Father O'Connor in the eye again."[78] It must be added, though, that Chesterton did play with Father Brown's death in his story "The Resurrection of Father Brown." Someone announced that the priest had died after being clubbed, to which a journalist confirms, "He's a goner." But as he lies in his coffin, the priest suddenly comes to and sits up. Was it a miracle? No, a planned sham. "Oh, you silly, *silly* people," Father Brown berates the mourning crowd. "God bless you all and give you more sense," he prays.[79]

The debate goes on. British mystery writer Dudley Barker did detect a "marked deterioration" of the stories that ended each volume as if Chesterton was bored with the current premise of the series and was eager to begin the next, a logical supposition if Chesterton did write the Father Brown stories only for financial profit.[80] It may also explain, as Professor White sees it, why Chesterton increasingly relied on "repetitive situations, characters and themes, and [seemed] to lose control of his constant temptation to the fantastic."[81] Martin Gardner, editor of the annotated *Innocence of Father Brown*, would argue that Chesterton did tire of Father Brown but carried on because the public wanted more and because he needed the royalties to fund his *G.K. Weekly*.[82] With that Chesterton biographer Ian Ker differs. He found that, for him, some of the best stories were from the later volumes.[83]

G.K. Chesterton died June 14, 1936. Whether he was speaking of Father Brown in "Errors about Detective Stories," Chesterton confessed that he had "written some of the worst mystery stories in the world.... I do not mean to speak in any superior fashion of the inferior stories. I am very fond of trash; I have read a great deal of it—I have also written a great deal of it."[84]

Since 1910, millions of readers the world over would disagree. Thus, it was inevitable that the Father Brown stories would eventually be adapted to radio, film, and television. As Chesterton authority Anthony Grist has recognized and BBC producer John Yorke would surely agree, "Faced with the need for a weekly crime the writers might even have had to fall back on Chesterton."[85]

2

The Many Faces
of Father Brown

"When a work of literature is translated into another
medium, the resultant gains and losses bring into focus the
peculiar virtues of the original."[1]

Fictional detectives have long made their way into dramatic adaptations, some shortly after they were birthed on the printed page. Characters created by authors such as Agatha Christie, Francis Durbridge, Arthur Conan Doyle, Georges Simenon, Raymond Chandler, and Dashiel Hammett found new life and new followers in movie theaters and, later, on television. Fictional clergymen (and women) detectives also proliferated in other media. Sean Connery starred as Friar William of Baskerville in Umberto Eco's *The Name of the Rose*, a historical mystery film. Ralph McInerny's Father Dowling, starring Tom Bosley of *Happy Days*, was a Chicago priest who found himself involved in mysteries aided by Sister Stephanie, a streetwise nun in television's *Father Dowling Mysteries*. Beginning with a made-for-TV movie, it then lasted for 43 more hour-long episodes. David Small, Harry Kemelman's rabbi in his literary series, teamed up for a short-lived TV series with the police chief in *Lanigan's Rabbi*. Anglican vicar Sidney Chambers is portrayed by James Norton in *Grantchester*, based on the book by James Runcie. Set in a real village near Cambridge in the 1950s, the television series includes Chambers' friend, local Detective Inspector Geordie Keating.

Current BBC producers were not the first, nor the only, to realize that dramatic reworkings of Chesterton's Father Brown stories would make for noteworthy entertainment. Perhaps realizing that his stories might someday find themselves enjoyed through another means than the printed word, Chesterton expressed his reluctance to accept the burgeoning medium of film in his essay "Errors in Detective Stories." He was unsure that a good mystery story would make good drama. The latter, Chesterton thought, depends on the audience knowing who the hero is and who the villain is; whereas in the detective story, the hero or villain is in the know while the audience is deceived.[2]

He had visited America on a lecture tour in 1921 when silent film was in its heyday, when the names of Hollywood stars like Buster Keaton, Charlie Chaplin, and Rudolph Valentino were household words. However widespread the relatively new medium was becoming, the previous year, Chesterton remarked in an essay to Britain's Society for the Protection of Ancient Buildings that he wasn't against cinema, but only that "it is a terrible waste of time." He would rather see a little boy climbing trees "and possibly really falling off, and possibly breaking his own neck" rather than the same child just watching the event in a theater.[3] He was questioned about his comments by an American journalist during a conversation about movies and morality. "This is my first visit to America and I am not acquainted with the saloon," Chesterton replied, but "if it was no worse than the English public house, I think it was far more preferable to the cinema. It's sad, don't you know, to have hundreds of people sitting in a cinema house, gaping away, and having ideas thrust into their heads."[4] He would much prefer that people think for themselves, an odd comment from a man not at all reluctant to profess his views on myriad topics in hopes of convincing his readers to think the same.

Then, in 1934, Hollywood's Paramount studios produced *Father Brown, Detective*, an amalgam of three of his stories, and invited him to a preview of the film. This was a risky move, since, given his penchant for drama and the theater, Chesterton had once opined that "in its origins, drama came down from heaven—from Olympus. It has descended step by step ever since until at last it reached Hollywood." Lest anyone misunderstand, he added, "The cinema did not come from heaven. It was born in a foul atmosphere—in the last swinish leavings of modern sentimentalism."[5] As a dramatist himself and fascinated as he was with all things theatrical, at seeing Father Brown in a format other than on the written page, he sadly left no comment for his readers except to tell biographer Maisie Ward that he liked the film as a film and the acting. Also, it had given him an idea for a new story about the priest.[6] After his death, the *Yorkshire Post* quoted an opinion he once expressed again detailing his dislike of film: "The cinema has broken up man." A man's eyes or nose may be on the screen, but he is not really there. With the advent of the talkies, Chesterton continued, "by modern necromancy the cinema is striving to put the man together again. It has already sent his voice after him in a separate parcel." Soon, he surmised, "it will no doubt send the smell of his cigar."[7] It is doubtful that he ever changed his mind, writing as he did in his autobiography, "I have ended by denouncing modern advertisements or American films even when they are beautiful."[8]

Despite Chesterton's staunch sentiments on the inconsequentiality of cinema, long after the last Father Brown story was published, the priest continued to sally forth solving mysteries, brought to life by some famous, and not so renowned, actors who brought their own interpretation to the character.

The first of these, that Chesterton previewed, was presented when Paramount studios purchased three Chesterton stories—"The Blue Cross," "The Flying Stars," and "The Paradise of Thieves"—and hired Metro-Goldwyn-Mayer's screenwriter C. Gardner Sullivan to adapt them for a big screen production.[9] Modifications are always necessary when literature is re-structured for a different medium. Combining three of the priest's adventures into one resulted in a longer script that kept the familiarity of the main characters but resulted in a whole new story. For the cinematic version, Sullivan added a romance to one of Flambeau's elaborate schemes: When the thief falls in love with the lovely and wealthy Evelyn Fisher after meeting her in a casino, he vows to obtain diamonds for her from the famous Flying Star necklace and from Father Brown's gold cross. With jewels in hand, he returns to her home and enters her bedroom, but she refuses to have anything to do with him and calls him an idiot for his thievery. Later, Evelyn realizes she loves him, so she and Father Brown devise a plan to reform him. But, still scheming to steal the priest's gold cross, Flambeau joins the Eucharistic Congress attended by invited clergy. Father Brown recognizes him and, acting irrationally, leaves bizarre clues for the police. He still hopes to save Flambeau from a life of crime by reminding him of Evelyn's love. When the police finally catch up to him, Flambeau escapes but afterwards he has a change of heart and turns himself in.[10]

Paramount was uncertain about casting the role of the priest, creating a whirlwind of speculation in the press. Was it better to use an experienced actor or a genuine cleric? At first, English actor Sir Guy Standing was considered for the role along with Episcopalian minister Henry Scott Rubel, but months later, neither man had yet to be approved for the role. Meanwhile, Paul Lukas, an Oscar-winning Hungarian actor, was cast as Flambeau with actress Gertrude Michael in the role of Evelyn. Alfred Worker was scheduled to direct the film. Standing remained in the line-up but seemed unlikely to be chosen. Days later, the *New York Times* announced that Irish actor J.M. Kerrigan would take the title role but, before the week was out, Paramount executives instead chose Shakespearean and Broadway actor Walter Connolly to play Father Brown under the direction of Edward Sedgwick.[11]

Shortly after filming began, Michael and Lukas were playing a scene in a gambling salon with 50 extras who were evidently selected from off the street to help populate the room. Having snuck out of her family's mansion, Evelyn is flirting with the wagering strangers. The action continued until actors costumed as police raided the den. Each extra made a hasty getaway, possibly having experienced that situation in real life, leaving Michael and Lukas the only two the police could lay hands on. According to the script, though, Michael and Lukas were the ones who were to escape.[12]

When Mr. and Mrs. Chesterton attended the film with Maisie Ward, Ward recalled thinking the stories had been "cleverly combined" and the cast "first rate" and predicted that Father Brown would become another Charlie Chan, a Hawaiian police detective in stories by Earl Biggers. Much like Father Brown, Chan also traveled the world solving crimes. However, Ward later wrote that the film failed and speculated that it was too short. The action was packed into only 68 minutes.[13]

The film rekindled public interest in the stories about the cleric detective and resulted in yet another characterization of the sleuth when the Mutual Broadcasting System's Sunday radio program, *Murder Clinic*, featured Chesterton's priest along with others among "the world's greatest detectives—men against murder." For more than a year from July 1942 to November 1943, the weekly dramatizations presented the stories of detectives by prominent mystery authors such as Edgar Wallace, Ngaio Marsh, and John Dickson Carr. Of the four Chesterton stories included in the line-up, two featured Father Brown.[14] Because Chesterton began many of his stories with a colorful description of the weather or landscape, formatting the stories for a listening audience required dialogue, not a long narration. So, the stock character of a housekeeper was introduced as someone with whom Father Brown could converse. The role of housekeeper, cook, or parish secretary has since survived as a staple in most Father Brown dramas, though the character does not appear in the original stories. Likewise, the former criminal mastermind Flambeau was made a police detective, which did have a precedent in Chesterton's stories when, after the first five, Father Brown converted the former thief. Without an explanation, readers were now to understand that Father Brown's saving tactics had finally worked on Flambeau. "Though his youth was a bit stormy," in the next story he was described as "a strictly honest man" who is now in business as a private detective.[15] Who better to know and understand the workings of a criminal mind?

Perhaps the Chesterton episodes on the *Murder Clinic* were popular enough that, two years later, the same Mutual Broadcasting System hired American actor Karl Swenson (after initially planning on Walter Huston or Spencer Tracy) to portray Father Brown in another radio version exclusively devoted to him. *The Adventures of Father Brown* ran throughout June and July 1945. Each 30-minute episode began with an organ prelude and an overview identifying the priest as "the best-loved detective of them all." In each story, Father Brown sits at his desk working on church accounts (or napping) and watched over by Nora, his fussy housekeeper, only to be interrupted when his assistance is needed in ferreting out the solution to a mystery or to prove a convicted person not guilty. With little difficulty, he helps the police, especially Detective Flambeau portrayed by Bill Griffis. Meanwhile, a "young Father Peter" takes over Father Brown's parish duties, and Gretchen Davidson played the housekeeper.[16]

In 1952, Columbia Pictures resurrected *Father Brown* with Alec Guinness in the title role, becoming one of the more famous Father Browns despite Guinness's tall thin stature being physically the opposite of Chesterton's short, rather frumpy, priest. But like the original Father Brown, Guinness's character thinks aloud and mumbles to himself about how he would commit the crime or how the criminal could be caught. Instead of a housekeeper, Father Brown shares his ramblings with the wealthy widow Mrs. Warren. The adaptation was closely tailored from "The Blue Cross" with only a few changes: Disobeying his bishop's orders, Father Brown carries St. Augustine's cross to the Eucharistic Congress and, in the process, audaciously foils the police's plan to capture Flambeau, once again cast as a bad guy. Running late and dropping his many packages, Father Brown encounters Flambeau disguised as a priest who switches one package for another when he picks them up to aid the clumsy cleric. Father Brown recognizes him as a phony priest who gives himself away by ordering a ham sandwich on Friday. Evading the police, Flambeau absconds with the valuable relic. Returning home, Father Brown must face his bishop who berates him for his folly, not recognizing that the priest had gambled on losing the cross in order to win Flambeau's repentance. Later, through an insignia on Flambeau's lost cigarette case, Father Brown tracks him through the catacombs of Paris to where Flambeau lives. The thief invites him to see all the objects of great wealth he has stolen and displayed for his own enjoyment. Looking around at the secret room, the priest laments that "even though I wear funny clothes and have taken certain vows, I live much more in the world than you do." Flambeau offers to return the cross to him, but Father Brown refuses to accept it unless Flambeau returns everything else he has stolen as well. "I thought you were a great sinner," the priest laments disparagingly. "You're only a small one."[17] As police arrive, Flambeau thrusts the cross at the priest and escapes. Back home, the bishop shows Father Brown a newspaper clipping touting the new "Flambeau Exhibition" at the Louvre, formerly his collection of stolen articles. On a Sunday morning, as

Father Brown reads the parable of the prodigal son to his congregation, a repentant Flambeau slips into a pew.

When producer Paul Moss bought the movie rights to Father Brown, he planned a comedic film then, if it did well, the potential was there for a series set in London and Paris. Studio executives wanted Guinness, known for his talent at playing quirky rogues, as Father Ignatius Brown and Charles Boyer as Gustav Flambeau. While Guinness agreed to portray the priest, Peter Finch eventually took the latter role.[18] Since then, producers have, almost always and for unknown reasons, cast the part of the French thief with a Brit.

Months before his death, Chesterton published another essay on films, leading to the conclusion that he would have immensely enjoyed this particular version of his sleuthing priest and of Guinness's characterization. He wrote,

> Mere slapstick pantomime, farces of comic collapse and social topsy-turvydom, are, if anything, definitely good for the soul. To see a banker or broker or prosperous business man running after his hat, kicked out of his house, hurled from the top of a skyscraper, hung by one leg to an aeroplane, put into a mangle, rolled out flat by a steam-roller, or suffering any such changes of fortune, tends in itself rather to edification; to a sense of the insecurity of earthly things and the folly of that pride which is based on the accident of prosperity.[19]

The film's London release in June 1954 garnered mixed reviews. The show business newspaper *Variety* praised the casting of Guinness as admirable. Likewise, story adaptor Thelma Schnee and director Robert Hamer were given kudos for having "fashioned a warm-hearted narrative."[20] After the film premiered in America in November as *The Detective*, another *Variety* critic credited the film as Guinness's best thus far and asserted that Schnee and Hamer had "turned out the gayest, liveliest cops-and-robbers opus that has been squeezed into 91 minutes in a long, long time." Bosley Crowther, the *New York Times* theater critic, found that Guinness proved his talent for slapstick comedy in his "hundred funny ways of dropping his packages, tripping over his feet, losing his hat, wildly clutching his belongings and scuttling off in a mass of disarray." On the other hand, as Crowther also pointed out, the film had trouble deciding whether it was to be a comedy or serious drama. He found the film confusing and derided Guinness for being too stern and "sanctimonious" in contrast to his usual comedic roles. Audiences who expected his mischievous, satiric side would be disappointed. The priest's disapproval of Flambeau's thievery came off as "smug" and "self-contented," so Crowther sensed that Guinness felt slightly uncomfortable having "gone moral."[21] Perhaps the reviewer was right, for, when Anthony Grist, a frequent contributor to *The Chesterton Review*, a quarterly journal of the G.K. Chesterton Institute for Faith & Culture, asked Guinness how he felt about the role, the actor replied that "he disliked the film, that it was false to the spirit of Chesterton, and that he himself was wrong in the part." Grist agreed that his "obsession with saving Flambeau's soul … comes across as pompous and priggish,"[22] the fault of which would seem to lie not with Guinness but with the script writer.

Despite Guinness's unease, an event occurred during production that ultimately influenced his future. In his autobiography, *Blessings in Disguise*, he remembered that, after a day's shooting, he was headed back to his hotel still costumed in a priest's black cassock when he heard footsteps behind him and someone calling "Mon père!" A small boy seized his hand and talked in a "non-stop prattle … although I was a total stranger he obviously took me for a priest and so to be trusted."[23] Guinness, at the time a devout Anglican, "reflected that a church which could inspire such confidence in a child, making its priests, even when unknown, so easily approachable could not be as scheming and creepy as so often made out." He "began to shake off [his] long-taught, long-absorbed prejudices [toward Catholicism]" which he, as a rule, omitted in his autobiography along with the "scheming and creepy" stories to which he referred.[24] Ironically, Father Brown's influence on Guinness roughly paralleled Father O'Connor's influence on Chesterton when, years later, Guinness was baptized a Catholic.

The next year, 1955, a short-lived West German television series *Die Galerie der großen Detektive* (*The Gallery of Great Detectives*) featured the works of mystery writers like Agatha Christie, Edgar Allan Poe, and G.K. Chesterton among others. In the fourth episode titled "Brown findet Daniel Boom" ("Brown finds Daniel Boom"), German actor Walter Janssen played the priest.

Chesterton begins the story with the death of an American millionaire, allegedly from handling or drinking from a cursed chalice known as the Coptic Cup. Despite Father Brown's "undistinguished countenance" and "rusty-black clerical clothes," he was besieged by journalists as soon as he stepped off the ship from England onto American soil, his reputation as crime-solver having preceded him. Norman Drage approaches and takes him to meet Peter Wain, whose uncle's business partner Brander Merton, is the third and current owner of the Cup. The two previous owners had received threatening letters from a "Daniel Doom" and shortly after were found dead. Merton is elaborately well-protected against a similar fate. However, when Father Brown enters the room to meet him, Merton lies dead from an arrow through his throat, and the cup sits on a table by the window. Father Brown searches for suspects, particularly those with a history of Red Indian war tactics (Chesterton had obviously been influenced by the history of American cowboys and Indians), including the use of arrows. In a surprise denouement, he identifies Daniel Doom and reveals how and why the man killed Brander Merton.[25]

The Germans also made two full-length films in the early 1960s inspired by Chesterton's stories. *Das schwarze Shaf* (*The Black Sheep*), starring Heinz Rühmann as Father Brown and Siegfried Lowitz as Flambeau, was filmed in Bavaria and Ireland. Following its release, Rühmann received Best Actor in the Deutscher Filmpreis (German Film Awards). This, despite reviews that criticized the popular German actor as not a "particularly credible clergyman," nor "a particularly convincing investigator" in a "not particularly successful Chesterton adaptation, neither a particularly thrilling thriller, nor a particularly intelligent comedy." The best thing that could be said about him was that he was "nice." In addition, Flambeau had been miscast; instead of the suave, lithe man Chesterton describes, Lowitz was rough and double-chinned with a receding hairline. According to film historian Michael Pitts, in the plot Father Brown, as became the norm in adaptations, ends up on the "bad side of his bishop, the local police, and his housekeeper" when he solves his latest murder.[26]

When a man is found dead in the churchyard, Rühmann's Father Brown, though it will be an "inconvenience" for him, promises to search for the killer. His accurate solution brings publicity in the press which angers his bishop. When he inquires why Father Brown must play detective, he replies that he's curious about the world, that he is a black sheep in a flock of whites. As a child he read two kinds of books, the lives of the saints and detective novels. As punishment for his un-priestly activity, the bishop sends him to replace a priest in Ireland. Coincidentally, a local police detective has also been banished to the same town as chastisement for *not* solving the previous crime that Father Brown did. In his new parish, manipulation of stolen stocks causes the death of an actor during a performance, so Father Brown puts himself in the mind of the murderer "to follow his crazy and confused thoughts." Flambeau is first suspected, but a more thorough study of the Biblical story of Cain and Abel enables Father Brown to deduce the criminal. For this unseemly activity, his bishop once more transfers Father Brown to an outpost where there is, as the previous priest tells him, a need not for a priest but for a detective.[27]

In the sequel, two years after *The Black Sheep*, Rühmann reprised the ecclesiastical role for *Er kann's nicht lassen* (*He Can't Leave It Alone*), directed by Axel von Ambesser. Following a cat into the church basement, Father Brown uncovers Van Dyck's painting of the Virgin and Child. When it is stolen, Father Brown, claiming to be a mere country priest and not a detective, nevertheless finds the men responsible, retrieves the painting, and invites the thieves to his church to confess. His bishop, once again upset over the fame that Father Brown has garnered and encouraged by his jealous secretary, sends Father Brown and his housekeeper to Abbott's Rock, a relatively crime-free locale, in hopes of dissuading him once again from his predilection for sleuthing. At his new assignment, Father Brown finds unexplained fatal accidents occurring in the fog and the legend of a ghostly curse at a medieval castle. When the heir to the castle arrives after a stint in rehab for drug addiction, Father Brown suspects that the ghostly legend is really a blind for smugglers and sends the young man away to the bishop's house for safety. When the priest is kidnapped by the same men who stole the Van Dyck painting, he escapes with a coffeepot full of their booty and drives off on a stolen motorbike pursued by the thieves and the police. Arriving at the bishop's office, he apologizes for solving another murder, then hands over the coffeepot full of drugs to the police.[28]

One reviewer found that the film's sarcastic and ironic humor "ensures a steady grin on the part of the audience." Another delighted in the funny but unrealistic car chases and the unpredictable ending when Father Brown arrives at his next far-flung assignment, a parish in Africa.[29]

The success of the first two films prompted an Italian-made production, *Operazione San Pietro* (*Operation Saint Peter*), in which Heinz Rühmann, now as Cardinal Erik Brown, tracks down a gang of thieves who have stolen the Pietà, Michelangelo's statue of Mary holding the body of the dead Jesus. Brown's old friend and member of the gang is the American Joe Ventura, played by Edward G. Robinson. The film, alternately titled in German *Die Abenteuer des Kardinal Braun* (*The Adventures of Cardinal Brown*), was not based on any of Chesterton's stories.[30]

On the other hand, "The Quick One," aired by the BBC in July 1964, *was* more faithfully adapted from Chesterton's original. In a five-year series titled *Detective* and featuring a variety of familiar literary sleuths, Mervyn Johns, who had played several priests over the course of a long acting career, starred in one episode as Father Brown. He solved the murder of a pub patron, Mr. Raggley, the local crank who complained about anything and everything. Based on Chesterton's story also titled "The Quick One," the priest, who asserts to the police inspector that "I don't often interfere with your business, which I know you do better than I should do it," finds a half-empty whiskey glass and deduces that the police need to find the man who had dashed into the bar and just as quickly rushed out again.[31] Paradoxically, the quick man was not the one who had poisoned Raggley's drink, but his testimony was valuable in locating the one who did.

From 1966 to 1972, German television broadcast 39 episodes of *Pater Brown*. Starring Viennese actor Josef Meinrad, who had wanted to become a priest before he took acting lessons that changed his mind about a vocation, the series was also fairly reworked from Chesterton's stories.[32] Instead of a Flambeau, however, this Father Brown was aided by Inspektor Smith, played by Guido Wieland for the first 10 episodes and by Ernst Fritz Fürbringer in the role of Inspektor Gilbert Burns for the last episodes. Many of the 25-minute programs bear original Chesterton titles, such as "Das unlösbare Problem" ("The Insoluble Problem"), "Das Auge des Apoli" ("The Eye of Apollo"), and "Das blaue Kreuz" ("The Blue Cross").

In the first episode, "Der Fehler Der Maschine" ("The Error of the Machine"), Inspektor Smith visits the priest because his "enlightenment" in a previous case was "simply brilliant." Due to his uncanny ability to solve mysteries, there are two opinions going around the police station about Father Brown, he says, either he is a "clairvoyant in league with the devil" or a "pastor who criminally neglects the souls of his community." Father Brown protests, claiming that he simply tries to get inside the criminal's mind and from there he can determine how the crime was done. After a suspect is wrongly accused through a policeman's prejudicial use of a lie detector, Father Brown shows how its results can often be mistakenly interpreted as they were in this case and clears the suspect of the crime.[33]

Italians also re-invented the English priest in their own image when comedian Renato Rascel starred in the 1971 television series *I racconti di padre Brown* (*The Tales of Father Brown*) along with Arnoldo Foà as Flambeau. Directed by Vittorio Cottafavi with credit given to G.K. Chesterton, the series only lasted for six 55-minute episodes. Many of those also bear Chesterton's titles. According to Italian sociologist Milly Buonanno, Italian police dramas were in the process of becoming more "homegrown" rather than international in settings and characterizations. But, even though Italians were beginning to emerge as national storytellers, non–Italian authors, such as Chesterton, still predominated.[34]

One of Britain's popular film stars of the 1950s, Kenneth More, was the next to don the cassock at the insistence of Sir Lew Grade, managing director of Britain's Associated Television (ATV). In his autobiography, More tells the story of Grade repeatedly phoning him and addressing him as "Father" until More finally relented into accepting the role.[35] In doing so, he became the most famous actor to play the priest since Alec Guinness. In 1974, ATV produced 13 episodes, each taken from a Chesterton story, including "The Secret Garden," "The Arrow of Heaven," and "The Dagger with Wings." Except for Dennis Burgess reprising his role as Hercule Flambeau, the thief-turned-private-investigator in five episodes, guest stars filled the remainder of the cast. Each program consisted of three parts introduced in some episodes by title cards as in silent films.

While critics remarked on the paucity of the sets, referring to them as "studio-bound" and "threadbare" as a result of a small budget and on actors who appeared to suffer from "hurried preparation and inadequate rehearsal," More was frequently praised for his charisma and "natural dignity." Anthony Grist, a *Chesterton Review* contributor, wrote that, despite Chesterton's "brightly coloured, boldly drawn" characters which usually become diminished when portrayed by a real person, "More's Father Brown radiates warmth, humour and humanity." Recalling specific scenes, Grist thought More did well at acting "self-deprecatingly nervous at the prospect of flying ... confidently reassuring at the deathbed of a penitent; agitated and broken-voiced" when confronting a man with a gun. "More's stature as actor and star ensure that the little priest still dominates the proceedings."[36] Mystery writer Hazel Holt agreed. Her opinion was that More was "a natural born actor" who could "breathe life into the most unpromising material." Father Brown, characterized by Chesterton as being unobtrusive, nevertheless, when More's Father Brown "was involved in the action the whole anaemic [*sic*] thing came to life."[37]

Adaptor Hugh Leonard and producer Ian Fordyce had ensured that scriptwriters remained somewhat faithful to Chesterton's priest by eliminating the housekeeper role so prominent in previous versions. The simple nature of the clerical sleuth established in the stories was maintained. "While others strut and loudly theorize he sits on the sidelines muttering things like, 'Oh dear, oh dear, it won't do, you know,'" described one *New York Times* reviewer while another likened More's Father Brown favorably to a "mild-mannered Columbo type" with his odd mannerisms.[38]

Though employed to adapt two of the stories, Leonard nevertheless felt that More had been terribly miscast. Apparently so did More. After visiting the set, Leonard reported that More had apologized to him. "I had it in mind to make a proper stab at being Father Brown, but I lost my nerve. Thing is I've played Kenny More for too long to make a change." The "Kenny More" he referred to was more comfortable in roles calling for a debonair leading man with a talent for comic timing when it was called for. In Leonard's opinion, the miscast put too much of a strain on More's fans so that the series "went down like a lead balloon."[39] The fact that Flambeau was no longer the notorious thief but has now been redeemed and is a successful private detective, may also have had something to do with poor ratings. In episodes where Flambeau is absent, Father Brown appears lost and lonely.

Despite his misgivings, More had played the part of a priest convincingly enough that, by chance, he had a similar experience to that of Alec Guinness. A few years after acting as Father Brown, More was working in Spain on another film when an old peasant woman approached him and asked him to hear her confession. He had to explain that he had only acted the role and was neither a Catholic nor a priest.[40]

On May 29, 1974, to celebrate the centenary of Chesterton's birth, BBC Radio 4 produced and broadcast five Father Brown stories with

British actor Leslie French as the priest, Willie Rushton as Chesterton, and Francis de Wolff as Flambeau. Rushton as Chesterton introduces the series in a way reminiscent of Dr. Watson introducing Sherlock Holmes' adventures.[41] Stories included the standard "The Blue Cross," as well as "The Queer Feet," "The Perishing of the Pendragons," "The Dagger with Wings," and "The Mirror of the Magistrate."

Sanctuary of Fear, variously titled *Girl in the Park* or *Father Brown, Detective,* was a 1979 made-for-American-TV movie broadcast on NBC that had little in common with Chesterton's Father Brown except the priest's name. Indecision on the part of studio executives led to the title changes as well as its failure to be greenlighted for a series to be produced by Marble Arch, the American division of Britain's ATV. Barnard Hughes played an American Father Brown with a Manhattan parish who considers himself an amateur sleuth. He befriends Carol Bain (played by Kay Lenz), an off–Broadway actress with a knack for finding dead bodies that happen to disappear after the police are called. After three or four such events, homicide detective Bellamy (Michael McGuire) becomes skeptical of her reports. However, he finally takes her seriously and even considers Bain a suspect when she misses a performance, and her understudy is killed onstage. Father Brown's offer of refuge in the rectory provides no safe sanctuary from her stalker.

Despite Hughes's Father Brown being quite remote from Chesterton's stories, the *Los Angeles Times* thought "he made the trip without a hitch" from an English country cleric of 50 years previous to a modern New Yorker. Chesterton may have even liked this characterization of Father Brown as "his mind [is] always on the intricacies of homicide and never on mundane matters such as his leaky church roof." Not so convinced, the *New York Times* critic figured out whodunit long before the denouement, saw through the extra scenes thrown in to pad the production, and finally concluded that "Father Brown has been stuffed, not quite whole, into a fairly typical decidedly mediocre format."[42]

Two seasons of the Father Brown tales were recorded for another new BBC Radio series in 1984 with Berlin-born Andreas (Andrew) Sachs as the priest in stories adapted from Chesterton's first collection, *The Innocence of Father Brown.* Already an experienced actor in television and film, Sachs enjoyed radio and, besides playing Chesterton's priest, he also portrayed another famous detective John Watson to Clive Merrison's Sherlock Holmes.[43] Flambeau was finally being played by a Frenchman, Olivier Pierre, after being portrayed by actors of almost every other nationality except French for years.

The voice of Welsh Shakespearean actor Emrys James portraying Father Brown was dubbed for Italian television in *Sei delitti per padre*

Brown (*Six Crimes for Father Brown*) in 1988. Like the Italian series with Renato Rascel (which the critic preferred because of Rascel's "liveliness"), this series also closely adhered to Chesterton's plots except for a few changes in titles, lest the plot or the villain's identity be given away. The time period remained early 20th-century Britain, but the setting was a large city instead of a small country village.[44]

Once again, Father Brown as a literary character successfully transitioned from 20th-century media to 21st and from an English country village to Germany with *Pfarrer Braun* (*Minister Brown*). Twenty-two episodes in the 2003–2014 German television series starred Ottfried Fischer as the maverick Bavarian priest Guido Braun; his sidekick is the inept Chief Inspector Albin Geiger. Aiding him in his investigations and to supplement the cast are the priest's talkative housekeeper Margot Rosshauptner and Armin Knopp, who was once falsely accused of a crime. When Pfarrer Braun gets Knopp released from prison, he becomes the priest's assistant; in return Pfarrer Braun serves as his parole officer.

Bishop Hemmelrath, aware that the Church's reputation rests on his shoulders, does not approve of Pfarrer Braun's investigating mysteries wherever he is stationed, especially when newspaper accounts begin calling Pfarrer Braun "God's Private Eye" or "Tabernacle Columbo."

So, the bishop transfers him to other parishes throughout Germany from Pfaffenberg to Potsdam in an attempt to discourage his sleuthing. But murder and death seem to follow Braun no matter where he's sent. Coincidentally, the bungling Inspector Geiger manages to get himself transferred to the same districts and assists the priest, while hoping to gain a promotion for himself based on Braun's solved cases. In turn, Geiger makes DNA or fingerprint analyses available to Pfarrer Braun.

In the first episode, "Der Siebte Tempel" ("The Seventh Temple"), Pfarrer Braun tells the Protestant police commissioner that "solving crimes is not a question of religion ... solving crime is a game for the mind." After mass at the prison, Pfarrer Braun confers with Bishop Hemmelrath who reprimands him once again for dabbling in mystery-solving and transfers him to a remote island where there are few Catholics and fewer crimes. He befriends an elderly lady who later dies from an accidental fall which Pfarrer Braun suspects is not so accidental, especially when there is a trust of 80,000 euros involved. Mindful of Hemmelrath's displeasure, he's hesitant to investigate but wonders, "What if the Lord sends me to places where there is a crime to be solved?"[45] Because of Ottfried Fischer's own diagnosis of Parkinson's disease, in the final episode—"Braun's Homecoming"—Braun learns that he suffers from a deadly disease. After solving his last case, the character dies in Rome, ending the series after 10 years.[46]

Ignatius Press, a Catholic Church–based company, published an audiobook version of Chesterton's first compilation *The Innocence of Father Brown* in 2008. Read by actor and Theater of the Word founder Kevin O'Brien, it features introductions written and read by Dale Ahlquist, president of the American Chesterton Society. O'Brien also teamed with the Chesterton Society to produce a 2009 made-for-TV movie based on Chesterton's story "The Honor of Israel Gow" in which he starred as Father Brown with Frank C. Turner as Israel Gow.[47]

Father Brown's popularity continued to flourish with the proliferation of audiobooks, podcasts, and local theater productions. For instance, in 2013, Boston's Colonial Radio Theater produced 16 Chesterton stories with J.T. Turner, an actor and voice-over artist, playing Father Brown. The production featured a complete cast, sound effects, and a musical score as in the early days of radio. In Spring of the same year, Little Candle Productions of Southern California, a community theater, performed "The Innocence of Father Brown," a script by Patrick Rieger that wove together stories from the collection. Blake Walker portrayed the priest-detective, Brandon Parrish as Flambeau was given a romantic interest, and Adam Daniel Elliott played Inspector Valentin.[48]

Merging two Father Brown stories—"The Invisible Man" and "The Curse of the Golden Cross"—John Goodrum created a whodunit for the Rumpus Theatre Company of Chesterfield, England. The company toured with the drama in Fall 2015 before staging the compilation drama "The Curse of the Invisible Man" at the London Theatre Royal in 2016–2017 with British television actor John Lyons as the clerical detective. The plot to Chesterton's fifth Father Brown story runs like this: John Turnbull Angus proposes marriage to Laura Hope. She tells him how, previously, when she had waitressed at her father's inn, two men—Isidore Smythe, a dwarf, and James Welkin who had an "appalling squint"—had proposed to her. She rejected them both because she found them ugly but, not wishing to hurt their feelings, she claimed she could only marry someone who made his living through his own efforts. Smythe went out and amassed a fortune by inventing robots to do domestic chores. Welkin instead harassed Laura: somehow she heard his voice when he wasn't there. He also hassled Smythe with threatening letters. After Angus enlisted the help of Flambeau and Father Brown to reassure Laura, Smythe's body was discovered in a canal. Father Brown realized that Welkin, costumed as a mailman, went about unnoticed. After murdering Smythe, he put his small body in his mail sack, later depositing it in the water. Welkin as a mailman was not truly invisible, instead he seemed part of the unremarkable scenery, someone no one ever noticed.[49]

In "The Curse of the Golden Cross," Chesterton told the story of how Father Brown met archeologist and lecturer Professor Smaill, world-traveler Lady Diana Wales, and journalist Leonard Smyth. Smaill had discovered a historical cross said to be cursed. Afterward, he was followed by a man who threatened to kill him if he didn't hand it over. Touring a tomb, Smaill stretched out to grab a similar-looking cross resting in a small coffin when his reach caused the stone lid to slam down on his head. Would the cursed cross destroy them all? Father Brown pointed out that the cross was rigged to a wooden peg, so when Smaill pulled the cross out, the lid was released, hitting him. Smaill recovered, but the man who had been pursuing Smaill committed suicide, thinking he had murdered the archeologist.[50]

In the composite of the two stories, Father Brown is called on to help Diana, an archeologist and good friend, when her niece Ella receives a letter from an old thieving boyfriend named James Welkin. As part of a plan to collect the entire set of five medieval daggers, Welkin hopes to steal the one that Diana has hidden in her house. With Ella and her new boyfriend Angus Turnbull, the four propose to capture the thief when he arrives. However, when Welkin's dead body is found in Ella's art studio, they realize they are all in great danger, especially since owners of the other daggers have all previously been killed.[51]

The Rumpus Theatre group toured during summer 2021 through spring 2022 with a new Father Brown drama titled "The Murderer in the Mirror." John Lyons reprised his role as Father Brown who is invited to watch the dress rehearsal of a West End production. Always in the right place at the right time, Father Brown is present when the director is shot in his dressing room, the plot based on Chesterton's story "The Actor and the Alibi." A shattered mirror and a cadre of possible suspects all onstage at the same time challenge the priest to find the murderer.[52]

When Father O'Connor, on whom Chesterton based Father Brown, wrote about his dear friend a year after his death in a book titled appropriately enough, *Father Brown on Chesterton*, it was clear from the first page how much mutual admiration had existed between the two men. Ranging from the topics they discussed throughout the years to their many shared adventures, at one point, O'Connor quotes the *Times Literary Supplement* to make the point about Chesterton's talent in communicating with his readers—"He is not a great teacher," wrote the *Times*. "He is a great entertainer. He is not a prophet. He is too entertaining."[53] Looking back, that genius became more obvious with every succeeding theatrical, cinematic, or audio presentation of the priest's tales. As Anthony Grist shrewdly observed, the gains of adapting stories such as the Father Browns to other mediums emphasize the good qualities inherent in the original. As much as they might have been tailored from Chesterton's works to make them compatible for a particular presentation, production companies worldwide simply found Chesterton's clerical detective too entertaining to ignore.

That insightfulness continues to this day. The most recent Father Brown program sets British actor Mark Williams in a BBC production. In this version, series creators Tahsin Guner and Rachel Flowerday incorporated Chesterton's literary Father Brown of 1910 into a cleric in a 1950s Cotswolds village. It was a potentially risky plan. As one Los Angeles reviewer had remarked about the disappointing Barnard Hughes' adaptation, "Updating and relocating famous literary figures is always chancy."[54]

Unlike previous interpretations which took the priest far and wide to Bavaria or New York City or Paris as in Chesterton's original stories, this Father Brown sticks close to home, tooling around his parish on a bicycle. Neither his message nor moral compass in condemning the sin but loving the sinner has veered off course. Over 10 seasons and 110 episodes (2013–2023), whatever the mystery or whoever the murderer is, Father Brown's first objective is to discover the criminal and convince him or her to repent. While such a righteous approach was judged "priggish" when portrayed by Alec Guinness, Williams' Father Brown offers sincere empathy for the lost souls he encounters and, through the actions of a simple priest, a mystery is solved and peace reigns once again, albeit temporarily, in the village of Kembleford.

Stepping into the priest's shoes after many wonderful performances by outstanding actors in the role, Mark Williams might be forgiven for wondering how earlier Father Browns handled the part. When a reporter asked if he had studied them as part of his preparation, Williams replied, "No—in fact quite the opposite. I'd never seen the Alec Guinness film but after I did the first series I did watch it and a bit of the Kenneth More series, but we're all radically different."[55]

From the United Kingdom to Italy to Japan, throughout Scandinavia and the United States, fans blog about eagerly anticipating the series to be shown on their local Public Broadcasting Stations or on BritBox. Father Brown continues to entertain, inspire, and charm, though, it must be admitted, not everyone views him in that light. In one episode, a police inspector accuses him of being "a loose cannon with delusions of grandeur. Meddlesome, recklessly foolhardy, morally dubious, yet possessed of a certain tiresome intelligence."[56]

Thousands of international fans would disagree with that negative assessment, but he gets the job done in such a charming manner, that's just the way they like him.

PART TWO

The BBC Production and Its Reception

3

The Newest Father Brown

"We don't always have murders [in Kembleford] but there
is a lot of crime."[1]

Journalist Sinclair McKay penned an op-ed in a 2009 edition of *The
Spectator*, a weekly British magazine, wondering when he could look forward to a new version of Father Brown. "Why," he wondered, "is Father
Brown not a part of that eternal ITV (Independent Television) Holmes/
Poirot/Marple television detective roster? ... [I]t's about time he became
a proper TV star."[2] Thirty years previously, a *New York Times* critic had
expressed similar sentiments in a review when, after Barnard Hughes had
portrayed Father Brown, he hoped for "further television dabblings into
the Chesterton character."[3]

With McKay's appeal in mind, producer and script editor John Yorke
was inspired by Ann Widdecombe's radio documentary on G.K. Chesterton to consider whether the Father Brown stories might be made into a
new television series. One of the first questions Yorke had to answer was
whether the subject matter might be too controversial. Protestant theologian Martin Marty, in his book on mass media and Christianity, believed
that, due to the expense of making movies and television, when profit was
paramount, such chancy subjects ought to be avoided lest they offend
viewers.[4] Instead, producers preferred to fund "safe" projects on general
or familiar subjects where large audiences and profits are more certain.
Yorke knew that Chesterton was one of the least offensive authors to modern audiences; any controversy surrounding social criticisms he may have
made died with the man in the mid–1930s. But what about making a Catholic priest the center of a series? During an era when reports of priests'
involvement in decades-long sexual abuse of children were being brought
to light in the media, Yorke had to think carefully about how to overcome
the risk. If any program with a Catholic priest as protagonist was to succeed, the character must be presented in a way that completely negates the
scandalous image associated with those reports.

Believing that Chesterton's clerical detective stories could be reworked to minimize the risk, Yorke proposed the idea to Liam Keelan, then the BBC's head of daytime television.

Yorke's cohort Ceri Meyrick, a BBC drama producer who had been associated with him at the Writers Academy, was on the lookout for work for newly trained writers. They approached Will Trotter, head of daytime drama, Birmingham Drama Village, and BBC Worldwide executives about subsidizing such a show that would appeal to international audiences.[5] They spoke to executives in the Daytime Television division because the Daytime division rather than prime time "had the vision and the bravery to commission us (Catholic priests aren't top of many drama controllers' go-to lists)," explained Rachel Flowerday, one of the new series' creators.[6]

Father Brown had not appeared on British television since Kenneth More's 1974 version, so it seemed an opportune time to bring him back. Given the green light, Meyrick approached Tahsin Guner and experienced writer Rachel Flowerday, former students at Writersroom, a BBC department that develops writers for dramas, comedy, and radio, and the BBC Writers' Academy, about creating Father Brown's world and populating it with supporting characters suitable for a television series.[7]

Shortly after commencing work on the new assignment, Flowerday blogged about its development and included an interview with herself and Guner wherein he confessed he'd never written a mystery drama nor had he even read Chesterton, facts that gave critics ammunition (and, no doubt, a few raised eyebrows) in their campaign to disparage the show from its inception. Flowerday was familiar with Chesterton but was apprehensive about adapting his beloved character and making the stories work for television.[8]

One consideration was whether to remain true to the priest as Chesterton wrote him. As *The Guardian*'s Michael Newton noted shortly after the series premiered, "Chesterton's protagonist is so humble a character, so unconcerned about his own self, that it's hard to make a show that focuses directly on him: Father Brown is comically unobtrusive."[9] The stories involved the activities of an unassuming cleric who occasionally does not appear until mid-story. In "The Oracle of the Dog," Father Brown doesn't even visit the scene of the crime. Ronald Knox, Chesterton's contemporary, had wondered how much mystery writers were constrained by the laws of probability. How unlikely is it that Father Brown would always be nearby when a crime was committed? It boiled down to simple "literary convention" that was not necessarily a good one, but one that was "well worn."[10] Father Brown's reasoning out the identity of the perpetrator is cerebral. He notices the tiniest clues—a wayward glance, an unconscious gesture, comments by others—on which the solution rests, and in that way, he identifies the villain, sometimes without a physical confrontation.

Such a device worked well in literature where the author could delve into the villain's motivations, but television drama requires action to hold the audience's interest. Thus, it was decided that the series would be *inspired* by Chesterton's original stories but would otherwise be very different. As Flowerday soon realized, "the tales themselves tend to follow an arc of brilliantly-described build-up with a final twist in the tale—perfect for bite-sized prose, but nowhere near twisty enough for ... TV drama."[11] Writing in his book *The Church on TV*, Lutheran theologian Richard Wolff argued that when television portrays the church, one of the first topics to occur is the conflict of the church with itself.[12] As several previous renditions of the Father Brown character had shown, the priest is often at odds with his bishop and the police regarding his penchant for sleuthing. The "twisty" bits for television were already present and just required fleshing out. However, because Chesterton most probably wrote the Father Brown stories when he was pressed for time and money, he increasingly relied on repetitive characters, situations, and themes, something that also had to be taken into consideration when writing for television, in case viewers became bored with recurring scenarios.

Flowerday maintained that another problem was copyright. In order to use Chesterton's stories, they had to be out of copyright in Britain and in the United States, which is usually defined as 70 or 75 years after the author's death. Because Chesterton wrote the Father Brown stories over the course of 25 years and because of the variances in copyright laws, many of the later stories were not useable. However, assuming no extenuating circumstances regarding copyright laws, it's curious that not more of the earlier stories were suitable. Chesterton died in 1936, making even his later works copyright-free in 2011.

The ATV productions of several of Chesterton's later stories by Kenneth More in 1974 had necessarily also fallen under copyright laws, such as "Arrow of Heaven," "Oracle of the Dog," "Curse of the Golden Cross," "Dagger with Wings," "Mirror of Magistrate," "Actor and the Alibi," and "The Quick One." In many of those, the situations and dialogue are taken directly from the stories. But the copyright status also explains the popularity and wide-spread dramatic use of "The Blue Cross," Chesterton's earliest Father Brown story from 1910. Several other of Chesterton's earlier stories were too short or too cerebral to be convertible to a 45-minute drama. As a result, more clues, more characters, and more dialogue was needed. So, only five Chesterton stories were considered adaptable, the rest had to be original scripts.

The two writers had a month and a half to create a first draft and a "bible," or series canon, which described the characters, how they would act, their values and relationships, and the overall feel of the series not only for themselves but for writers of future episodes. As with many television shows, since multiple writers and directors worked on different episodes, this was necessary to maintain a consistent style.

Jude Tindall wrote several scripts for the series, the first being Season 1's "The Bride of Christ." A lot of her ideas comes from daily newspapers, she said in an interview, but script writers for mysteries usually start with the murderer, then the reason for the murder and then continue on from there.

She explained the process of writing for *Father Brown.*

> The episode was commissioned in January so [the turnaround] is roughly around five months…. You pitch [your ideas] first then do a scene-by-scene breakthrough. You do six or seven drafts before you end up with the finished script, so it takes anywhere between 12–16 weeks … it is quite a long process![13]

Next to be determined was location. Unlike Chesterton's globetrotting Father Brown, the developers decided to set *Father Brown* in the Cotswolds.[14] With the relatively small budget available to them, there had to be one stationary location that included permissions to use nearby country estates, churches, and the villages proper. Commercial reasons warranted the location, executive producer Will Trotter clarified; historical adaptations were quite costly to film.

Trotter should know, having worked in television since the 1990s and as a producer since 2003. In his role as executive producer for several series, one of his priorities was dealing with funding, assuring that the money allotted for the project is spent wisely and making certain the episode or series comes in on time to avoid any overages. He also may acquire scripts and hire the cast and film crew. Whereas other people involved in a production do their jobs and leave, like writers or guest stars, executive producers stay with the show, providing a sense of continuity. Always keeping in mind the BBC's goals and function in UK (and worldwide) viewing, Trotter is the man to most heartily endorse each season before it begins as well as to recap it at its completion.

Also, since the BBC is not permitted to have a program with advertising commercials to sell a commodity or service in the UK, it needs to make its productions attractive to foreign audiences. Because BBC Worldwide co-funded the series expecting a global sales market, they expected to display the best of England to the world, and the Cotswolds had some of its most beautiful scenery. As Sorcha Cusack, who played Mrs. McCarthy, commented after several seasons of filming: "You can't say it's the worst place in the world to work."[15] Trotter was enthusiastic as he continued: "It's timeless: you can almost shoot through 360 degrees once you've moved the [modern] cars out of the way. And, second, it has these amazing houses— quite moneyed and full of antiques and looking lovely—that we can tell the mysteries in."[16]

Tom Chambers, who played Inspector Sullivan, was equally enthusiastic about the Cotswolds locations. "Everywhere you look, you feel as though you're in a novel … you turn up to these incredible mansions that you would never normally get to see because they're tucked away behind long driveways and woods and trees."[17] About 80 miles northwest of London, the scenic area of old villages built from local honey-colored limestone was ideal. Its 800 square miles luxuriant with quaint homes and rural landscapes provided a setting that did indeed show off the best of England to the world. The fact that it was close to Birmingham, the production base, was a plus.

So, Father Brown was to be firmly ensconced as the parish priest of St. Mary's Church in Kembleford, a fictional Cotswolds village. Blockley's Anglican church of Saints Peter and Paul served as the setting for church scenes. Several seasons in, journalist Kate O'Hare interviewed Mark Williams and mentioned,

> Originally built in the late Norman period, it wasn't always Anglican. "Sorry," says Williams…. "Of course, it was Catholic." It's an irony of historically Catholic England that its ancient Catholic churches were taken over by the Church of England, and many current Catholic churches were built in the 20th century. So, if you want to shoot a Catholic show in a beautiful old English church, you're probably going to be in an Anglican parish.[18]

Around the village, a local vicarage was renamed a Catholic presbytery (what American Catholics might call a rectory); the Great Western Railway (GWR) was pressed into service as were other neighboring churches, castles, schools, mansions, and police stations. One such building was the former Moreton-in-Marsh hospital, now owned by the National Health Service. It closed to patients in 2009, but the NHS made it available for the filming of *Father Brown*. Besides serving as a medical facility in those episodes where such a setting was needed, the building's various areas also functioned as the police station, the presbytery kitchen, and Father Brown's study. Set designer Francis Boyle loved the look of the old building. After making sketches of how he wanted the final venue to look, he set builders to constructing rooms apropos to the series.[19] And so, to the quiet village came a production crew that unfortunately brought an element of (fictional) wrongdoing.

Over lunch with executives John Yorke, Will Trotter, Ceri Meyrick, series producer Sam Hill, and script editor Neil Irvine, Guner and

Flowerday also chose a time period and the supporting characters.[20] Instead of adhering strictly to Chesterton's protagonist who had entertained readers from 1910 to 1935, they updated the stories to a 1950s Britain recovering from World War II under the governance of the newly crowned Queen Elizabeth II.

The decade worked because, like Chesterton's detective, this new Father Brown also solved crimes based on his knowledge of human nature without relying on modern technology, like DNA, cell phones, or criminal databases. Prospective themes could now include the 1950s' concerns of threats of the atom bomb, obsolete and brand-new medical practices, recovery from World War II, immigration, and race relations. Trotter believed that Chesterton would be okay with the differences because he, too, was passionate about social issues.[21] Mark Williams also thought the 1950s setting was a good decision because the decade "was the incubation period for a lot of things … [t]he beginning of television, the beginning of popular music available to everybody, the beginning of being able to use your car at will, the beginning of feminism, the beginnings of increased understanding of what racism meant."[22] Too, with the limited budget allocated for the daytime program, modern costumes and sets more closely resembled those of the '50s decade than those of 1910.

The all-important step of casting came next. In his 2009 article, McKay had suggested Martin Clunes of *Doc Martin* fame as a good choice to play Father Brown. But, similar to Kenneth More being tapped to play Father Brown with no warning or audition, so it happened with then 59-year-old Mark Williams. He was on location in Northern Ireland filming the first season of another BBC series, *Blandings*, in which he played the butler Beach, when his agent phoned to report that BBC Birmingham was offering him a role in a new mystery television program. "I said: 'Oh brilliant—what's the part? A murderer? A kindly doctor?'" When she informed him it was the title role in *Father Brown*, Williams thought for 10 seconds, then said yes. "I knew instantly what I'd do with the role."[23]

After playing the priest for several seasons, Williams recollected,

> After *Harry Potter* [in which he played Arthur Weasley], I didn't need the money, but the idea of having my own series was very seductive. Also, G.K. Chesterton's Father Brown stories are so fascinating. Most whodunits are about conundrums and intellectual problems, but Father Brown is more about an emotional reaction, and how this priest believes people should respond to extremity.[24]

Williams was perfect for the role. Will Trotter thought he "is a really good actor in terms of the range that he can do…. He can do comedy, and he can do really intelligent character acting."[25] Mark Williams was once described as one of Britain's best comedians, but he insisted, "I am not a comic, not even a comedy actor.... I can't do stand-up."[26] His reputation doubtless came from the numerous shticks he had performed on Britain's *The Fast Show*, a comedy sketch program. Trotter explained what the BBC looked for in Williams that convinced them he'd be perfect for the role: "What you don't want is a two-dimensional comedy priest; that would be really uninteresting. But, at the same time, you need someone who can be a bit irreverent, because Brown is a maverick in the way that he deals with the world."[27]

Appearing in a historical drama suited Williams just fine. In a later interview, he revealed that he had had a passion for history since he was a youngster. Before becoming Father Brown, he had made three documentaries on industrial history for the BBC and had always preferred reading books over watching television; reading was "a massive part of my life," he said.[28] Being extremely well read, Williams filled a bookshelf on the set for Father Brown's study with volumes he had collected over the years that included references, books on poisons and death, almanacs, and other 1950-era books, "Everything I could get hold of on the Catholic Church, pre- and post–Vatican II." He admitted to being "quite proud of it really."[29] Rachel Flowerday recalled how he "totally took the ball and ran with it. He did masses of research, he really engages with the Latin, he really engages with the books, so he's really properly become Father Brown."[30]

After only one season, Williams' co-stars agreed. Alex Price, who plays Sid Carter, remarked, "I've never come across a fierce intelligence like Mark Williams.... [The show] needs someone who has the intelligence to lead it the way he does." Nancy Carroll, as Lady Felicia Montague, quickly realized, "He's brilliant. And if there's a book to be read about the subject on which the episode is based, he will read it. He knows his stuff. You know, I think like all of us, he's passionate about getting it right, and about good storytelling." Tom Chambers, Inspector Sullivan, observed that "he's a perfect fit for Father Brown. He looks the part, I'm sure he's really worked out for it. He's got just the right look."[31] When Emer Kenny joined the cast in Season 5, she found that Williams "has such a brilliant mind and has totally made Father Brown his own: modern, eccentric and loveable."[32]

At the same time as his co-actors were crediting him with leading the team, Mark Williams saw it as a collaborative effort, modestly sharing the acclaim. "The sort of television we're making, which is quick—and quick is often good—it's nimble, it's light on its feet."[33] Doubtless, Williams was referring to the limited budget and its attendant constrained filming time frame where there was little chance of multiple takes of a scene. Actors must be on their mark and ready when the director called, "Action!"

While Mark Williams does look the part of a kindly village priest in his long black cassock, his resemblance to the literary Father Brown is not so apparent. The myriad brown paper wrapped packages are gone, though the commonplace black umbrella accompanies him everywhere.[34] In a "Behind the Scenes" snippet from 8.3 "The Scales of Justice," Williams talked about the umbrella. When Father Brown is working a case, he carries the umbrella pointed to the side so that it resembles a question mark. When the case is solved, he carries it with the curved handle facing backward or forward.

Williams' height (six feet) and sophistication cannot compare to Chesterton's short, clumsy little man with "a face as round and dull as a Norfolk dumpling." One reporter asked Williams how he felt about being considered the perfect actor to fill the role. "Doesn't bother me," he answered, obviously not caring about the lack of physical resemblance. "Part of what makes this character work is that you under-estimate him when you look at him.... Really, what casting is all about is that they want you to solve a problem, namely—how do you translate what the writer wants, and also what the director wants, onto the screen. Every part I've ever been chosen for is because someone's decided I can probably do that pretty well."[35]

Playing the fictional priest has often affected actors in unexpected ways. Alec Guinness was inspired to convert to Catholicism; four years after he appeared in the television series, Kenneth More was approached by a woman to hear her confession.[36] Mark Williams found that playing Father Brown "has taught me to be more accepting. I wasn't particularly judgemental of people before; but now I am not at all. It has also made me a better detective." Williams is not Catholic and didn't want to label himself. He revealed that he was raised in the Church of England but doesn't practice any particular religion. In another interview, he referred to himself as a "pantheistic humanist" who finds Father Brown interesting for his "huge appetite for the detail of life and for humanity." He considered that Father Brown "believes in redemption, and he believes that we're all God's children, and he's a man of faith, so I respect him."[37]

Williams repeated in a separate interview: "That's the most interesting thing about [Father Brown] as a sleuth: it's not him solving a conundrum or a crossword, he's dealing with what he sees as people's eternal damnation." He resumed, "Brown is relevant in a way that anybody is relevant who has clarity. It doesn't mean that his personality isn't in conflict, but he doesn't shift his attitude: people are people and faith is faith. He's one of those people who's fed by life. It doesn't feed on him."[38]

Acting the priest is one thing; looking like one is something else. Williams remembered being fitted for his costume at J. Wippell, a clerical outfitter.[39] The cassock, he said, is the "real deal. It buttons all the way up and down and the costume designer said, 'Do you want us to put Velcro on it?' And I said no. So every time I do a take and finish the take I have to unbutton the whole cassock and button it back up. Recently I was talking to another priest … and he said, 'Ah yes but if you use Velcro the cassock never hangs properly' and he's right."[40] Viewers may also have noticed that, for special occasions, he wears an elbow-length cape called a pelegrina over the cassock.

Despite any initial clumsiness involved in getting accustomed to wearing a priest's long robe, Williams admits he grew "surprisingly fond of Brown's trademark shabby robes and misshapen hat. 'I have to say that the dress of a Catholic priest is brilliant. Apart from bicycling, which is tricky.'"[41] He continued, "When you read the script and it says, 'Father Brown cycles really quickly up to the front door,' and you go like, uh, no."[42] But, after several seasons, Williams offhandedly remarked, "I've never been one of those walk-on-stage-and-stand-still actors…. So riding a bike wearing a cassock, you just work out how to do it, and there's a lot of pleasure in solving problems, because that's a lot of what acting is about."[43] Still, to capture the feat, there is a "tracking vehicle, a rickshaw driven by cameraman Richard Hines, who cycles alongside me to get the shot. It's very exciting doing stunts and crashes."[44]

However, Williams didn't realize how warm the cassock would be in summer when the episodes are filmed. A New Zealand interviewer thought, "The simplest solution, surely, would be to simply take off his pants. After all, who would know? … [H]e'd still be wearing the flowing robes of a Catholic priest over the top, like an airy kaftan." But Williams would not hear of it, even if it does get "bloody hot." "There's the crew, standing around in shorts and sandals, while Williams swelters in black trousers, black shoes, socks, long-sleeved shirt, wide-brimmed hat, overcoat, and long black cassock…. 'We talked about losing the pants,' [Williams said,] 'but I just couldn't bring myself to do it. No one else could tell if I was just in my Jockeys, but I would know, and it would fundamentally alter the character.'"[45] But, he added, "I have to be very zen to get through it."[46]

Father Tony Nye, a London-based priest of the Society of Jesus, could relate. In the third season, he replaced Father Gwilym Lloyd, the first real priest/advisor brought in to certify that scripts and settings were authentically Catholic pre–Vatican Council II. Father Brown's hearing confessions, his pronunciation of Latin, and the quotes of Biblical verses needed to be true to the period. However, Fathers Lloyd and Nye have allowed scripts enabling this Father Brown to be much more politically correct than a 1950s priest might have been. In episodes dealing with the Church's failings, homosexuality, or other less mainstream religions, for instance,

Mark Williams' Father Brown is quite enlightened and liberal in his reactions that more generally reflect the 21st-century way of thinking rather than the mid–20th century. But Father Nye neglected to teach the cast several mandatory Catholic practices such as genuflecting in front of the tabernacle on the altar and speaking softly when in the church. The set designer should have been informed of having a red sanctuary light burning to indicate the presence of the Blessed Sacrament and of the fact that women in those years were required to wear hats in church and men were required to remove theirs.

As appearances go, Father Nye thought that perhaps "[Father Brown's] cassock and soup plate hat wouldn't be the regular gear of many priests of the time, but I let that pass for its dramatic value of character recognition."[47] Another part of a priest's garb is the stole that's about eight feet long and two to four inches wide that hangs around the priest's neck for Mass and other services. Father Lloyd presented Williams with a shorter pocket stole to use when he finds a dead body or hears an impromptu confession. Viewers will often see Father Brown kiss the cross sewn onto the back of it as a sign of Christ's yoke. "It's a kind of spiritual emergency kit," said Williams. To get the character authentic, Williams said, "I also wanted to ask him about how you deal with the dead, what obeisance you would make for a dead body that had just been stabbed, for instance—that kind of detail."[48] To complete the costume, Williams also added a pair of round glasses. In several of Chesterton's stories, Father Brown wears moonlike spectacles and cannot read without peering closely at the printed word as though he were very near-sighted.[49]

Viewers see Father Brown greet his congregants before or after Mass, a common practice. Though hearing confession—usually from the crime's perpetrator—is *de rigueur* for a series with a sleuthing cleric, television or movie priests may prepare sermons, perform baptisms or weddings, or officiate at funerals, but audiences seldom see them and their parishioners during a service. This may not be so unusual, Richard Wolff points out. Rarely are the church's rituals broadcast as entertainment.[50] Previous adaptations of the priest, particularly in the German films, showed Father Brown processing in to say Mass, genuflecting before the altar, facing the congregation to intone "Dominus vobiscum" ("The Lord be with you"), and preaching from the pulpit but stopped at actually re-creating the Mass. Occasionally, Father Brown's deep faith is explored, and he is seen lighting a candle or kneeling before the altar meditating or praying, particularly when he is most puzzled by a mystery.

Aside from the challenging work of acting in an unaccustomed role, Williams found doing the series "seductive." It's obvious he thought about the character a great deal.

There are no vague grey areas for this guy. If you lie to God, you risk eternal damnation. He doesn't judge because he thinks people will be judged in the afterlife. Criminals are making decisions about what will happen to their very souls.... Father Brown is more about spirituality and intuition. He's endlessly fascinated by human nature and incredibly nosey, and there's absolutely nothing that's not worthy of attention.[51]

The series' writers put Father Brown in situations to which all Catholic parish priests could relate. He worries about parish finances, presides over weddings and funerals, and hears confessions. Occasionally he's in trouble with his bishop, not for uninspiring sermons or sloppy liturgy but, like other Father Browns before him, for his determination to solve the mystery of whodunit.

Fortunately, Father Brown has a band of unlikely collaborators to aid his investigations. Traditional detectives have had their sidekicks— Holmes had his Watson, Poirot his Hastings—relationships which Neil McCaw in his *Adapting Detective Fiction* refers to as symbiotic,

in which individual inspiration has less of a part to play. Truth and meaning are revealed ... through group participation.... Criminals stand much more clearly in opposition to a collective national identity, with the prevailing morality reinforced by more than a single outrider.[52]

Commonly called "stock characters," previous Father Brown adaptations included a housekeeper, a disapproving bishop, and inept police. After viewing an episode or two, and, perhaps from personal experience, audiences are conditioned to understand the motives and tendencies of such characters. Alden Dalia, an executive at WME talent agency, believes that characters "you become completely entranced with" who inhabit a world you want to spend time in make the show. Interesting and complex television is centered around such characters and their development; thus, a diverse cast "provide[s] the greatest potential for maximizing viewership and boosting ratings."[53] Fortunately, in the BBC's *Father Brown*, even the "extras" are well-drawn with distinct personalities and serve a real purpose in helping Father Brown solve the mystery *du jour*.

The censorious Mrs. McCarthy acts as parish secretary and unofficial personal assistant. She ensures that Father Brown is treated with respect, has clean cassocks and hot meals, and reminds him of his appointments. Flowerday recalls that she pitched an idea for a "doughty, no-nonsense 60-something lay second-in-command who's kind of a mother-figure but who probably also slightly fancies him/dotes on him ... someone to check facts for him, to protect him from the wrath of the diocese, to make sure he eats."[54] And, just like that, the presbytery housekeeper gossipy Mrs. Bridget McCarthy was born.

Played by Irish actress Sorcha Cusack (American pronunciation sor-kuh cue-zuk), she and Father Brown are like an old married couple though he always respectfully refers to her as Mrs. McCarthy, even when she's been poisoned and is near death.[55] Several times, when she's come through with a particular insight or has provided an important clue, he praises her as being "an angel and a saint rolled into one." Relying on local gossip for facts as village busybody, she is unafraid to speak her mind and share her ill-gotten stories with other ladies of the same character. Unfortunately, her oft-expressed critical opinions of others and her holding to strict Catholic tradition when justice or mercy should prevail instead gets her in trouble with Father Brown and, in the end, she is forced to retract, or contradict, her own comments, usually insisting she never said any such thing in the first place. Nevertheless, she is flattered when the priest requests her sleuthing assistance. In episode 6.4, he assures her she is "completely irreplaceable." Indeed, though he censoriously acknowledges her indulgence in gossip, he does occasionally find her a useful font of village information.

Mrs. M, as she is affectionately called, occasionally tries to temper his enthusiasm for dubious schemes to catch a criminal and repeatedly warns him to be careful. While many Catholics have kindly memories of the parish secretaries of the 1950s who cleaned the rectory and cooked for the resident priests, Chesterton devotee Kevin O'Brien stoutly criticized the addition of Mrs. McCarthy to the cast, despite the appearance of the housekeeper role in nearly every previous adaptation of *Father Brown*. O'Brien wrote in his blog, "I personally feel that most parish secretaries fit somewhere below DRE's [digital rectal exams] and somewhere above Parish Nurses in the Hierarchy of Hell."[56] In that, he agrees with Mrs. McCarthy's long-lost husband who returns to denigrate her role as parish secretary, thinking she must be bored with her life to do such work.[57] To these two men, Mrs. M would surely take umbrage by refusing either of them any of her award-winning strawberry scones.

In contrast to the Mrs. McCarthys of 1950s society, Nancy Carroll regards her character—the posh socialite Lady Felicia Montague—as "very saucy" who is always willing to lend a hand and her social connections in any investigations.[58] Lady Felicia occasionally is in the right place at the right time to discover a corpse; her screams at finding one are legendary. Why? Because "she just has that sort of personality, and partly because it just gets written into lots and lots of different episodes."[59] Though she occasionally mentions him, the viewing audience never meets her husband Lord (Monty) Montague until the 100th episode in Season 9. Wherever he's off to on official government business, she has no qualms about brazenly flirting with any handsome guest star in his absence, including the thief Flambeau. Lady Felicia and Mrs. McCarthy have a love/hate relationship, and most of the time they manage to co-exist peacefully, even lovingly. Felicia acknowledges early on that Mrs. McCarthy is disadvantaged when it comes to controlling her tongue, but once, after a tiff between them, Mrs. M conceded rather bluntly to Felicia, "You think I'm a foolish old woman with ideas above my station … and I think you're a stuck-up madam with too much time on your hands."[60] They reconciled, although later Mrs. M thoughtlessly blurts out that Lady Felicia is more decorative than useful, a comment that is followed shortly thereafter by an apology.[61]

Alex Price plays former small-time con man Sidney Carter who comes complete with lock-picking tools which he teaches the mechanics of to his priestly friend. Sid effortlessly discards his conscience when it comes to aiding and abetting any of Father Brown's dubious schemes. He doubles as Lady Felicia's chauffeur and still can hustle with the best of them, though Father Brown attempts to keep him on the straight and narrow and mostly succeeds. In an emotional moment in episode 5.11 when Sid is ready to use violence in his search for vengeance, Father Brown tries desperately to foil his plans, wondering if this might be the one mystery he will be unable to solve. The priest admits that he tries to save Sid from himself, because Sid is "the closest thing I have ever had to a son."[62] Price left the series after Season 6 to perform on stage as the aged Draco Malfoy in *Harry Potter and the Cursed Child* but, like Nancy Carroll, reappears occasionally in later episodes.

Kasia Koleczek played Susie Jasinski, Mrs. McCarthy's housekeeping aide. As a Polish immigrant, her character provided a historically accurate storyline as well as emphasizing one of the various ethnic diversities that the church served. After the first season, Koleczek left to star as the female lead in the thriller *Albert and Elizabeta*.

In a blog essay, Professor of Religious Studies Pamela Milne observed that none of the characters have any other real family nearby: Father Brown's family is not mentioned at all.[63] Mrs. McCarthy's long-lost husband reappears in one episode hoping she will care for him in his last illness (she won't); her sister visits from Ireland following a gypsy fortune-teller. Lady Felicia is childless and is left alone to dally with available men while Monty is away. Sid has occasional girlfriends, but his birth family is not mentioned; like Lady Felicia, her niece Bunty has flings with several men but also is mostly alone. Even Flambeau has a daughter whom he rarely sees and has just recently come to know, but because of their chosen occupations, they go their separate ways. As a result, the close-knit friends of St. Mary's parish have formed a sort of spiritual family in their care for each other.[64] Viewers don't learn about the families of Inspectors

Valentine or Sullivan, but the longest-running Inspector Mallory has a wife and children which tend to cause him aggravation at times; at other times he shows immense pride in them. Sergeant Goodfellow refers to having a wife waiting for him at home, and she is seen in several scenes when he is out of uniform.

Stereotypically, the police officials in crime dramas are either fastidious in their investigations or hopelessly bungling. When an ordinary citizen is able to discover clues and solve a mystery, the official stance is one of resentment and frustration. This is also reflected in the current proliferation of "cozy" mysteries wherein a local librarian, knitting shop owner, or baker concludes that they alone can find out who killed the mayor, do-gooder, or Boy Scout leader because they know the community and its residents, allegedly much better than police professionals. Uncovering the mystery of the criminal and his motive often involves the clash of opposing abilities. Chesterton recognized this in his story titled "The Mirror of the Magistrate." In it, Detective Bagshaw complains,

> Ours is the only trade … in which the professional is always supposed to be wrong. After all, people don't write stories in which hairdressers can't cut hair and have to be helped by a customer; or in which a cabman can't drive a cab until his fare explains to him the philosophy of cab-driving.[65]

In the BBC series, various police inspectors toe the law-and-order line, but most often, they're one or two steps behind Father Brown and, for that, persist in their resentment of his intrusion. All in all, unlike Chesterton's Father Brown whose interactions with the police seem to run on parallel tracks rather than competitively, Williams' sleuth is not looked upon kindly by Kembleford's police inspectors, nor by others he may target in his investigations. He's been called "an interfering priest," "a puppet of the Vatican," and "a pain in the proverbial …" among other slights.[66]

The first of the police officials was the French Inspector Valentin from Chesterton's stories. However, despite his playing an important role in "The Blue Cross," in the second story, "The Secret Garden," Chesterton surprised his readers by making Valentin himself a murderer who eventually commits suicide. As an "anti-clerical of some note," Valentin was dismayed to learn that a multi-millionaire was in the process of converting to Catholicism, after which he would likely bequeath much of his wealth to his new church. As a man gone mad, Valentin "would do anything, anything, to break what he calls the superstition of the Cross."[67]

With the slight, but significant, addition of the final e after Valentin's name, the BBC writers changed the inspector's nationality from French to British and hired a British actor to fill the role. The new Valentine was not so desperate, not so insane, and was in turn admiring and frustrated in his interactions with the priest. When Hugo Speer was hired for the role, he (and the succeeding police inspectors) was given second billing in each episode's introduction, right after Mark Williams. The writers knew he was already contracted for a role in *The Musketeers;* as a result, when Speer left after the first episode in Season 2, it was explained that Inspector Valentine had been promoted within the police ranks and was headed to London. His leaving this way also created the opportunity for Valentine to return to Kembleford at some point in the future.

Tom Chambers, as Inspector Sullivan, replaced Speer. The second police official to grace the BBC series, Sullivan's attitude toward priestly interference in his criminal cases followed even more steadfastly his predecessor's approach. In an interview, Chambers fleshed out his interpretation of his character: "[Sullivan]'s well read, a gadget man up to speed with science and forensics—he goes in with reason and rationality as the primary tools of his enquiring mind…. Father Brown is constantly outdoing him and Sullivan finds that very irritating…. They're constantly at loggerheads because he doesn't want Brown's interference…. He just wants to solve the cases and be the hero."[68] The debonair Sullivan often must hold his temper in check when Father Brown points out a wound or other significant detail that Sullivan inadvertently overlooked. Happily, many episodes later, Inspector Sullivan finally appreciates the priest's unique talent and suggests they work together.

But, with no explanation to the viewing audience, Chambers too was gone after Season 3 to be replaced by Jack Deam as the irascible Inspector Mallory.

Deam admits that he enjoys playing Mallory because "I can just get to be grumpy all day … the baddie or the grumpy characters are far more entertaining to play."[69] Mallory, costumed in suit and overcoat à la Columbo, finds police work tedious and rarely conducts thorough investigations or, as Father Brown observed, "the Inspector sometimes comes to a conclusion, and then looks for evidence to support it."[70] As a result, those conclusions are frequently invalid, illogical, or simply incorrect. Nevertheless, he resents the "Padre's" interference. In one episode, he urges Father Brown out of his office with the suggestion that he get on with his work, like "souls to save, sinners to punish, children to indoctrinate."[71] Like his predecessors, Mallory does not appreciate Father Brown's setting forth the correct solution before he does.

Mallory's second-in-command, Sergeant Goodfellow, is portrayed by John Burton, and it doesn't take long for long-suffering Goodfellow to become frustrated and irritated at his new boss. Originally a background character without a lot to do or say, the writers have allowed Goodfellow to become a character in his own right, one who is increasingly sympathetic to Father Brown and less loyal to his superior in the police force.[72]

Lady Felicia's niece Penelope Windermere, better known as Bunty and played by Emer Kenny, joined the Kembleford team when Nancy Carroll left the series after season 6 to allegedly be with her husband, now a government official in Rhodesia. Bunty provides a younger face and, as Kenny succinctly puts it, "drives Jags and solves crimes."[73] Since she feels she's stuck in Kembleford, besides attending parties when and where she can find them, Bunty enjoys participating in Father Brown's mystery solving. Kenny claims to love playing Bunty because she's "really outspoken, brave, and always bold…. Bunty will always pick the most exciting, slightly dangerous option."[74]

Chesterton had confided by his fifth story—"The Invisible Man"—that Flambeau was the priest's "only friend in the world" and afterward became the only recurring character.[75] In Kenneth More's version, the writers had transformed the master thief into a detective and, possibly with a nod to Chesterton, the only person Father Brown could trust. As with adapting the French *Valentin* to the British *Valentine* in the newest BBC series, the producers continued the tradition and hired British actor John Light as Flambeau and changed his nationality from French to British. Nevertheless, with ostensibly no conscience, instead of being a confidante, Light's Flambeau endures as a thorn in Father Brown's side. The two lock horns, going up against each other again and again in a battle of wits, a battle that Father Brown hopes will eventually result in Flambeau's repentance and salvation. For being such an important character in all previous adaptations for radio or television, Light's Flambeau only appears in one episode in each season.

Clifford Stumme discusses the role of the secondary characters in his thesis on didacticism in Chesterton's *Father Brown*. While the detective's role is "truth seeking," the "underappreciated" rest of the cast gave Chesterton—and those in the BBC's *Father Brown*—"the perfect opportunity to enlighten while entertaining." When Father Brown explains his plan to Mrs. McCarthy, Lady Felicia, or Bunty, he can show or teach them, and simultaneously the audience learns what he has in mind.[76] In general, Mark Williams' Father Brown looks very kindly on his extended spiritual family, but occasions arise where he must gently nudge, with a verbal cue or eyebrow raising, the indiscretion of one of them. He might look the other way when Sid deftly employs his lock-picks so as not to be a party to the crime (that is, until he acquires a set of his own) or glare over the top of his glasses at Mrs. McCarthy's gossip, a look that delivers the subliminal message that she is doing something wrong.

Stumme continues his assertion that Chesterton also created

antagonistic relationships between his characters so he could explore the contrast between them.

> [T]hese direct binaries are relationships between two characters that have opposing views on the philosophical, economic, religious, etc. The characters interact with each other in a parable of how their philosophies interact, and Chesterton often comes to a conclusion on which idea is right, a conclusion supported by those characters' dialogue or actions.[77]

The most obvious binaries are, of course, Lady Felicia and Mrs. McCarthy. As for Father Brown and Flambeau, the priest's incessant reformation tactics only serve to amuse the thief who has no intention of giving up his chosen criminal profession.

With characters defined and cast hired, by January 2012, scripts were readied, and production was moving along. Flowerday remembers, "The read-through of our first two episodes was magical—Mark Williams *was* Father Brown, Sorcha Cusack made Mrs. McCarthy emphatically her own … their faith in the scripts couldn't fail to excite us."[78]

If there were problems facing the production, at the top of the list would be that each episode's allowance was only £250,000 (about $317,000), compared to a primetime drama with a £1 million ($1,300,000) budget.[79] The actors quickly learned to deal with the reality of having little money for extras, like the luxury of postponing scenes to another day to avoid bad weather or of having the opportunity for Father Brown to travel outside Kembleford. Jack Deam's experience had taught him that "with television now you don't get rehearsals; you turn up and hit the ground running," particularly when the budget allowed limited preparations.[80]

Mark Williams took it all in stride: "We have budget problems, we're constrained. I mean, we can make virtues out of them, this is amusing, not a symphony. But then we like that. We get tired, but we don't get bored." Tahsin Guner also looked at it optimistically and gave credit to all those working behind the scenes: "It doesn't *look* like it has a low budget … a lot of that has to do with the costume designing, the locations, everything that goes into—the sort of the love that goes into—the making of the show."[81]

A secondary problem quickly became obvious when the exterior shots were filmed during warm, and occasionally wet, British weather. Williams reported, "When [the rain] lashes down[,] the Cotswold mud is very fine and slithery and it can be really difficult for the production guys to move things around. And the wind is not helpful for sound." As an example of a scene shot in the rain, see episode 8.3 "The Scales of Justice." When Bunty approaches her car in the lane in one of the early scenes, raindrops are visible. Perhaps a tarp was stretched over the location because the actors themselves don't appear to get more than slightly misted. Filming a period piece in a modern village could also grind to a halt to allow for the occasional sound of a plane flying over or a nearby gardener cutting the lawn.[82]

Overall, Williams is proud of the way the show turned out: "I think Father Brown is extraordinarily good, and not because I am in it.... We do the English detective genre very well. There's a satisfying sense that people look normal then stab each other to death, but nicely."[83] One only needs to google a search for British crime dramas to verify Williams' comment: *Agatha Christie's Poirot* ran 24 years and *Midsomer Murders* 25 years, just to name two.

As the BBC intended, the effort and quality were appreciated worldwide; the first series had been viewed in 232 countries with 2.5 million viewers in the UK alone.[84] One of the valued aspects of the Father Brown series is that the episodes can be watched in any order. This allowed the BBC to sell any variety of episodes to international networks. Except for the two episodes (5.6 and 6.2) involving convicted murderer Katherine Corven, there is no chronological sequence from one episode to the next.

Before the second season began filming, executive producer Trotter was touting the virtues of the program. "This wonderful series gives us a great opportunity to build on BBC Birmingham's drama expertise in creating popular returning period drama series, featuring lavish locations, classy artistes and telling compelling stories."[85] Richard Wolff had found that programs based on the church often did not do as well in the ratings as series focusing on other institutions such as law, medicine, or education. *Father Brown* was about to prove him wrong.[86]

Caution: The president of the American Chesterton Society quoted Chesterton saying, "The man who tells the ending of a detective story 'is simply a wicked man, as wicked as the man who deliberately breaks a child's soap-bubble.'"[87] For fear of the present author being accused of such daring wickedness, what follows in the next chapter are teasing quotations, synopses of the episodes, and "British-isms" of *Father Brown*, perhaps best not read until after viewing the episode.

4

The Episodes

Daniel—"You've a keen mind. You're wasted out here."

Father Brown—"On the contrary, I think that you've proved that this is where I should be."[1]

Season 1 began on January 14, 2013, with a totally re-written and expanded adaptation of Chesterton's ninth Father Brown short story, "The Hammer of God." The episode introduced threads that continued throughout the series: Mrs. McCarthy's pride in her award-winning strawberry scones, Lady Felicia's pitch-perfect scream at finding a dead body, Father Brown's unwelcome and barely tolerated intrusion into police affairs, and the inspector's reluctant admission that the priest has solved the mystery long before the police. Each episode begins with a teaser that featured the victim, followed by a series of potential murder suspects for the audience and Father Brown to narrow down.

Viewers are introduced to the unique settings of St. Mary's presbytery, the stations and tracks of Britain's Great Western Railway, and the lovely buildings of Kembleford. Experts on hand ensured accuracy in all aspects of the show: Dr. Bob Bushaway, a recognized authority on World War I, served as historical advisor, and John MacDonald gave advice as police consultant. Mark Williams had occasion to use Father Gwilym Lloyd's mini-stole and to wear Catholic ritual garb such as the decorative chasuble worn when celebrating Mass. Its colors varied according to the occasion or the church's calendar: purple for Advent and Lent, white for weddings or baptisms, black for funerals, green for ordinary times.

Shortly after the greatly anticipated program premiered, critics wondered why it was shown at 2:10 on weekday afternoons when it appeared much more suitable for a Sunday evening time slot. This exasperation continued throughout the run of the series with the question posed not only by critics, but by the actors themselves once it became clear just how popular the show was.

Season 1

1.1 "The Hammer of God"

Father Brown—"I don't so much look for mysteries as they come looking for me."

Original Air Date: January 14, 2013
Writer: Tahsin Guner
Director: Ian Barber
Father Brown investigates the motives of four suspects when a cruel man is killed during a church fete.
Guest Stars:
    Barry Sloane as Simeon Barnes
    Oliver Ryan as Philip Walker
    Bryony Afferson as Elizabeth Barnes
    Sam Hoare as Norman Bohun
    Adam Astill as Rev. Wilfred Bohun

- Homosexuality had been illegal in Britain since the 16th century. Recently it came to be considered a pathological or psychological condition requiring treatments such as chemical castration, i.e., drugs used to lower the sex drive. In the original story, the vicar's brother was guilty of cruelty and adultery; Chesterton did not include the topic of homosexuality. If he had, his Father Brown's reaction would have been one of abhorrence. Even in the more modern 1950s, it is doubtful that a priest would be compassionate.
- Susie Jasinksi, the presbytery housekeeper, lived in a Polish resettlement camp. After World War II, more than 200,000 Poles who had allied with Britain and France against Germany and the Soviet Union remained in Britain. Because their homeland was to be annexed by the Soviet Union, they were allowed to live in barracks vacated by the Americans and Canadians. Through the 1947 Polish Resettlement Act, they were offered British citizenship so they could stay and work, helping the country to get back on its feet economically.
- The Anglican church in Blockley near Chipping Campden was transformed into Catholic with the addition of confessionals in the rear and Stations of the Cross on side walls.
- The scriptwriters eliminated one of the suspects in the original story: "Mad Joe" is a mentally challenged individual that Norman Bohun teases unmercifully. If Joe had been arrested and charged with the murder, he would not have been hanged because of his disability, making him a good scapegoat.

1.2 "The Flying Stars"

Father Brown—"It seems like everyone is hiding something."

Original Air Date: January 15, 2013
Writer: Rachel Flowerday
Director: Ian Barber
The theft of a valuable piece of jewelry and a tragic drowning may be related in a case of murder.
Guest Stars:
  Josephine Butler as Anne-Marie Adams
  Julian Wadham as Colonel Adams
  Amy Morgan as Ruby Adams
  Ryan Hawley as John Van Ert
  Dan Fredenburgh as James Trewlove

- In the early 1950s, the Cold War between the United States and the Soviet Union grew even colder, resulting in persecution of thousands suspected of being Communist sympathizers. Private citizens, government officials, and Hollywood celebrities were targeted. Being blacklisted meant card-carrying Communists, or even those only accused of such, could be denied employment, forcing them to leave the country.
- When Inspector Valentine learned that the Adamses fought over the colonel wanting a divorce, he asked Father Brown if Anne-Marie would have been granted it. "Not as a devout Catholic," he answered. In the 1950s, divorce was condemned by the Church as a serious sin.
- In Chesterton's original story, financier Leopold Fischer brought Ruby three white African diamonds called the Flying Stars because they'd often been stolen. Flambeau, the jewel thief, arrived, posing as an unfamiliar uncle. During a tussle in the play, the diamonds were stolen. Father Brown found Flambeau at whose suggestion the play was performed because he realized he could easily steal the jewels in the confusion. He was about to escape, but the priest convinced him to end his crime spree and return the gems.
- The British Socialist Party had recently been organized when Chesterton's story was first published in 1910. Its leaders recommended that the party attempt its reforms through the ballot box. Union leaders deplored this idea, and a wave of strikes embroiled the country. Chesterton described socialism as the proposal that all property should be nationally owned so it could be fairly distributed. He explained through one character, "A radical does not mean a man who lives on radishes … and a Conservative does not mean a man who preserves jam. Neither, I assure you, does a Socialist mean a man

who desires a social evening with the chimney-sweep. A Socialist means a man who wants all the chimneys swept and all the chimney-sweeps paid for it." Father Brown finished the clarification, "But who won't allow you to own your own soot."[2]

1.3 "The Wrong Shape"

> Father Brown—"God created man in his own image. It's my vocation to remind people of that."

Original Air Date: January 16, 2013
Writer: Nicola Wilson
Director: Dominic Keavey
Father Brown is visiting a home for a poetry recital when a man is found hanging. The priest deduces that it was not suicide as first supposed, but murder.
Guest Stars:
    Ramon Tikaram as Umesh Varma
    Ruth Gemmell as Martha Quinton
    Robert Cavanah as Leonard Quinton
    Jennie Jacques as Violet Parnassus
    Simon Thorp as Mr. Harris

- In Chesterton's original story, Father Brown found a crooked oriental knife in the grass, but its shape was unsuitable for cutting. Squinting at a note left by the dead man, Father Brown demonstrates his myopia. He puzzles over the case, particularly the piece of paper, more crooked than the dagger that killed him. The missing corners contained quotation marks which altered the note's meaning.
- The priest advisor, or set designer, neglected to notice that candles in the altar's candelabra were burning, an unnecessary expense when no service was being held.
- Father Brown prays over the deceased cat. "All creation, O Lord, is in your care. Give us eyes to see that every living creature speaks to us of your love."
- The drug Mrs. Quinton had taken was Thalidomide. However, it wasn't until the late 1950s that doctors prescribed it for morning sickness, unaware that it could cause severe birth defects. First developed by the German pharmaceutical company Grünerthal, it is now used to treat some diseases like leprosy and leukemia. It works on the immune system to reduce inflammation.
- The poem that Mrs. Quinton reads to her daughter is quoted from "Death is Nothing at All" by Henry Scott-Holland.

- At Olivia's grave, Father Brown recites in Latin the opening lines from Psalm 130: "De profundis clamavi ad te, Domine. Domine, exuadi vocem meam. Fiant aures tuae intendentes, in vocem deprecationis meae." "Out of the depths, I cry to you, O Lord; Lord, hear my voice. Let your ears be attentive to my voice in supplication."

1.4 "The Man in the Tree"

Father Brown—"None of us are holy, and we all have battles to face."

Original Air Date: January 17, 2013
Writer: Rebecca Wojciechowski
Director: Dominic Keavey
Lady Felicia discovers a bleeding man stuck in a tree. When Father Brown's friend is suspected of attempted murder, Father Brown solves the crime.
Guest Stars:
  Jonathan Sidgwick as Franz Prepffler
  Steffan Rhodri as Christy Nolan
  Rod Hallett as Father Franc/Wilhelm
  Katherine Dow Blyton as Annie Mace
  Keith Osborn as Sergeant Allbright
  Mike Eastman as Policeman

- That British trains run on time, Father Franc credited to the industrial revolution. Throughout World War II, Germany conducted extensive bombing, primarily targeting Britain's industrial cities. With ubiquitous reminders of the damage remaining, the English felt long-lasting animosity toward all Germans. After Poland was invaded by Nazi Germany, an Army and Air Force consisting of displaced Poles was formed in England. The war remained a painful memory, particularly for Susie who lost her father in the confrontation.
- In the early 1950s, there was concern about the number of prostitutes in London, so a committee headed by Sir John Wolfenden recommended stricter controls (as well as the decriminalization of private homosexual activity between consenting adults). The result was the 1959 Street Offences Act, which found it an offence for a person 18 or older to persistently loiter or solicit for prostitution in public places. A guilty person would be fined between 10 and 25 pounds (equaling more than £500 or $700 in 2022). If convicted, a woman could serve as much as seven years.[3]

- Father Brown was aghast at seeing Wilhelm begin chest compressions, or cardio-pulmonary resuscitation, to bring the injured man back to life after cardiac arrest. The method had first been used in 1903 but was not promoted as a useful technique until experiments on dogs in 1958 led to more precise information about the speed, and where and how to press. Mouth-to-mouth resuscitation was also adopted as a life-saving measure at this time.

1.5 "The Eye of Apollo"

> Father Brown—"The transcendence of the spirit I'm all for, but turning someone's grief into a theatrical event, that I find somewhat dubious."

Original Air Date: January 18, 2013
Writer: Tahsin Guner
Director: Matt Carter
Shooting location: Sudeley Castle, Sudeley, Gloucestershire
The Church of Apollo comes to Kembleford. Susie becomes transfixed
   by its theology and falls under the spell of its charismatic leader.
Guest Stars:
   Michael Maloney as Kalon
   Camilla Power as Dominique Baxter
   Ben Starr as Adam Watkins
   Tara Coleman-Starr as Rose
   Adrian Mitchell as Villager

- In Chesterton's story of the same name, wealthy Pauline Stacey fell under Kalon's spell. When Kalon began his prayers to the sun from his balcony, Father Brown looked up at him from across the street. Suddenly there was a crash, and people rushed out of the building. Pauline had fallen into the elevator's open shaft. Before police arrive, Kalon announced that Pauline had made a will leaving a fortune to his church, but he could not have caused Pauline's accident because people saw him on the balcony when she died. Therefore, she must have committed suicide. Father Brown announced that Pauline was going blind from following Kalon's teaching about staring at the sun. When there was a crash and scream as the priest of Apollo prayed, he was not startled; he had been expecting it.
- In Greek mythology, Apollo was worshiped as the god of light and truth. Daily, he harnessed four horses to his chariot to move the sun across the sky.
- Sudeley Castle, the episode's location, had been a POW camp for

Italians and Germans during World War II. King Henry VIII's sixth wife, Katherine Parr, is buried on the grounds.[4]

1.6 "The Bride of Christ"

Sister Gregory—"Our Lord asks for poverty, chastity and obedience. He never said anything about sobriety."

Original Air Date: January 21, 2013
Writer: Jude Tindall
Director: Ian Barber
Shooting location: Princethorpe College, Warwickshire
Father Brown investigates the deaths of two nuns at Saint Agnes's convent.
Guest Stars:
  Penny Downie as Reverend Mother Augustine
  Roberta Taylor as Sister Paul
  Selina Cadell as Sister Gregory
  Keith Osborn as Sergeant Allbright
  Paddy Wallace as Tom Evans
  Lorna Watson as Sister Boniface
  Joanna Horton as Joyce Evans
  Jenny Galloway as Sister Thomas

- Sister Mary Magdalene, about to become "a bride of Christ," wore a wedding dress. Women aspiring to be nuns begin as postulants to become familiar with a sister's life. As novices—in some orders wearing white veils—they make a temporary profession, renewed annually for three or five years. Afterward, novices profess final vows of poverty, chastity, and obedience.
- Father Brown greets the bride with the Latin "Dominus vobiscum"— "The Lord be with you." The congregants' response is "Et cum spiritu tuo"—"And with your spirit."
- The girls from Princethorpe college portraying the other nuns were not properly instructed.[5] Nuns in those years kept their hands tucked demurely into their sleeves, they would not refer to each another as "girls," but as sisters. When St. Bridget's warden is called away, she clomps down the hall, another offence in sisterly decorum.
- Agatha Christie's training in pharmaceuticals during World War I gave her insight into the use and misuse of poisons. Sister Boniface was not only familiar with Christie's mysteries, but also with Dorothy L. Sayers' Lord Peter Wimsey stories.
- When Sister Boniface was caught snooping, she claimed she lost her

rosary. Reverend Mother urged her to thank Saint Anthony after she finds it; Catholic tradition holds that he can find lost objects.
- At Father Brown's persistence, Inspector Valentine finally calls out, "Will no one rid me of this turbulent [or troublesome] priest?" The line echoes that of King Henry II over his frustration with his enemy Thomas Becket. Lest his officers actually kill Father Brown as Henry's knights killed Becket, Valentine warns them not to take him literally.

1.7 "The Devil's Dust"

> Father Brown—"Anger can take us to countries we never knew existed."

Original Air Date: January 22, 2013
Writer: Dan Muirden
Director: Dominic Keavey
Father Brown joins the search when a young girl suffering a skin condition from radiation goes missing.
Guest Stars:
    Pip Torrens as Geoffrey Bennett
    Stirling Gallacher as Emily Bennett
    Holly Earl as Ruth Bennett
    Jamie Glover as Dr. Michael Evans
    Melanie Kilburn as Alice Murphy
    Don Gilet as Douglas Taylor
    Mike Eastman as Policeman
    Tobias James-Samuels as Police Officer

- The horrors of World War II were not far from the minds of 1950s Britons. More than 100,000 people had died when the United States dropped atomic bombs on Nagasaki and Hiroshima, Japan, others died from radiation-caused cancers years later. Paranoia about radiation's effects and the possibility of a Soviet atomic attack during the ensuing Cold War fueled hysteria. Unknown at the time were occupational dangers related to exposure to asbestos and lead. Painters, foundry workers, and plumbers worked with toxic materials that later caused skin diseases or led to organ damage.
- German physicist Hans Geiger at the University of Manchester discovered a way to count alpha particles emitted from radioactive materials by using sound. In 1908 he was able to use his detector to identify the nucleus of the helium atom.
- When Bennett used the Geiger counter to detect radiation from yellow or orange enamel in Susie's Cloisonné necklace, the exposure

was very small. But the glaze on the dishes contained uranium oxide in greater quantities because red contains higher levels of the mineral.

- Devil's Dust is also the name of a mix of hot and spicy chile pepper seasonings used to add zest to soups or grilled meats.

1.8 "The Face of Death"

Father Brown—"I always think that solitude and thinking are the best bedfellows."

Original Air Date: January 23, 2013
Writer: Lol Fletcher
Director: Matt Carter
Shooting location: Rous Lench Court, Evesham, Worcestershire
After an automobile accident that killed his father, his son is suspected in a vengeful murder at a charity event.
Guest Stars:
    Peter McNeil O'Connor as Daniel Walsh
    Stella Gonet as Lady Margaret Galloway
    Stephen Boxer as Professor Patrick Galloway
    Flora Spencer-Longhurst as Lucia Galloway
    Mark Dexter as Captain Clarence Clifton
    Jack Baggs as Thomas Dillcot
    Graham Burton as Arthur

- Lady Galloway and her daughter Lucia suffer from dyslexia in which the aptitude to read and write numbers and letters in their proper order is difficult. Poor spelling, the inability to distinguish left and right, and the avoidance of reading because of the difficulty are symptoms of the condition.
- Jazz was not new to Britain, having been heard in clubs and recordings since the 1920s. The war years had occasioned an increase in bands to entertain the troops. After World War II, however, the BBC attempted to broaden the musical taste of the British public when "modern jazz," influenced by American bebop, began to emerge. One of the more prominent performers was a talented trumpet player named John "Dizzy" Gillespie, for whom the dog in the episode is named.
- By the 1950s, the clothes rationing of World War II had ended wherein coupons had been required to buy any garment. Women were interested in more feminine styles than the industrial look of the war years. The introduction of Christian Dior's "New Look" motivated a

generation of fashion designers so, despite her dyslexia, it's likely that Lucia's talent could secure her career in the fashion industry.[6]

- Galloway's retort that "God is dead" was an oft-repeated quotation of Friedrich Nietzsche, a 19th-century German philosopher, who believed that, in a life that denied God, development of one's own intellect and creativity could thrive. Instead of striving toward a supernatural kingdom, a person would better value the world as it is. The phrase was occasionally used to explain an increase in atheism.

1.9 "The Mayor and the Magician"

Father Brown—"It's never too late to seek forgiveness."

Original Air Date: January 24, 2013
Writer: Nicola Wilson
Director: Dominic Keavey
Location: Ashdown World War II Camp, Evesham
Shortly after the mayor's speech at a fundraiser for the Polish resettlement camp primary school, a death occurs. It's up to Father Brown to discover if the murderer was someone at the fete.
Guest Stars:
  Sam Crane as William Knight
  Louise Brealey as Eleanor Knight
  Fern Deacon as Kathleen Knight
  Emma Hiddleston as Matilda Newell
  John Lightbody as Edwin Bloom
  Frank Grimes as Franc McCarthy
  Mike Eastman as Policeman
  Steve Hunt as Coconut Shy Operator
  Keith Osborn as Sergeant Allbright

- The mayor's speech referenced William Beveridge whose 1942 report foresaw a wide-ranging insurance system that would assure security for all Britons from cradle to grave. Three years later, Prime Minister Clement Attlee announced establishment of the welfare state outlined in Beveridge's report, including the National Health Service which offered free medical treatment. A national system of social security was also founded.
- At the fete, Father Brown's job was to count "humbugs"—hard, minty candies—as he put them in a jar for a guessing contest. It was indeed a treat to win such a prize because candy and chocolate rationing during World War II had recently ended in February 1953. The rationing had been put in place by the Ministry of Food in July 1942.[7]

- Edwin Bloom claimed to be a founding member of the Peace Pledge Union, Britain's oldest pacifist organization. Supporters pledged to renounce war and to work for removal of all causes of war.
- During World War II, women aged 19–30 had to register for possible conscription in the military. Matilda had served in the Women's Royal Naval Service. Seventy-four thousand Wrens, as they were called, worked as telegraphers, aircraft mechanics, drivers, pilots, and any man's job that a woman could do, thereby freeing males for combat. They served on the home front as well as overseas.[8]

1.10 "The Blue Cross"

Father Brown—"Thieves respect property. They merely wish it to be their own."

Original Air Date: January 25, 2013
Writer: Paul Matthew Thompson
Director: Ian Barber
Father Brown takes it upon himself to carry the blue cross to Newbury priory but is pursued by the international thief Flambeau.
Guest Stars:
Malcolm Storry as Bishop Talbot
Keith Osborn as Sergeant Allbright
Christopher Villiers as Justin De Vey
Patrick Brennan as Mr. Dawson/Quip
Graham Pavey as Stationmaster
John Light as Captain Flynn/Hercule Flambeau

- The adaptation for this episode closely follows Chesterton's popular story of the Blue Cross in several aspects: the need for Father Brown to take the cross to safety, the brown-paper wrapped packages and the recurrent switching of them, the leaving of clues for the police to follow, the priest's insistence on wanting to forgive Flambeau, and finally the flummoxing of Flambeau. However, in the original story, the thief steals seemingly for the fun of it; in the Alec Guinness version, Flambeau wants it simply to add to his collection of beautiful things; scriptwriter Paul Thompson has given this Flambeau perhaps the most selfless reason, to avenge his father's death and the Church's neglect in coming to his aid.
- Mark Williams' Father Brown reveals that he served in the Gloucestershire regiment in the Flanders trenches during the Great War before he became a priest. Flanders is an area of Belgium, Ypres a

town that had changed between the Germans and Allies throughout World War I.
- The episode introduces John Light as the master thief Flambeau. He will return at least once in each season to match wits with Father Brown. It also marks the final appearance of Kasia Koleczek as Susie Jasinski.
- Doppelgänger usually refers to a living person's look-alike. However, Father Brown uses the term to refer to the worthless parcel that Flambeau repeatedly swaps with his valuable one holding the cross. The characters also use some other distinctly British terms: "ponce" (a fancy man); "nicked" (caught committing a crime); "charmless spiv" (con man); and "caught on the hop" (caught unexpectedly).
- Father Brown ponders Saint Dismas, patron saint of criminals, who was crucified with Christ. Dismas was known as "the good thief" who said to Jesus, "Remember me when you come into your kingdom." Jesus answered him, "This day you will be with me in paradise."[9]

Season 2

Shortly after the last episode had been broadcast, BBC executives studying the ratings were pleased with viewers already numbering 2.5 million in the UK and with the options to sell the program to Australia, the United States, Japan, Sweden, and Denmark.[10] Reflecting on those millions of viewers, Kate Harwood, head of drama, remarked, "[Executive producer] Will Trotter's Birmingham team created a little bit of sunlit magic during a wet English summer and we're delighted that the show had such a warm response and a swift recommission. How wonderful that the brilliant Mark Williams will get to ride his bicycle into action yet again."[11]

Trotter predicted, "It's going to be a big show for the BBC worldwide. For a period drama it works really well. It's iconic."[12] Early on, one critic hailed it, "one of the under-recognised crown jewels of quality."[13] Believing the same, Christopher Stevens of the *Daily Mail* railed against the program being broadcast in the afternoon. "With its Cotswold settings, witty scripts and undercurrents of religious philosophy, Father Brown is crying out for a Sunday evening berth." Not everyone, he wrote, has the luxury of sitting down for 45 minutes in the afternoon with a sherry.[14] However, Jude Tindall, who wrote five of the scripts in the first three seasons, revealed that the *Father Brown* series was not conceived specifically for the daytime British audiences, but for the overseas market. When writing a program script, she pictures "middle America" or ABC Australia audiences watching from their sofas.[15]

If reviewers found any fault with the new adaptation, it was that the show strayed somewhat from Chesterton's Father Brown. One cleric found that "the English anti–Catholicism regularly satirized in Chesterton's stories is essentially moot here. Rather than a good-will ambassador of Romanism to Anglican and modernist readers, this Father Brown is a genial representative of enlightened faith to secular postmodern viewers—no bad thing in itself."[16]

As to how critics viewed Mark Williams as a clerical detective, the same cleric observed that "amiable" Williams fared very well in the role and was the "new show's best asset."[17] "Williams as the wise and wily Father Brown," continued Christopher Stevens, "is one of the best things currently on television." Those writers should be applauded who "give Father Brown stern principles, endless patience and lashings of common sense. One look of disapproval from his quivering jowls would be enough to make any murderer confess."[18] Yet another critic "loved" Williams' "portrayal of a pugnacious and interfering clergyman despite how very different it is from Chesterton's more meek and mild priest on the printed page."[19]

Viewers familiar with the Cotswolds might recognize familiar sites throughout the series, such as the Warwickshire village of Ilmington; the 11th-century Berkeley Castle in Gloucestershire; and the Kenilworth Castle dating from the 1100s. Princethorpe College, now a school in Warwickshire, was built as a Benedictine convent in 1792 and served in an episode as the nun's chapel. Ashdown, Evesham in Worcestershire replicates a World War II camp, complete with military vehicles and Nissen huts.

2.1 "The Ghost in the Machine"

Father Brown—"There's no such things as ghosts."

Original Air Date: January 6, 2014
Writer: Rachel Flowerday
Director: Matt Carter
Charlotte McKinley calls on Father Brown to exorcise the spirit of her sister. Hers is one of three disappearances that Father Brown must solve.
Guest Stars:
    Lizzy McInnerny as Charlotte McKinley
    Andrew Havill as Victor McKinley
    Poppy Drayton as Selina McKinley
    Paul Warriner as Seth Wake
    Keith Osborn as Sergeant Allbright
    Tom Chambers as Inspector Sullivan

- The McKinleys' cat's name was "Marmite." Marmite is a brown, salty British food paste made from yeast extract often spread on crackers.
- Mrs. McCarthy reminds Father Brown that he had been on a pilgrimage to Lourdes, a French town where Jesus' mother Mary appeared to Bernadette Soubirous in 1858.
- Father Brown offered Mrs. McCarthy a pear drop, a pink or yellow boiled candy in the shape of a pear.
- The priest hole at Cudely Manor was quite large in order to accommodate the actors, the camera, and the cameraman but in reality they were very cramped and unsanitary quarters, built mainly in the latter part of the 16th century. During Queen Elizabeth I's reign, Catholics were persecuted, and priests, when found, were executed. Many manor houses installed a priest hole to conceal clerics and the trappings of Catholic ritual including vestments and Mass accoutrements in case the house was searched. Because "priest hunters," known as pursuivants, were thorough in their searches, priest holes were cleverly concealed behind fireplaces, staircases, walls, or under floors.
- With Hugo Speer leaving the show to assume his role as Treville in *The Musketeers*, his Inspector Valentine has been promoted to a detective chief inspector of the Metropolitan Police in London. Officers holding the rank are charged with investigating serious crimes like murders. Taking his place in Kembleford is DI Sullivan, played by Tom Chambers.
- The dates on Elspeth's grave indicate she died in 1944. Since her disappearance was nine years previously, this episode takes place in 1953.

2.2 "The Maddest of All"

> Mrs. McCarthy—"I always suspected you were a few pints short of a milk churn."

Original Air Date: January 7, 2014
Writer: Tahsin Guner
Director: Matt Carter
Shooting location: Hatherop Castle School, Cirencester, Gloucestershire
After appearing to die, Felix miraculously returns to life. To find out what's going on, Father Brown gets himself committed to the hospital.
Guest Stars:
   Peter Bramhill as Felix Underwood

Terence Booth as Dr. Ernest Miller
Laura Main as Dorothy Underwood
Tessa Parr as Sarah Mulgrew
Helena Lymbery as Nurse Bridget Farrow
Adrian Rawlins as Dr. Walter Henshaw
Kenny Wyton as Jeremy
Keith Osborn as Sergeant Allbright

- The blue and cream teapot and cups that Mrs. Underwood used to serve the priest and detective feature later in the series in the presbytery kitchen.
- Father Brown's throwing soup at the wall was a nod to Chesterton's Father Brown doing the same in the story of "The Blue Cross." Mark Williams thought it was a nice detail to add in. "Those are the kinds of moments that I like … where he does something very shocking in terms of social behaviour. We tried to get a few of those in there."[20]
- When Father Brown found a listing of drugs and the patients who received them, the records were dated May through October 1953.
- Dr. Henshaw's treatment center cared for veterans suffering from what is now known as Post-Traumatic Stress Disorder. Sufferers of PTSD often re-live the trauma they endured through flashbacks and nightmares. Such a facility can be helpful by providing counseling and medication in a setting that avoids the people and places that caused, or are reminders of, the initial shock.
- Father Brown leaves Sarah with another Biblical reference—Matthew 9:22 in which Jesus says to a suffering woman who touched His cloak in hopes of being healed, "Courage, daughter. Your faith has restored you to health." In an interview for a Wales newspaper, Williams revealed that he, too, knew his Bible from his study of English literature at Oxford University.[21]
- The title derives from a quote by French philosopher Voltaire: "Men will always be mad and those that try to cure them are the maddest of all."

2.3 "The Pride of the Prydes"

Father Brown—"Hell is only the absence of God."

Original Air Date: January 8, 2014
Writer: Jude Tindall
Director: Paul Gibson
Shooting locations: Chastleton house, Moreton-in-Marsh (Pryde family home interior); Berkeley Castle, Berkeley, Gloucestershire (castle)
A local historian dies after uncovering an ancient curse. Father

Brown's realization that the key to the death lies in the past leads him to determine who killed the historian and why.

Guest Stars:

Marcia Warren as Audrey Diggle

Robert Boulter as Alan Archer

Guy Williams as Arthur Danby

Richard Hope as Sir St. John Pryde

Caroline Blakiston as Lady Lavinia Pryde

Susannah Fielding as Bunty Pryde

Angus Imrie as Jago Pryde

Keith Osborn as Sergeant Allbright

- Sir St. John was required to pay death duties or inheritance tax because tenants worked his land in exchange for living on it. In 1950, the tax could be more than 70 percent. Whether he should sell or allow foreclosure was "Hobson's choice," a phrase referring to Thomas Hobson who, in the 17th century, rented out horses. His stable was full, but he told customers to take the horse nearest the door. That way, the choice was his, not the customer's as most customers inevitably took the closest one.
- Bunty consulted Father Brown about wedding banns. In traditional Catholicism, announcements were made from the pulpit or posted in the church bulletin about upcoming marriages, providing an opportunity for anyone with good reason to say why the marriage should not take place.
- Bunty asked Mrs. McCarthy to make her wedding cake, after all, she is a WI champion. The WI (Women's Institute) was formed during World War I for women to socialize and learn from one another. The organization goes strong today, still enabling women to be a force in their community.[22]
- Each of the Prydes were skilled in using a longbow, a traditional bow with a string drawn by hand that shoots a long, feathered arrow. In the 1415 Agincourt battle, England's Henry V's army using longbows defeated a much larger and better equipped French army.
- Jago is between Scylla and Charybdis, a rock and a hard place, or, in his case, between incarceration or death. Homer's *Odyssey* tells of two sea monsters: Scylla, a supernatural creature with 12 feet and six heads whose sharklike teeth devoured whatever came near. Charybdis was personified by a whirlpool that caused shipwrecks.
- Simon was MI6, a spy working for a government agency that collected information worldwide to protect the United Kingdom. Its official name is the Secret Intelligence Service.

- The castle would be handed over to the National Trust, a charity founded in 1895 to preserve special places, including historic houses, throughout the United Kingdom.

2.4 "The Shadow of the Scaffold"

Father Brown—"How many more people have to die before you listen to me?"

Original Air Date: January 9, 2014
Writer: Rachel Flowerday
Director: Paul Gibson
Father Brown has three days to prove a woman innocent or she will surely be hanged.
Guest Stars:
  Emma Stansfield as Violet Fernsley
  Stuart Laing as Charlie Denham
  Susan Brown as Ethel Fernsley
  Joe Sims as Wilf Fernsley
  Adam Sopp as Archie Fernsley
  Adrian Dobson as Dr. Phillips
  John Burton as Sergeant Goodfellow

- In the 1950s, a pregnancy test meant waiting for a "rabbit test." A woman's urine sample was injected into a rabbit causing ovulation. Unfortunately, the rabbit was killed in order to obtain the test's results. Shortly after the 1960s, pregnancy tests using the woman's blood or urine could detect the increase of a hormone known as hCG (human chorionic gonadotropin) that occurs six days after fertilization.
- Ethel Fernsley faked a psychological paralysis in which a person pretends to be ill. Her alleged inability to move about qualified her to call on and receive comfort, aid, and sympathy from her family and neighbors. Unable to do housework, she depended on Violet, thus her anger at Piotr's effort to take Violet away.
- This episode marks the first appearance Sergeant Goodfellow played by John Burton who would become a regular in later seasons.

2.5 "The Mysteries of the Rosary"

Father Brown—"You can never run far from God, no matter how hard you try."

Original Air Date: January 10, 2014
Writer: Paul Matthew Thompson

Director: Ian Barber
Shooting location: Bloxham School, Banbury, Oxfordshire;
  Kenilworth Castle, Warwickshire (location of the rosary)
A friend of Father Brown researches the Lannington rosary that is
  alleged to have healing powers. Flambeau is also after the relic, but
  there's a glitch in the tale.
Guest Stars:
  James Laurenson as Professor Hilary Ambrose
  Malcolm Storry as Bishop Talbot
  Anton Lesser as Father Ignatius
  Ben Wilby as Peter
  Sylvestra Le Touzel as Verity Penhallick
  Stephen Thompson as Jacob Spender
  Keith Osborn as Sergeant Allbright
  John Light as Flambeau

- A rosary is a Catholic devotion in which Our Fathers, Hail Marys, and Glory Be's are recited as one fingers beads. Users meditate on each decade that commemorates an event in Christ's life ranging from Gabriel's Annunciation through Jesus' death to His ascent into heaven.
- Professor Ambrose lectured at Oxford university for the Newman Society, founded to promote Catholic education. He had discovered the Penhallick prayer book in the Ashmolean archives, Oxford's Museum of art and archaeology.
- Inspector Sullivan was proud of the recently discovered tape-lift method of pulling fingerprints from a crime scene. It involved using a piece of adhesive tape to capture trace evidence which could then be viewed under a microscope, saved on a card, or viewed on a projector.
- Sid was sure that Flambeau would be off "like the hare at Harringay," a greyhound racing track and motorcycle speedway. He also said he'd been on and off the khazi, the toilet. When Sullivan told him to stay put, Sid did only for a minute. Then he said, "Sod that for a game of Soldiers," meaning he wasn't going to obey.
- In the mid–16th century when Henry VIII wanted to divorce Catherine of Aragon so he could marry Anne Boleyn, the Catholic Church refused and was obliged to excommunicate him. Pope Clement VII rejected giving him a papal dispensation. Instead, the Archbishop of Canterbury granted the divorce, leading to England's break from the Roman Church. In revenge, the king then ordered monasteries and convents dissolved.
- Father Brown suspects that Father Ignatius suffers from epilepsy, a neurological condition that causes seizures and convulsions.

2.6 "The Daughters of Jerusalem"

Father Brown—"God wants sacrifice, but not suffering."

Original Air Date: January 13, 2014
Writer: Jude Tindall
Director: Matt Carter
Father Roland efficiently resumes Father Brown's duties while he
is laid up with a broken leg. It doesn't stop Father Brown from
investigating a crime committed 25 years previously.
Guest Stars:
  Clare Higgins as Dinah Fortescue
  James Rastall as Father Roland Eager
  Janet Henfrey as Vera Thimble
  Annette Badland as Judith Bunyon
  Justin Edwards as PC Hywel Pugh
  Nick Owenford as George the Postman

- The episode's title came from the Old Testament's *Song of Songs*. The
  phrase is also used in the New Testament when Jesus, on the way to
  Calvary, exhorts the women of Jerusalem not to weep for him but for
  themselves and their children (Luke 23: 27–28).
- Once ordained, a man is a priest forever. However, he can be released
  from clerical duties so he is free to marry but he cannot celebrate
  Mass or expect support from the church.
- When Father Brown asks if he wants to confess, PC Pugh says he's
  "chapel," meaning a Protestant Christian who belongs to a church of
  nonconformists who did not abide by the Church of England.
- Chesterton's second collection of Father Brown stories was titled
  The Wisdom of Father Brown. That book "dwell[s] mainly on the
  intellectual aspect of detection…. [H]is role is to interpret correctly
  the assumptions others make."[23] With Father Brown dependent
  on Mrs. McCarthy and Lady Felicia, he was forced to rely on their
  observations and intel gathering.

2.7 "The Three Tools of Death"

Father Brown—"Don't tell the bishop, but I'm not very
keen on sermons—too boring."

Original Air Date: January 14, 2014
Writer: Lol Fletcher
Director: Paul Gibson

Alice didn't mean to kill her mother while they were hunting, but electric shock treatments for memories of the horrid accident are equally traumatizing. When another death occurs, to identify the killer, Father Brown puts together various clues.

Guest Stars:
Alice Henley as Alice Armstrong
David Calder as Sir Aaron Armstrong
Nick Moran as Eddie Monk
Andrew Knott as Peter Royce
Martin Fox as Psychiatric Doctor
Matthew Ashforde as Jim Magnus
Lynne Verrall as Hilda Magnus
Keith Osborn as Sergeant Allbright

- Alice was treated with electroconvulsive therapy, used in the 1940s and 1950s to treat mental illnesses like severe depression and schizophrenia. Today's patient is anesthetized, electrodes are attached to the scalp, then small electric currents are passed through the brain triggering a brief seizure. Unfortunately, side effects of such procedures can include memory loss, confusion, and heart problems.
- Alice compared the treatments to those of Joan of Arc being burned at the stake. In the 1400s, teenaged Joan had visions from God urging her to speak to the weak-willed French leader. Joan then led the French army to victories over the English. Afterward, she was put on trial for witchcraft and was condemned to death.
- Father Brown named his bicycle Bucephalus, also the name of Alexander the Great's black horse.
- In Kenneth More's Father Brown television episode based on the same story, he is referred to as Father *John* Brown, S.J. (Society of Jesus, aka a Jesuit).
- Architectural Consultant Dr. Nancy Sheridan was added to credits, perhaps to verify that Armstrong could die falling out of a window at that height.

2.8 "The Prize of Colonel Gerard"

Father Brown—"What a strange compulsion man has to try and conquer nature. I fear someday we will reap the whirlwind for such arrogance."

Original Air Date: January 15, 2014
Writer: Dominique Moloney
Director: Ian Barber

Shooting location: Cornbury Park Estate, Charlbury, Oxfordshire
After a welcome home party for a former POW, a death occurs, and
everyone in the household is suspected. Father Brown finds the
answer in a most unlikely place.
Guest Stars:
   Nicholas Jones as Colonel Cecil Gerard
   Simon Ginty as Edward Gerard
   Katie Leung as Jia-Li Gerard
   Emma Fielding as Ada Gerard
   Tim Wallers as Rupert Digby
   Philip Delancy as Henri Chapel
   Keith Osborn as Sergeant Allbright

- Korea split into two countries in 1945. Five years later, North Korea
  attacked South Korea. The British government, at the time still
  recovering from World War II, nevertheless realized that it faced
  an undesirable commitment to support its allies—mainly the
  United States—in the newly created NATO (North Atlantic Treaty
  Organization) to combat the cancer of Communist aggression.
- Because tiger hunting was regarded in India as a royal sport, the
  taxidermized tiger proved the stalking skill of Colonel Gerard. He
  would have been one of thousands of military men stationed in India
  after the imposition of British imperialism in the mid–18th century.
- Mr. Digby says he could be found in the cupboard in an "Eton Mess."
  The phrase means disheveled, but also refers to a meringue and fruit
  dessert.
- This episode was a reunion of sorts for Mark Williams and Katie
  Leung (Jia-Li) who both appeared in the *Harry Potter* movies.

2.9 "The Grim Reaper"

Father Brown—"Never forget, the professionals built the
Titanic, but an amateur built the ark."

Original Air Date: January 16, 2014
Writer: David Semple
Director: Matt Carter
It looks like Dr. Crawford is guilty in a farmer's death, but are the
rumors going around Kembleford the truth or pulp fiction?
Guest Stars:
   David Troughton as John Tatton
   Adam Long as Alfred Tatton
   Maureen O'Connell as Oona Crawford

James Fleet as Dr. Adam Crawford
Charles Armstrong as Clerk of the Court

- Death by threshing machine was a real danger ever since it was invented by a Scottish mechanical engineer in the late 18th century. Its teeth and rotating blades separated husks from grain, and hands or feet caught near the blades could easily be severed. Clothing pulled into the blades could drag in one's entire body.
- In Britain, a doctor's office is known as his surgery.
- Mark Williams had mentioned in previous interviews how hot the costume of a priest can be. During the filming of this episode, the temperature in the Cotswolds hovered at 36°C degrees (97°F). No one would have blamed him for losing his pants or shirt under the cassock, but he wouldn't have. "It would fundamentally alter the character. And besides, acting's not really about comfort," he said.[24]

2.10 "The Laws of Motion"

Father Brown—"I know lust when I see it."

Original Air Date: January 17, 2014
Writer: Tahsin Guner
Director: Paul Gibson
At Kembleford's car rally, the racetrack owner is accused of murder. After an accident with a racecar, Father Brown follows the clues to find out who tampered with it.
Guest Stars:
    Tracy-Ann Oberman as Audrey MacMurray
    Amelia Lowdell as Harriet Welsby
    Cian Barry as Gary Bakewell
    Oliver Mellor as Walter MacMurray
    Lisa Jackson as Phyllis Stanwyck
    John Burton as Sergeant Goodfellow

- Father Brown mulled over Audrey's overbearing personality, Gary's admission of damaging the brake line, and the affair between Phyllis and Walter. Only one final clue was needed. This priest, like G.K. Chesterton's Father Brown, "could not help, even unconsciously, asking himself all the questions that there were to be asked and answering as many of them as he could; all that went on like his breathing or circulation."[25]
- Walter finally realized that Phyllis would double-cross him to further her own ends. Sid rolled his eyes and remarked, "The penny drops."

The idiom, meaning "now I understand," originated with the British newspaper *The Daily Mail* in August 1939. According to the Oxford English Dictionary, the phrase alluded to an automaton that required a penny to run. If the coin got stuck, the operator would have to wait for it to drop before the machine would work again.

- The character names are a throwback to the 1944 film *Double Indemnity* in which Barbara Stanwyck and Fred MacMurray starred as Phyllis Dietrichson and Walter Neff.
- Father Brown's sleuthing is finally recognized in an official commendation honoring him as a "chief constable" in the Gloucestershire constabulary.
- The Shelsley Walsh Hill Climb near Worcester was the scene for three days of filming. The incredibly steep course is the site of one of the oldest motorsport events.[26]

Season 3

Will Trotter was pleased, and most likely surprised as well, with the continued positive audience reaction to *Father Brown*, now calling it "compulsive viewing" on BBC One Daytime. It proved that "viewers have really taken Mark Williams as Father Brown to their hearts." He was "delighted that we can continue to bring such a well-loved character to life."[27] Trotter had assumed that *Father Brown* would last about three seasons but was unwilling to admit that he did not hold out high hopes for the series; hence, it's being relegated to daytime television instead of prime time. But its popularity in the UK and, more importantly, its popularity overseas resulting in sales to PBS stations and eventually to Netflix and Britbox, promised to keep it on the air for many more seasons. Still, it remained an afternoon program instead of being moved to prime time. Why?

One anonymous BBC source answered succinctly: "Too religious,"[28] a curious comment given that the main character is a priest. Was that not expected? The subject is so pronounced as to nearly qualify as religious programming. Mark Williams agreed that a Sunday nighttime slot was deserved. "But I'm not really allowed to say. There are lots of well-paid people at the BBC who tell us what they want and when they want it. I think the reason it looks good is that we know what we're doing. We don't spend time messing around with shots of people driving through villages. Our scripts are very tight, and our actors are exceptional."[29]

As the production team was filming episodes for Season 3, Bill Young of the Tellyspotting blog and his crew spent a week in Moreton-in-Marsh in the Cotswolds observing. They were fortunate to have access behind the scenes as well as meetings with the primary actors. The result was an hourlong television special titled "Father Brown: Saving Souls, Solving Crimes." Pertinent to the episodes being filmed, the Tellyspotting team also learned the history of cricket, visited the church in Blockley, and viewed the set for the Kembleford Police Station.[30]

One thing they may not have noticed from the two previous seasons is that the kitchen in the presbytery was different. The new setting is much larger, making it easier in which to film. The table is longer; the wall shelves still hold decorative dishes. The presbytery's delicate blue and white tea set is often in evidence. The kitchen table remains a gathering place where talk of the mystery, the direction the case might take, and the next step to its solution is debated among the group. The kitchen was the domain of Mrs. McCarthy who was frequently seen in an apron but always seen wearing a hat. Several of her myriad hats feature a wide brim with fake flowers or other decorative touches which flatter her face. At other times, the costume department might put her in a smaller crown hat for everyday wear. While head coverings were on the way out of fashion for younger women, those of more mature years would not have gone without one. It is a rare scene—usually only in her own home or if she's hospitalized—where Mrs. McCarthy goes hatless.

By now, any faithful viewer will recognize the haunting *Father Brown* musical theme written by Debbie Wiseman, who had also written scores for other television series. In the beginning, after reading a *Father Brown* script and watching a rough cut, she offered several themes, each with a different mood. She, Trotter, and producer Ceri Meyrick easily decided to use the one now familiar to audiences with its strong basses and violins. It had an "Ealing Comedy" feel, Wiseman says, meaning it sounded like themes of films produced by Ealing Studios of West London from 1947 to 1957. Wiseman wrote a new score for each episode to suit the action, create background for the red herrings, or highlight the malevolence of the villain. For starters, she composed using electronic instruments. Once it was approved, she wrote and conducted the full score performed by a 25-piece orchestra. "Music really helps to tell a story," Wiseman believes. "You never hear a film or TV drama without it."[31]

3.1 "The Man in the Shadows"

Father Brown—"I am a bumbling idiot, but I see patterns to things."

Original Air Date: January 5, 2015
Writer: Rob Kinsman

Director: Paul Gibson
Shooting location: Ditchley Park, Enstone, Oxfordshire
Fake historians, Lady Felicia's reputation, Sid's arrest, and a spy game
   figure into the secrets in an old manor house.
Guest Stars:
   Christopher Webster as William Sheppard
   Florence Hall as Marion Sheppard
   John Bett as Hugo Masters
   Daniel Flynn as Daniel Whittaker
   Nigel Lowe as Butler
   John Burton as Sergeant Goodfellow

- After World War II, Soviet espionage was of primary concern.
  The Soviets wanted to keep control of eastern Europe to safeguard
  against more German attacks; British, American, and Soviet spies
  were employed to gather information. If such classified data became
  public, it could cause serious military or political damage. Today,
  MI5's top priority remains national security and the countering of
  any threats of terrorism, espionage, or sabotage.
- Sid claimed he can keep schtum about what he saw, meaning silent,
  but Sullivan put him in the chokey (jail) anyway.
- To keep the series authentic, several new consultants came aboard
  starting this season: Dr. Matthew Francis as historical advisor; priest
  advisor Father Tony Nye, S.J.; and police advisor Dave Cross.

3.2 "The Curse of Amenhotep"

Father Brown—"Confession is good for the soul."

Original Air Date: January 6, 2015
Writer: Jude Tindall
Director: Matt Carter
Shooting location: Spetchely Park, Worcester, Worcestershire
Father Brown investigates how Sir Raleigh's new bride died in a
   locked room after looking at an ancient mummy.
Guest Stars:
   Chris MacDonald as Young Raleigh
   Genevieve Gaunt as Young Evelyn
   David Bamber as Walter Hubble
   Geraldine Alexander as Valerie Oliphant
   Nicholas Farrell as Sir Raleigh Beresford
   Poppy Corby-Tuech as Caterina Beresford
   Josh O'Connor as Leo Beresford

Richard Price as the Mummy
John Burton as Sergeant Goodfellow

- Sir Raleigh planned to donate Amenhotep's mummy to Chicago's Oriental Institute, a prominent museum that showcases the art and archeology of the Near East.
- Tutankhamen's curse also forebode death to whoever disturbed the Pharaohs. Members of Howard Carter's 1922 expedition, which discovered King Tut's tomb, did die unexpectedly, but perhaps from mold or bacteria found in the ancient tombs.
- The doctor prescribed camphor oil for Father Brown for anti-inflammation to relieve pain. It can be found in popular medications like Vicks VapoRub and BENGAY. Atropine eyedrops are often used to dilate the pupil of the eye for an eye exam. They contain the drug tetrahydrozoline which can cause slow heart rate and gastrointestinal irritations if ingested.
- Sir Raleigh wondered if he needs to be a "Left Footer," i.e., a Catholic to confess. It's an insulting phrase applied to Roman Catholics that comes from the difference between left- and right-handed spades found on Irish farms. Older spades had a footrest on one side instead of the newer two-sided footrests. Therefore, if one was from Catholic Ireland, he might distinguish himself by digging with the wrong foot.
- The episode nods to Agatha Christie, several of whose books contain the characters of Tuppence and Tommy Beresford. Christie's second husband Max Mallowan was an archaeologist, and she traveled with him to excavations in Egypt, which provided the setting for at least six of her mysteries, including *Murder in Mesopotamia*, *Death on the Nile*, and *Death Comes as the End*.

3.3 "The Invisible Man"

Father Brown—"You don't deserve hell on earth or anywhere else."

Original Air Date: January 7, 2015
Writer: Tahsin Guner
Director: Matt Carter
When a circus comes to Kembleford, waitress Laura flirtatiously agrees to marry the hypnotist or clown. But them taking her seriously was not in her plans.
Guest Stars:
    Joe Layton as Nicholas Wallis
    Justine Cain as Laura Hope

Sevan Stephan as Reggie Smythe
Kiruna Stamell as Enid Flay
Kobna Holdbrook-Smith as Marvin Morris
Guy Henry as Arthur Welkin
Isabeau Bentley as Circus Hostess
John Burton as Sergeant Goodfellow

- In Chesterton's story "The Invisible Man," two men wanted to marry Laura Hope, but she would not marry someone who had not made his own way in the world. After a while, Smythe did make a fortune. Welkin doesn't show his face, but Laura feels his presence. Smythe is secured in his flat; his cleaner, doorman, a policeman, and a chestnut-seller are asked to keep watch for strangers. Later, when Smythe's body is found in the canal, the sentinels swear that no one had come or gone, despite obvious footprints on the stairs. Father Brown explains that people, when asked, answer what is expected. The four men saw nothing out of the ordinary. A postman is a person who can come and go with no one acknowledging his presence, so Welkin disguised himself as a postman and carried a sack in which he could carry out Smythe's dwarfish body yet be "invisible" to anyone not looking for him.
- Smythe utters a dying declaration, one that is considered credible based on the belief that if a person believes he is about to die, he does not lie.
- Sullivan supposed that Welkin was in the pub singing "Knees Up Mother Brown," a tune with bawdy lyrics popularized in East End pubs in the 1800s.
- When Father Brown walked Laura down the aisle, the organist played Mendelssohn's *Wedding March*, a familiar secular piece not used in Catholic weddings. Mendelssohn composed the piece for Shakespeare's *A Midsummer Night's Dream*, a play which includes fairies, spells, love potions, and pagan gods, themes antithesis to the Catholic faith.

3.4 "The Sign of the Broken Sword"

Father Brown—"You can dress it up as justice or revenge but murder is murder."

Original Air Date: January 8, 2015
Writer: Stephen McAteer
Director: Ian Barber
Father Brown investigates a death at an army barracks, finding clues in another murder at Dunkirk 13 years previously.

Guest Stars:
   Craig Whittaker as Major Desmond Murray
   Jamie Ballard as Major David Rawlings
   Steven Miller as Lieutenant Anthony Graham
   William Ash as Regimental Sergeant Major Reginald Davis
   Angus Wright as Colonel Laurence St. Clare
   Grace Cassidy as Simone Murray
   John Burton as Sergeant Goodfellow

- The battle of Dunkirk raged throughout May and June 1940, a miracle and a tragedy. More than 200,000 British troops were rescued from the advancing German army by boat but were forced to leave behind thousands of guns and ammunition. Prime Minister Winston Churchill called it a "colossal military disaster. Wars are not won by evacuations."[32]
- In Chesterton's story of the same name, as Father Brown and investigator Flambeau wander through a cemetery, the priest asks, "Where does a wise man hide a pebble?" "On the beach." He explains that St. Clare was a great general commanding a force in Brazil whose President Olivier was magnanimous to prisoners, often letting them go free. Indignant at "any needless waste of soldiers," St. Clare killed Olivier. St. Clare, normally prudent, was desperate for money and turned traitor to get it. When Major Murray guessed his secret, St. Clare plunged his sword through Murray's body, breaking off the tip. Afterwards, he led 800 English soldiers to their deaths, hiding Murray's body in a "hill of corpses." St. Clare was later hanged with his broken sword.
- Chesterton wrote, "I once wrote a short story called 'The Sign of the Broken Sword.' It is, as a modern military episode, very melodramatic and improbable, for the simple reason that I originally planned out the plot as that of some medieval skirmish, with spear and battle-axe, and then translated it back into modern life in order to make it contemporary." Chesterton's own walking stick concealed a sword "in case he ever needed it to save a lady in distress."[33]

3.5 "The Last Man"

> Father Brown—"Hell is merely the absence of God. I wouldn't wish it on my own worst enemy."

Original Air Date: January 9, 2015
Writer: Jude Tindall
Director: John Greening

Shooting location: James Barrie Cricket Pavilion, Stanway, Oxfordshire

The Kembleford cricket team is in trouble, but Father Brown is on the case. A recorded list of dates, money amounts, and initials indicate blackmail is involved.

Guest Stars:

Tom Chadbon as Major Peter Wallander

Perdita Avery as Daphne Wallander

Haydn Gwynne as Professor Jane Milton

Robbie O'Neill as Vince Lennon

Darrell D'Silva as Max Scullion

Abhin Galeya as Doctor Raj Chandraty

Colin Deaney as Hornby

Marc Esse as Blacksmith Bill

John Burton as Sergeant Goodfellow

- Cricket is a ball and bat game played by opposing 11-person teams. The positions of thrower, square leg, first slip, wicket keeper, and captain refer to their angle from the batsman. The other team members are on the field. The goal of the batsman is to score runs.
- Prejudice toward people from India was common in the 1950s. After World War II, Britain welcomed immigrants to help rebuild the country. However, the hope was that white immigrants from eastern Europe would come, not "colored" immigrants from the West Indies or India. In 1955, the Colonial Office realized that restricting entry, particularly since many migrants were unskilled and non–English speaking, was racially prejudicial. Inflammatory fearmongering, even 20 years later, resulted in fewer than two percent of immigrants being non-whites.[34]
- Mrs. McCarthy quotes from Proverbs 14:19: "The evil will fall down before the good, and the wicked before the gates of the just." Father Brown quotes Psalm 22:14: "My heart is poured out like water. My bones are scattered. And my heart, like wax, is melted."
- Added to the list of consultants for this episode was Dr. Terry Quinn, M.D., as medical advisor.

3.6 "The Upcott Fraternity"

Father Brown—"Murder ... is not the shedding of blood for remission."

Original Air Date: January 12, 2015

Writer: Paul Matthew Thompson

Director: Paul Gibson
Shooting location: Worcester Cathedral; Stanbrook Abbey Hotel,
   Worcestershire
Students and staff at the Upcott Seminary mourn the death of
   a student priest. Father Brown needs a spy at the seminary
   to learn what is going on. It's Sid, unlikely as it seems, to the
   rescue.
Guest Stars:
   Dudley Sutton as Father Francis Palfreyman
   Ed Brody as Ciaran Wolfe
   Daniel Easton as Hugh McKenna
   James Dryden as Clarence Risley
   Tim Treloar as Father Emlyn Lewis
   Matthew Tennyson as Thomas Potts
   Leo Chell as Acolyte
   Laura Fleming as Sid's One-Night Stand
   John Burton as Sergeant Goodfellow

- A small error: In the 1950s, the priest celebrated Mass in Latin with
  his back to the congregation and only the altar boys responded to the
  prayers as the congregation followed along in missals.
- Men might study for the priesthood at a seminary for four to eight
  years, depending on whether they entered with a college degree. The
  time of study would also depend on whether they chose a parish
  ministry or a contemplative order. Holy Orders is the sacrament in
  which a man is ordained a priest.
- Catholics are, or were, advised to engage in mortification,
  particularly during Lent, the 40-day period before Easter. Wearing a
  cilice or a hair shirt or enduring self-flagellation was often a method
  of penance. Penitents used knotted ropes or sharp objects to inflict
  pain on themselves in imitation of Christ's scourging. Propitiations
  such as cold showers, fasting, or sleeping without a pillow are milder
  forms.
- On August 15, the Catholic Church celebrates the Assumption in
  which God took the Virgin Mary into heaven upon her death.
- Douglas Hitchens shares a surname with Christopher Hitchens,
  a well-known atheist famous for his book *God Is Not Great: How
  Religion Poisons Everything.*
- Father Brown was hoping that Sid would have a Damascene
  conversion, a reference to Saul who, on the road to Damascus as
  a torturer of Christians, was converted to a disciple of Christ. He
  became Apostle Saint Paul (Acts 9:1–23).

3.7 "The Kembleford Boggart"

Father Brown—"I never did have much luck with my bishops."

Original Air Date: January 13, 2015
Writer: Jonathan Neil
Director: John Greening
Shooting location: Chastleton House, Oxfordshire
When gypsies gather outside Kembleford, antagonism between them and some villagers is apparent. A book written by one of the villagers features a boggart, an unwelcome imp who causes trouble.
Guest Stars:
    Polly Hemingway as Aggie
    Simon Williams as Jeremiah Moxley
    Philip McGinley as Alfons
    Nathalie Buscombe as Hannah Moxley
    Ben Deery as Harry Grandage
    John Burton as Sergeant Goodfellow

- Mrs. McCarthy comes to the gypsy camp to accuse Alfons of stealing a chalice off the altar in the church, but chalices were used during Mass and would not have been left out on the altar at any other time.
- Harry Grandage says he was in Belgium when he first read Hannah's work, then later claims he was in Korea. Father Brown did not pick up on the discrepancy.
- The North Sea flood that Grandage reported occurred January 31–February 1, 1953. As the sea's worst storm on record, it affected not only Belgium, but the Netherlands, Scotland, and England. More than 2,000 people and thousands of cattle perished.
- At episode's end, Grandage is about to drive off with Hannah in a very nice sports car. Mark Williams told a reporter, "We get all these amazing '50s cars because we shoot in the Cotswolds which is quite near Birmingham and Coventry which were essentially [the home of] the British car industry after the war.... I never get to try them. There are lots of publicity pictures of me in a car because I go and say, 'Can I sit in it?'"[35]

3.8 "The Lair of the Libertines"

Father Brown—"Happiness is an unexpected gift. It is evasive. If we pursue it, we will never achieve it."

Original Air Date: January 14, 2015
Writer: Lol Fletcher
Director: Matt Carter
Father Brown and his friends find themselves unexpectedly staying
at a residence where playboys have gathered for a weekend of
debauchery. But someone is killing the guests, and everyone is in
danger of being the next victim.
Guest Stars:
Ace Bhatti as Syrus
Nicholas Le Prevost as Count Fiskon
Michael Culkin as Dr Barashi
Ronni Ancona as Madame Chania
Rae Baker as Mimi
Trudy Coleman as Nurse
Rebecca Neal as Daisy
John Burton as Sergeant Goodfellow

• Mimi caters to libertines, i.e., men who prefer an unrestrained,
  sexually immoral life. She claims to be a "hedonistic existentialist"
  trying to cope with the nightmare of living with the joy of killing.
• Mrs. McCarthy compares the situation to Sodom and Gomorrah, two
  sin-filled cities referenced in the book of Genesis 19:1–26 which God
  threatened to destroy because of their wickedness.
• Father Brown's ending quote: "And God said, let the earth bring forth
  the living creature in its kind ... and it was so done" comes from
  Genesis 1:24.

3.9 "The Truth in the Wine"

> Father Brown—"In my experience, the truth will always
> out."

Original Air Date: January 15, 2015
Writer: Kit Lambert
Director: Ian Barber
Father Brown sets out to find the truth, including that some people
are not who they claim to be, when a murder is discovered in a
vineyard.
Guest Stars:
Gareth Jewell as Henry Gibbs
Georgina Leonidas as Emily Fletcher
Emma Cunniffe as Mabel Grayson
Sheila Reid as Lady Edna Forbes-Leith

Daniel Ryan as Colonel Anthony Forbes-Leith
Edward Akrout as Gregoire Bisset
John Burton as Sergeant Goodfellow

- Lady Felicia thought the Colonel resembles a hero from a novel by H. Rider Haggard who set many of his books in Africa and is famous for writing *King Solomon's Mines* and *Allan Quartermain.*
- The Biblical story of the prodigal son can be found in Luke 15:11–32. Father Brown refers to Rahab who saved spies and was herself saved (Joshua, chapter 2).
- Dionysus was the god of winemaking and the grape harvest. The dog Bacchus was named after the god of agriculture and wine.
- Is it sometimes all right to lie? St. Augustine's treatise, *De Mendacio,* indicated that lying depended on believing something was true yet saying something else. He wrote that some arguments prove that we may sometimes tell a lie if, in doing so, we are also doing good.[36]

3.10 "The Judgment of Man"

Father Brown—"There is always redemption for those who truly seek it."

Original Air Date: January 16, 2015
Writer: Paul Matthew Thompson
Director: Ian Barber
Shooting locations: Worcester Guildhall; Spetchley Park, Worcestershire (Montague estate, exterior)
Flambeau arrives in Kembleford with nefarious intent, as does Rebecca Himelbaum from whose father the Nazis stole a painting during the war. Father Brown finds himself involved with several guilty parties.
Guest Stars:
    James Dreyfus as Binkie Cadwaller
    Martin Docherty as Mirren McConnell
    Anna-Louise Plowman as Rebecca Himelbaum
    Samantha Phelps as Frau Himelbaum
    David Gant as Claude Chabrol
    John Light as Hercule Flambeau
    John Burton as Sergeant Goodfellow
    David Gant as Claude Chabrol
    Colin Deaney as Hornby
    Adrian Dobson as Security Guard

- The Vatican's archives hold the Church's extensive and richest private collection of 12 centuries of documents and sacred art. Ironically, the Vatican Apostolic library may be entered through the Belvedere courtyard.
- Modern artists are referred to in the episode: Scottish Eduardo Paolozzi, who founded the Independent Group which led to the American Pop Art movement, and the American Ernest "Robert" Rauschenberg, whose works incorporated common objects as art.
- The recovery and return of art and property owned by the Jewish people and stolen by the Nazis continues to this day. For more on stolen artwork, see https://www.ushmm.org/collections/bibliography/looted-art.
- The Gestapo took Rebecca's parents to Theresienstadt, a waystation before they were deported to the concentration camps.
- The painting was titled "The Final Judgement." There exist several paintings of an artist's interpretation of God's ultimate, or final, judgment. "The Last Judgement," a similar scene by Michelangelo, hangs behind the altar of the Vatican's Sistine Chapel in Rome.

3.11 "The Time Machine"

Father Brown—"It's never too late to return to the fold."

Original Air Date: January 19, 2015
Writer: Tahsin Guner
Director: Ian Barber
Shooting locations: Alscot Park, Stratford-upon-Avon, Warwickshire
Father Brown visits a young physicist who invented a time machine to prove who killed his father a year ago.
Guest Stars:
Alexandra Gilbreath as Georgina Francis
Mark Lewis Jones as Arnold Francis
Gabrielle Dempsey as Sarah Francis
Lucy Chappell as Angelica Francis
Will Attenborough as Jacob Francis
John Burton as Sergeant Goodfellow

- Based on context clues, the time period of the episode is 1953 since Sarah and Angelica train for the track events "in Vancouver next year." The 1954 British Empire and Commonwealth Games were held in Vancouver, British Columbia, July 30–August 7, 1954.
- In the 17th century, the Roman Catholic Inquisition condemned Galileo for teaching correctly that the earth and other planets

revolved around the sun. Aristotle's viewpoint that the earth was the center of the universe had been accepted doctrine until his time. With the production of better telescopes, astronomers eventually verified Galileo's findings. The century before, Giordano Bruno had anticipated Galileo's teachings, arguing his infinite universe theory. For this, he was also condemned and burned at the stake.

- Strychnine is a strong poison that, because it is a white, odorless, crystalline powder, can be ingested, inhaled, or injected. Overdoses produce deadly effects, but a minimum amount acts as a stimulus that can prove advantageous in endurance races. Today it is often used as a pesticide.

3.12 "The Standing Stones"

Father Brown—"Oddball does not equal murderer, or they'd have arrested me."

Original Air Date: January 20, 2015
Writer: Rachel Flowerday
Director: Matt Carter
Father Brown investigates the ritualistic murder of a woman at a mystical site in a village where polio has struck down several children.
Guest Stars:
Holly Lucas as Ginnie Godden
Maya Grant as Sylvia Swann
Mark Benton as PC Walt Everett
Nigel Cooke as Malcolm Driscoll
Sandy McDade as Marjorie Shipton
Richard Hawley as Alf Gastrell
John Burton as Sergeant Goodfellow

- Stonehenge, besides being a prehistoric place of worship or a calendar, was a healing site. Bones excavated nearby show the intense trauma suffered by some people who had come to be healed.
- Mrs. McCarthy quotes the first commandment, "Thou shalt not have strange gods before me" (Exodus 20:3). Father Brown prays Psalm 23:4, "I will fear no evil for Thou art with me. Thy rod and Thy staff comfort me."
- Poliomyelitis is a crippling and potentially deadly infectious disease. The virus spread from person to person and could invade the brain and spinal cord, causing paralysis. The tank respirator, the iron lung, was used to treat patients whose paralyzed chest muscles left them

unable to breathe. In one year alone, thousands were paralyzed and more than 3,000 died.
- Mrs. McCarthy informs Sergeant Goodfellow that Father Brown cannot be out on a call because his pyx bag was still in the presbytery. The pyx is used to carry the Eucharistic host outside of the church.
- In the 1950s, the Last Rites of the Catholic Church (Viaticum) was called Extreme Unction. A Catholic in danger of dying was given holy communion and anointed with consecrated oil meant to offer healing and strength and to prepare the receiver to depart this life.
- Nigel Cook, who plays Malcolm, is Sorcha Cusack's husband.

3.13 "The Paradise of Thieves"

Father Brown—"I am a man of God, I am never alone."

Original Air Date: January 21, 2015
Writer: Rob Kinsman
Director: Diana Patrick
Father Brown is forced into being a witness when two men rob the bank in which he's doing business. Since he's involved, when a murder also soon occurs, Father Brown needs to find out how the two crimes are connected.
Guest Stars:
    Kirsty Besterman as Julia Flanders
    Michael Jibson as Martin Wheeler
    William Gaminara as Samuel Harrogate
    Michael Jibson as Martin Wheeler
    James Burrows as Thomas Brandon
    Alexander Rain as Stephen Browning
    Johnathan Garratt as Bank Robber
    Jayc O'Neill as William "Billy" Flanders
    John Burton as Sergeant Goodfellow

- Mrs. McCarthy and Father Brown figured that the new church roof would cost £247, or £6,012 ($7,010) in today's currency.[37] A leaky church roof seemed to be a common purpose for fundraising in several films featuring the Catholic church.
- For the episode's filming during August 22–28, 2014, Tewkesbury provided Watson Hall and the Corn Exchange in the Town Hall as a setting. Filming inside a bank is not permitted, but the large white pillars of the Exchange resembled a 1950s bank.[38]
- Mrs. M laments that people are tired of buying Victoria sponge cakes. The fluffy sandwich is made by combining two sponge cakes layered

with jam or vanilla cream between them. It was named after Queen Victoria; allegedly it was one of her favorites.
- Despite the seriousness of the crime, there was humor in the episode. As Sid and Father Brown prepare to break into the vault to find clues, Father Brown appears in his cassock.

SID—"You could have worn something more practical."
FATHER BROWN—"It's black."
SID—"It's a dress, you cannot rob a bank in a dress!"

3.14 "The Deadly Seal"

Bentley Duke—"So, this is why the Bishop calls you his 'blackest sheep.'"

Original Air Date: January 22, 2015
Writer: Dan Muirden
Director: Diana Patrick
Shooting locations: Everyman Theatre, Cheltenham (the foyer was Cheltenham's Pittville Park)
When a penitent confesses that the bishop will be assassinated the next day, Father Brown hustles to deter the killer and save his superior.
Guest Stars:
　　Yolanda Kettle as Natasha Farrango
　　Malcolm Storry as Bishop Talbot
　　Aden Gillett as Bentley Duke
　　Bill Buckhurst as Peter Redhill
　　Kate Anthony as Ethel Davies
　　Tom Knight as Winston Grater
　　Chris Wilson as Albert Davies
　　John Burton as Sergeant Goodfellow

- Father Brown praised the bishop's Corpus Christi sermons. The feast, honoring Jesus' body and blood in the Eucharist, was celebrated on the Thursday after Trinity Sunday, eight weeks after Easter.
- For 231 years previously, the most senior officer of the Royal Household of the United Kingdom, the Lord Chamberlain, had the authority to repress the performance of any new play for any reason. Since 1968, he was no longer empowered to censor dramas.
- As in Chesterton's fondness for theatrical effects, Father Brown plays a role in the creation of a literal scene of the crime. The "West End" refers to London's theater district, relatively comparable to New York City's Broadway.

- Sid learns that Davies was betting on horses at the Kempton Park Racecourse in Surrey, England, even though he was "skint," slang for broke.
- Father Brown quotes Romans 12:19–21 to Ethel, "'Revenge is mine, I will repay,' saith the Lord. 'Be not overcome by evil but overcome evil by good.'"

3.15 "The Owl of Minerva"

Inspector Trueman—"According to Inspector Sullivan, you're a loose cannon with delusions of grandeur."

Original Air Date: January 23, 2015
Writer: Jude Tindall
Director: Matt Carter
Inspector Sullivan is himself on the run, suspected of murder, and seeks Father Brown's help in proving his innocence.
Guest Stars:
    Adrian Scarborough as Clive Trueman
    Harry McEntire as Frank Albert
    Ron Donachie as Jock Hamilton
    Natasha Little as Harriet Greensleeves
    Jay Villiers as Sir Jeffrey Greensleeves
    Gareth Hale as Commissioner Busby
    Jerry Willey as Norman Finley
    John Burton as Sergeant Goodfellow

- This episode marked the final appearance of Tom Chambers as Inspector Sullivan. Unlike the departure of his predecessor, no explanation was given for his leaving.
- Locard's principle states that in any contact between two items, there will be an exchange. A perpetrator wittingly or unwittingly brings something to the crime scene and leaves with something that can be used as forensic evidence.
- The Greensleeves, according to Harriet Greensleeves, were playing Bezique, a two-player card game.
- Sodium pentothal, known as "truth serum," can incapacitate a person so his defenses are down, causing him to be unable to lie. In actuality, it can cause a person to *believe* he is telling the truth, even if what he says is false. Thus, in most cases, a confession produced by its administration is not admissible in a court of law.
- The Illuminati, meaning "enlightened," was a secret society founded in 1776 by German philosopher Adam Weishaupt. Its members

opposed the Catholic Church's power and sought to free themselves from the church and government.

- Philosopher G.W.F. Hegel, in his *The Philosophy of Right*, wrote that the "owl of Minerva spreads its wings only with the falling of the dusk," denoting that only retrospection at the end of day can bring wisdom after an analysis of the day's lessons.[39]

Season 4

Ironically, near the end of the last episode, Sergeant Goodfellow remarks to Inspector Sullivan after his misadventure that it was good to have him back. To which Sullivan replies that he was glad to be back. Unfortunately, as Season 4 begins, Sullivan is gone when Tom Chambers was cast in the film *Meet Pursuit Delange*. John Burton remains the constant at the police station in his role as Goodfellow, but Kembleford has a new police inspector from Durham in the person of Inspector Mallory played by Jack Deam. Viewers are given no warning for Sullivan's departure or Mallory's unexplained presence, but both he and Father Brown carry on in the season's first episode as though they've known each other all along. Mallory's fierce brook-no-interference attitude, even more so than that of Inspectors Valentine or Sullivan, does nothing to engender a compromising association with Father Brown.

How Mark Williams got on with Jack Deam off-set is unknown, but he was thrilled to be portraying Father Brown for another season. Up until he was offered the role, Williams had had a successful career as a character actor in theaters and in British and American films, but he loved acting and so, when asked, had eagerly accepted the role. He understands how Father Brown is about "spirituality and intuition. He's endlessly fascinated by human nature and incredibly nosey, and there's absolutely nothing that's not worthy of attention." As for Williams' own spirituality, he says,

> Well, we know we have a soul, because we talk to it inside our heads. Where it came from and where it might go after we die is up for debate, but when it's in our head, we all know it's there. While you're alive, you have custody over your soul. Religion is a complex issue, of course. But the whole point with Father Brown is that it matters! Crime isn't about an intellectual puzzle or an anagram.... It's somebody's soul that's at stake, and however you want to frame it, that's a thing we all have.[40]

Before Season 4 aired, Ann Widdecombe, whose documentary on Chesterton and Father Brown inspired its newest adaptation, visited the Gloucestershire village where the series was filmed. She was accompanied by Father Tony Nye who had been tasked with ensuring the accuracy of the Catholic portrayals like converting the Anglican church used for filming into the Catholic church of St. Mary's and Father Brown's dress, attitude, and actions. Using consultants helped producers avoid any conflict with the church and, in this capacity, Nye had to research old Latin and the Catholic translation of scripture used in the 1950s.

4.1 "The Mask of the Demon"

Father Brown—"I think you should love yourself as much as He loves you."

Original Air Date: January 4, 2016
Writer: Jude Tindall
Director: Paul Gibson
Shooting location: Coughton Court, Alcester, Warwickshire
When a film company comes to Kembleford, its obnoxious director is found murdered. Father Brown finds that many on the set had a motive to want him dead.
Guest Stars:
   Molly Hanson as Paulette Swain
   Jonathan Firth as Rex Bishop
   Deirdre Mullins as Bebe Fontaine
   David Schofield as Vivian Wolsey
   William Ellis as Billy Neville
   John Burton as Sergeant Goodfellow

- The 1950s saw many wonderful movies released, such as *A Streetcar Named Desire* and *High Noon*. However, there were also some terrible B movies, such as *Attack of the 50 Foot Woman* and *Bela Lugosi Meets a Brooklyn Gorilla*.
- When they enter Wolsey's office and find him dead, Paulette screams, puzzling Lady Felicia. Screaming at finding a corpse was her shtick.
- Mallory thinks that wax on a horror film set is as common as coal from Newcastle, a center for coal mining. "Carrying coals to Newcastle" was a common metaphor meaning something useless.
- Lady Felicia compared Bebe Fontaine to Muriel Box, a passionate feminist and talented director, producer, and screenwriter. She and husband Sydney Box won an Oscar for *The Seventh Veil* (1945).
- Alan Turing, mathematician and *Enigma* codebreaker, was perhaps the most infamous homosexual in the 1950s when homosexuality was illegal. Alternatives to prison included aversion therapy treatments,

electric shocks, chemical castration, religious counseling, and psychoanalysis. During the war, prosecution for homosexual activity had increased, worrying officials that homosexuals dealing with government secrets could be blackmailed into giving away those secrets. Finally, by 1957, Sir John Wolfenden's report advised the British government that homosexuality should not be illegal. Ten years later, homosexual acts between men older than 21 were finally decriminalized.

4.2 "The Brewer's Daughter"

> Father Brown—"It would certainly be a surprise to the global theological community if [the Holy Grail] was found in a brewery in Kembleford."

Original Air Date: January 5, 2016
Writer: Kit Lambert
Director: Paul Gibson
Shooting locations: Donnington Brewery, Donnington near Stow-on-the-Wold, Gloucestershire; the Coach & Horses Inn (a brewery pub) in Longborough, near Moreton-in-Marsh, Gloucestershire
Father Brown untwists intricacies of the plot when a fire kills a brewery owner whose daughter is involved with Sid.
Guest Stars:
  Rosemary Boyle as Grace Fitzgerald
  Sean Blowers as Martin Cartwright
  Tristan Beint as Harry Fitzgerald
  John Hogg as Owen Brunt
  Katie Griffiths as Rose Kane
  John Burton as Sergeant Goodfellow

- In a brewery, a cooper was one who made and repaired barrels or casks.
- Rose claims she was a "cuckoo in the nest" when her father remarried, meaning she felt unwelcome and in the wrong place.
- Father Brown discovered evidence which has upset Inspector Mallory once again. "Give me one good reason not to arrest you for removing evidence from a scene of a crime." Father Brown replies, "The paperwork."
- Sid was morose that Grace was not to be the love of his life after all, particularly since her father owned a brewery. "All that glisters is not gold," Father Brown told him, quoting Shakespeare's *The Merchant of Venice*.

4.3 "The Hangman's Demise"

Father Brown—"Come now, Mrs. McCarthy. Not every man who invites you out to lunch will turn out to be a murderer."

Original Air Date: January 6, 2016
Writer: Dan Muirden
Director: David Beauchamp
Shooting locations: Broad Campden Quaker Meeting House, Chipping Campden, Gloucestershire
Father Brown gets involved in solving two murders after a retired hangman is poisoned.
Guest Stars:
Liam Jeavons as Thomas Lightman
Rob Jarvis as Henry Lee
Adie Allen as Iris Lightman
John Duttine as George Hammond
Charlotte Randle as Edie Lee
John Burton as Sergeant Goodfellow

- At Henry's death, Father Brown quoted Alfred, Lord Tennyson's poem *Inevitable*: "The stream will cease to flow, the wind will cease to blow. The clouds will cease to fleet, the heart will cease to beat. For all things must die."
- Lady Felicia doubted that Mrs. McCarthy ever read anything by Constance Spry, the legendary British floral designer.
- Father Brown called hemlock a "strange choice of poison, it paralyses the body, slowly, but leaves the mind untouched." All parts of the plant are toxic even in small amounts, and there is no antidote.
- The last people to be hanged in the UK were Peter Allen and Gwynne Evans in August 1964. In the 1950s, two men were hanged, then were later found to be innocent, turning public opinion against capital punishment.
- Unlike in today's judicial system where appeals after a conviction of guilt can take years to come to fruition, anyone found guilty of a capital crime could be hanged within three weeks. The law extended back to Victorian times when it was thought that that was enough time for any new evidence to come to light and for the guilty one to make his peace with God.[41]

4.4 "The Crackpot of the Empire"

Lady Felicia—"You know what [Father Brown's] like, he's probably sleuthing somewhere."

Original Air Date: January 7, 2016
Writer: Lol Fletcher
Director: David Beauchamp
Two years ago, ventriloquist Uncle Mirth was hospitalized. When
    attendees at his Welcome Home party begin to die, Father Brown
    finds out who set up the deadly practical jokes to get revenge.
Guest Stars:
    Toby Longworth as Julius "Uncle Mirth"
    Richard Braine as Henry Kirkov
    Oona Kirsch as Annabelle Marcel
    Laurence Kennedy as Sir Mortimer
    Reanne Farley as Eve Telford
    Sam O'Mahony as Jacob Doyle
    John Burton as Sergeant Goodfellow

- As Mrs. McCarthy rests, Lady Felicia reads an erotic lesbian novel by
  Lucia Morell, titled *Lulu and Lucia*, also found in episode 3.8 "Lair of
  the Libertines."
- According to the *BBC News Magazine* of May 25, 2010, about 400
  ventriloquists were working in the UK in the 1950s and 1960s. It was a
  major branch of show business.
- Uncle Mirth's dummy was named Kafka, sharing his name with
  Franz Kafka, a German novelist whose books include *The Trial*, *The
  Castle*, and *The Metamorphosis*.
- The title derived from Uncle Mirth's theme song: "I'm loony, loopy,
  hooky, kooky, I'm the crackpot of the empire."

4.5 "The Daughter of Autolycus"

Father Brown—"My God sets no store by earthly treasures."

Original Air Date: January 8, 2016
Writer: Jude Tindall
Director: Paul Gibson
Shooting locations: Great Parlour, Chastleton House, Moreton-
    in-Marsh, Oxfordshire; Gloucester Cathedral, Gloucestershire
    (Bishop's palace)
When Marianne Delacroix, Flambeau's daughter, is kidnapped, he
    asks for Father Brown's help in stealing the ransom object.
Guest Stars:
    Gina Bramhill as Marianne Delacroix
    Jo Stone-Fewings as Nero Hound
    Colin McFarlane as Cardinal Papillon

Roger Ashton-Griffiths as Cardinal Bonipogio
Michael Pennington as Bishop Reynard
John Light as Hercule Flambeau
Gerry Cannell as the Pope
Chris Cowlin as Receptionist
Adrian Dobston as Chauffeur
Colin Murtagh as Swiss Guard
Rock Salt as Terry
John Burton as Sergeant Goodfellow

- Nero Hound identified Autolycus as son of the god Hermes who inherited his father's skill for theft and trickery; he could never be caught when he was stealing.
- The Pope at the time of Queen Elizabeth's coronation on June 2, 1953, was Pius XII, which dates the episode to just prior. The Swiss Guards, in their colorful red, blue, and yellow uniforms with plumed helmets, are a corps of Swiss soldiers charged with the pope's safety, much like the Secret Service guards the U.S. president.
- Bishop Talbot had called Father Brown the "Eleventh Plague of Egypt." The others involved locusts, boils, hail, darkness, lice, water turning to blood, and the murder of firstborn children (Exodus, chapters 7–11).
- When Bishop Reynard worried that he'll be literally "sent to Coventry," an industrial blue-collar city in Warwickshire, the phrase also meant he'll be ostracized. Allegedly, in the 17th century, Cromwell, an enemy of King Charles I, sent soldiers who were loyal to the king to Coventry where they were shunned by the townspeople. Nazi bombs destroyed the entire city in World War II. Flambeau mentioned that the city will be getting a new cathedral to replace the one bombed in 1940, and in 1962, the new cathedral was consecrated.
- Playing Nero Hound, Jo Stone-Fewings is the real-life husband of Nancy Carroll, Lady Felicia.

4.6 "The Rod of Asclepius"

Sid Carter—"Father Brown is not your average priest."

Original Air Date: January 11, 2016
Writer: Jude Tindall
Director: David Beauchamp
Lady Felicia and Mrs. McCarthy are hospitalized after a car accident. When murders start occurring in the same hospital, Father Brown intervenes to save his friends.
Guest Stars:

Sarah Ball as Matron Baxter
Rachel Teate as Peggy Fletcher
Dominic Mafham as Sir Malcolm Braithwaite
Faye Castelow as Flora Honeywell
Gillian Bevan as Mrs. Steel
Ben Mansfield as Dr. Tony Fairfax
Jules Woodman as Mrs. Garrity
John Branwell as Albert Garrity
John Burton as Sergeant Goodfellow

- Lady Felicia wishes to be treated by a doctor from Harley Street in London, an area known for its numerous medical specialists. Doctor Braithwaite was fearful that attention drawn to Kembleford's hospital vagaries would detract from the newly instituted National Health Service. In 1948 the NHS was created with the tenet that health care should be available to all, regardless of a patient's ability to pay. It remains free at the point of use for UK residents.
- In the 18th century, carbon dioxide, oxygen, and nitrous oxide were discovered by Joseph Priestley. Inhaling a combination of the gases during surgery kept the patient unconscious and pain free. To ensure that the medical terminology and procedures were accurate to the 1950s, Jonathan Reinarz, a professor of medical history, advised on this episode.
- After speaking with Father Brown, Nurse Honeywell said the hospital matron would have her "guts for garters" if she were late. The phrase may have come from an era when thieves were drawn and quartered as punishment. Their intestines could theoretically have then been used for garters to hold up men's stockings.
- In Greek mythology, Asclepius, the son of Apollo, was honored as the god of healing. A serpent wrapped around a rod symbolized a snake's ability to quickly go from lethargy to activity and signified progression from sickness to health. Legend has it that Moses used a bronze serpent on a pole to cure snakebites.
- Doctor Braithwaite denounces his first wife as a "Tiller girl," meaning a dancer in a troupe known for its synchronized kicks, much like the Rockettes of Radio City Music Hall.
- Nurse Honeywell planned to become a doctor, a lofty goal. By 1950 only one in 20 medical students were women.

4.7 "The Missing Man"

Father Brown—"Not for me, aircraft. I get wobbly legs on ladders."

Original Air Date: January 12, 2016
Writer: Rachel Flowerday
Director: David Beauchamp
A RAF pilot missing for eight years returns home only to die in
   mysterious circumstances. Father Brown must determine if it was
   suicide or murder.
Guest Stars:
   Leah Whitaker as Meg Le Broc
   Oliver Le Sueur as Geoffrey Le Broc
   Madeleine Harris as Milly Le Broc
   Rupert Vansittart as Arthur Le Broc
   Oliver Dimsdale as Ned Le Broc
   Ashley Margolis as Jackie
   John Burton as Sergeant Goodfellow

- The small plane that Milly flew was an Auster Autocrat, a single
  engine three-seater used by individual pilots for charter flights
  and photography. With a wingspan of 36 feet and length of 23
  feet, it had a maximum speed of 120 mph. In this episode, its
  registration number was G-AIGD and was flown by stunt pilot
  Andrew Dixon.
- Father Brown anointed Ned's eyes, ears, nose, lips, hands, and feet
  with holy oil. However, according to Catholic doctrine, he would not
  have anointed Ned since he was already dead. Extreme Unction (last
  anointing), as it was known, or the Sacrament of the Anointing of the
  Sick, is meant to offer healing and strength and prepares the near-
  death receiver to depart this life.[42]
- Relief at landing the plane, Father Brown quotes Psalm 18:11, "And he
  ascended upon the cherubim and He flew. He flew upon the wings of
  the winds."
- A plot point in the episode is reminiscent of a Sherlock Holmes
  mystery in which he refers to the curious incident of the dog in the
  night-time. The fact that it did nothing was the curious incident.
- When Mrs. McCarthy wondered who would want to hang in the air
  in a "glorified tin can," Lady Felicia replied that Amy Johnson made
  it look glamorous. Johnson's career in aviation began in 1928 when,
  after flying solo, she became the first British-trained female ground
  engineer. She was also the first woman to fly solo to Australia in
  1930. In World War II, she joined the Air Transport Auxiliary
  ferrying aircraft from factories to RAF (Royal Air Force) bases.
  During one of these flights, her plane crashed into the Thames, and
  she drowned.

4.8 "The Resurrectionists"

Father Brown—"It's never too late to ask for forgiveness."

Original Air Date: January 13, 2016
Writer: Rob Kinsman
Director: James Larkin
The day after his funeral, Alex's grave and coffin are found empty.
It could be grave robbers or Alex back from the dead. Father
Brown must figure out how he really died and how he managed his
resurrection.
Guest Stars:
   Paul Lacoux as Dr. Harris
   Eleanor Wyld as Catherine Blackstone
   Pooky Quesnel as Ruth Moore
   Will Richardson as Alexander Moore
   Ryan Watson as Ian Moore
   Richard Lumsden as Peter Blackstone
   John Burton as Sergeant Goodfellow

• Resurrectionists was an elite term for grave robbers and body-
snatchers. At a time when bodies were needed by medical schools
for dissection, removing a corpse from a grave became a dangerous
and difficult, but lucrative, business. It was reprehensible, though
not illegal, to steal a corpse; nevertheless, the majority of bodies used
in medical schools was supplied by resurrectionists. With the 1832
Passage of the Anatomy Act, Britain, recognizing the need of bodies
for research, allowed medical schools to use unclaimed bodies or
those where the family gave permission. In the 1880s, the regular
practice of embalming ended body snatching because it enabled the
schools to keep bodies on hand for months.
• The difference between a casket and a coffin is that a casket is a
traditionally built rectangular box. A coffin, in which Alexander
was buried, has six sides allowing it to be wider at the shoulders and
narrower at the feet, thus saving wood.

4.9 "The Sins of the Father"

Father Brown—"I've always been fascinated by civilization
and its discontents."

Original Air Date: January 14, 2016
Writer: Al Smith
Director: Paul Gibson
A letter warns a local aeronautics magnate that his son will be

murdered. Father Brown uncovers events in all the suspects' pasts that influence their current actions.

Guest Stars:
Robert Daws as Robert Twyman
Paul Bown as Mordaunt Jackson
Amy Noble as Rosie Everton
Oscar Dunbar as Calvin Twyman
Dean Williamson as Lester Wallace
John Burton as Sergeant Goodfellow

- A locked-room mystery is one in which a murder is committed in an inaccessible area by someone with no logical means of escape afterward. The Twyman house was locked, therefore, Twyman or Wallace had to be the murderer, yet neither had motive to kill Calvin. Only after Wallace admitted that he had allowed a visitor in does an alternative suspect appear.
- Calvin claims that the piano competition is a doddle, i.e., something easy to attain. His father accuses Rosie of "sailing close to the wind," that is, becoming obnoxious.
- When Lady Felicia developed a sore throat, she sent Sid to find a pineapple whose enzymes have anti-inflammatory properties known to reduce throat irritation. Also, its vitamin C boosts the immune system. Pineapples grow in the tropics, so after transport, they were expensive to buy in the UK, making them a treat for the wealthy only. Lady Felicia was familiar with them, but Sid wasn't.
- Rosie Everton had covered the "Belcher scandal." In 1948, the Labour party's John Belcher fell in with a lobbyist who plied him with expensive gifts at a time of rationing for ordinary citizens. In return, Belcher was to prevent prosecution of a company that had breached paper rationing rules. Belcher used his position as Parliamentary secretary to the Board of Trade to receive gifts and other favors. The resulting scandal led to his resignation.
- Dr. Jackson relied on Freud's methods in psychoanalysis and hypnosis. Rather than cure Twyman's guilt over manufacturing faulty aircraft for profit, the unscrupulous Jackson used Twyman's fear of discovery to avenge the death of his son. Both doctor and patient could benefit from true psychoanalysis, and the deaths of two people could have been avoided.

4.10 "The Wrath of Baron Samdi"

Father Brown—"'Mrs. McCarthy was right.' Never expected those to be my last words."

Original Air Date: January 15, 2016
Writer: Tahsin Guner
Director: James Larkin
When a group of jazz musicians find themselves in Kembleford after their car breaks down, Father Brown ends up in the middle of a conflict between the singer and a voodoo priest. It soon appears that there is a homicidal poisoner in the presbytery targeting a main character.
Guest Stars:
Cornelius Macarthy as Emmanuel Jannitte
Claire Prempeh as Voodouisant
Michelle Asante as Yveline Lafond
Paul Thornley as Joseph Sinclair
Tosin Olomowewe as Lloyd Bennett
Tom Morley as Tommy Sinclair
John Burton as Sergeant Goodfellow

- In Haitian Voodoo, Baron Samdi was a mysterious god of death and black magic. He watched over the spirits of the dead, admitted souls to the spirit world, and could cure humans of diseases. So the dead do not return as zombies, he ensured that corpses rot in the ground.
- Several Haitian terms are used in the episode: Emmanuel calls Joseph a "cochon"—a pig; Yveline refers to Emmanuel as her houngan—her voodoo priest. Voodoo's creator god is Bondye. Tommy explains that Voodoo is syncretic, meaning a combination of two religions. Yveline exemplifies this in her illuminasyon, that is, devotion to the Virgin Mary as Lwa and prays the Hail Mary to her in French.
- Mrs. McCarthy exclaims over the cost of staying in the luxury hotel for £20 a night, equal to approximately £580 today. In 2022 U.S. dollars, that's more than $750.
- Sid angrily referred to Mallory as a Keystone Cop, an incompetent (though comic) police force in silent film slapstick.
- Inspector Mallory, certain that all came out right in the end, calls the situation "swings and roundabouts." The phrase, mostly used in the UK, means balancing. Americans might say "six to one, half dozen to the other." What is lost in one instance would be equaled by pluses in another.

Season 5

Despite statements by Dan McGolpin, controller at BBC Daytime, that "Father Brown goes from strength to strength and continues to be the most popular drama series on daytime television," after last season, fans might be forgiven for expecting that the series was in danger of being cancelled. Riveting scenes in two of the episodes had dealt with the near-deaths of main characters Father Brown and Mrs. McCarthy. On the other hand, two other episodes dealt with someone returning from the dead. Will Trotter, however, had no intention of letting the show lapse despite any suspicions to the contrary. He was "delighted with how well audiences have taken to the shows.... Father Brown [is] a real gem of a programme and this is highlighted by its global popularity."[43] So, perhaps to reassure viewers that all was well in Kembleford after all, and that the next season was indeed on tap, the fifth season began with a Christmas special in December, two or three weeks before the customary season premiere in January.

Mark Williams was eager to get back to work. He told one interviewer, "It's going to sound so twee (quaint), but it's the truth. Working with the same team over 45 episodes, it really is like a little tribe. And I'm actually getting excited about seeing everyone again. The nearer we get, the more I'm thinking 'Yeah! We're going to play with Father Brown again.'"[44]

In this season, the Chief Inspector's subordinate, Sergeant Goodfellow, played by John Burton, is promoted to the regular cast and gains a place in the introductory list. Jack Deam was moved to third on the list under Sorcha Cusack. Unfortunately, as Burton gained a larger role, two of the favorite regulars would be missing for most of the season. Alex Price who plays Sid, Lady Felicia's chauffeur, is missing, but viewers don't learn the reason for his absence until the 11th episode, "The Sins of Others." In reality, Price was cast in the role of Draco Malfoy in *Harry Potter and the Cursed Child*, a West End theatrical production. Happily for him, he reprised the role when the show played in the United States on Broadway. Lady Felicia appears in only two of Season 5's episodes before purportedly leaving Kembleford to join her husband, Lord Montague, in Rhodesia where he has been promoted to a government post. She was off the set working in a German drama called *Woyzeck*.[45] Replacing her, actress Emer Kenny joins the cast as Penelope Windermere, nicknamed Bunty, Lady Felicia's niece. Flambeau would later describe Bunty in episode 7.10 as "a firework, charming, but all color and show and gone in a flash." As series developer, Tahsin Guner keeps his hand in and is credited as writer on three of Season 5's episodes.

5.1 "The Star of Jacob"

Father Brown—"The thing about miracles is that they do happen."[46]

Original Air Date: December 23, 2016
Writer: Jude Tindall

Director: Paul Gibson
Shooting locations: Cornbury Park Estate, Charlbury, Oxfordshire
Festivities at Lady Felicia's Christmas ball at Montague mansion are
    marred by the kidnapping of a duke's son.
Guest Stars:
    Roger May as Canon Damien Fox
    Raymond Coulthard as John Langton
    Zannah Hodson as Diana Langton
    Harriet Layhe as Amy Jones
    Isla Blair as Nanny Langton
    Elliott Jordan as George Parkin
    Cooper and Austin Curtis as Baby Jacob
    Colin Deaney as Hornby
    Dean Andrews as Michael Negal
    Christos Lawton as Basil Urquhart
    Maddy Hill as Hannah Parkin
    Mary Keegan as Matron

- Hobbling about on crutches with gout, a form of painful arthritis that often affects the big toe, Inspector Mallory jokes that he didn't even get a "red card," a reference to a soccer rule in which the referee shows a red card to a player who disobeyed a rule and is therefore ejected from the game.
- Canon Fox assumes everything is "shipshape and Bristol," from the nautical term meaning organized and in good order.
- Mallory believes that Parkin is "as guilty as Bluebeard." According to legend, Bluebeard was a wealthy man who left his wife the keys to all the castle doors but forbade her to open one of them. When he leaves, she disobeys and finds the bodies of his former wives. On his return, Bluebeard threatens to behead her as punishment for her disobedience, but she is saved by her brothers.
- Baby David was returned in the manger because, as Father Brown says, "the church is never locked." Unfortunately, in modern times, Catholic churches are often locked to discourage vandals or thieves. Michael hints that "Jochebed" left the baby in the church. Father Brown recognizes the name from Exodus 2:1–10 and 6:20 as the mother of Moses, who put him in a basket in the bulrushes where he was found and raised as a prince by the Pharaoh's daughter.
- Script writer Jude Tindall revealed that she had been wanting to do a nativity scene, but the cost (thousands of pounds) and the Cotswold's spring and summer temperatures (higher than 70°F) made it impractical, plus the "animals and children, all the things

you're not supposed to work with." Producer Caroline Slater thought it was fun to organize the scenes even though the actors, 40 extras, and 12 children were wrapped in winter garb. As a sort of reward, the caterers served Christmas dinner during the breaks.[47]
- During the filming in May, the crew of Snow Business created a "snow" base of recycled wood pulp over a membrane which gave the fake snow some depth and also made clean up easier. Because of the dialogue, a noisy machine that usually created falling snow was not used. Instead, a snow product was burned, and its ashes floated down, convincingly giving the illusion of falling snow.[48]
- The episode was watched by more than 2.2 million viewers.[49]

5.2 "The Labyrinth of the Minotaur"

Father Brown—"You need to tell the truth and save your soul."

Original Air Date: January 2, 2017
Writer: Jude Tindall
Director: Paul Gibson
Locations: Stanway House, Stow-on-the-Wold, Gloucestershire
Lady Felicia's niece Bunty needs a place to lie low after a certain indiscretion, so Father Brown and Mrs. McCarthy take on "babysitting" the 25-year-old.
Guest Stars:
Emer Kenny as Penelope "Bunty" Windermere
Max Beesley Snr as Norman Vanderlande
Claudia Jessie as Joan Vanderlande
Frances Barber as Davina Malmort
Caitlin Drabble as Ruby Jewel/Smith
Ed Cooper Clarke as Robert Malmort
Jonathan Ryland as Chester Logan
Philip Barker as Arthur Malmort
Colin Deaney as Hornby

- Bunty describes the Malmort mansion as being like Gormenghast. Beginning in 1946, author Mervyn Peake wrote three fantasy novels about the residents of Castle Gormenghast, an ancient deteriorating manor.
- Bobby Malmort carries a figure of Robert Craufurd, a Scottish Major-General of the early 19th century. His violent outbreaks earned him the nickname "Black Bob" but, as commander of the Light Brigade, he turned it into a famous fighting unit. He was one

of Field Marshall Arthur Wellington's best commanders of the Napoleonic era.

- Ruby Jewel used to dance at the Windmill club in Soho, a striptease club that opened in the 1930s. Bunty gave her a stole that cost 60 guineas (about £63 or $81).
- Bobby suggests that Bunty stay overnight lest she drive home "half cut," meaning drunk.
- The Malmort maze, similar to Pisani's maze designed by Frigimelica, was a circular path with nine layers and many dead ends. Pisani's consisted of hedges so high it was nearly impossible to find one's way out. Legend has it that Hitler was afraid to enter it. Father Brown finds red yarn that Joan used to find her way—"Ariadne's thread." Ariadne was Theseus's lover, who gave him a ball of red twine, so he could find his way out of the Minotaur's labyrinth. King Minos had built the labyrinth to contain the monstrous Minotaur creature.
- Because Joan is an intellectual, Bobby calls her a Blue Stocking, a derogatory term for an intelligent woman.

5.3 "The Eve of St John"

Mrs. McCarthy—"Sometimes men are just more trouble than they're worth."

Original Air Date: January 3, 2017
Writer: Jude Tindall
Director: Gary Williams
Father Brown steps in when a coven of witches comes to Kembleford and one of them gets killed.
Guest Stars:
  Hara Yannas as Lilith Lafitte
  Oliver Gilbert as Reverend Peter Allsworthy
  John Sessions as Reverend Adam Gillespie
  Sally Dexter as Selina Crow
  Ken Bones as Eugene Bone
  Estella Daniels as Dione Moon

- St. John's Eve and the summer Solstice coincided on June 23, 1950.
- Bunty suggests the villagers should consider the Germans' Greiköperkultur (public nudism), to which Reverend Allsworthy retorts that they want neither Germans nor nudists. Father Brown, who usually finds himself in conflict with either his bishop or the police, instead clashes with the leaders of other religions in his acceptance of, and curiosity into, the witches.

- Bunty also indicates that the invitation to dinner will be a "knees up," meaning a party and not, presumably, Christians on their knees. Mallory calls the young girl a "tearaway," a hell-raiser.
- Several biblical verses are quoted in the episode: "Offer hospitality to one another without grumbling" (1 Peter 4:9); "There shall not be found among you any one that makes his son or daughter pass through the fire, or that uses divination, or an observer of times, or an enchanter, or a witch" (Deuteronomy 18:10); "Oh ye of little faith" (Matthew 8:26); "A man or a woman that has a familiar Spirit, or is a Wizard, shall surely be put to death" (Leviticus 20:27); "Be sober, be vigilant; because your adversary the devil, as a roaring lion, walketh about, seeking whom he may devour" (1 Peter 5:8); and "Had they stood in my council and did they but proclaim to my people my words, they would have brought them back from evil ways and from their wicked deeds" (Jeremiah 23:22).
- Unsuccessfully hunting for mushrooms, Bunty claims she'd have more luck searching for the Scarlet Pimpernel, a mysterious Englishman and his men who rescued aristocrats in France before they could be guillotined. The Pimpernel is the protagonist of Emma Orczy's historical novel set during the French Revolution. Later, Bunty avows that Crows Wood is a hundred-acre wood and finding something in it would be as difficult as finding a bear with very little brain, a reference to Winnie the Pooh stories by A.A. Milne.
- Selina Crow willingly offers Eugene to Dione rather than put up his "whinging," his complaining.

5.4 "The Chedworth Cyclone"

Father Brown—"Redemption is real, if you truly seek it."

Original Air Date: January 4, 2017
Writer: Paul Matthew Thompson
Director: Paul Gibson
Shooting locations: Upton House, Banbury, Warwickshire; Earle's Spit 'n' Sawdust Gym, Banbury, Oxfordshire
When a local boxer is found dead under suspicious circumstances, Father Brown must uncover the murderer to ensure a fair fight.
Guest Stars:
Chris Gordon as Jeb Cornish
Samuel Rush as Connor McNeive
Bill Fellows as Teddy O'Connell
Ewa Jenson as Rita Simmons

Nicholas Cass as Roy Tomkins
Martin Kemp as Dennis Nelson
Pablo Raybould as Master of Ceremonies
Mens Sana Tamakloe as Devon Hoyle
Jonathan Rigby as Commentator

- The boxing agreement that Dennis Nelson negotiated (by blackmailing a councilman) was dated Thursday, June 6, 1953; however, that date fell on a Saturday.
- The Marquess of Queensbury Rules of boxing were written by John Graham Chambers in 1867. The 12 rules include, among others, the size of the boxing ring, the length of each bout, what happens if a man is down for 10 seconds, the quality of the gloves and shoes.
- Racketeering is defined as a crime involving attempts to get money from a person or organization through intimidation.
- Teddy confesses that he sold Jeb down the river for a figurative 30 pieces of silver, coincidentally the same amount Judas was given to betray Jesus.
- During filming, Martin Kemp spoke to an interviewer. To prepare for the part, he said, "You use bits and pieces from everything you've ever done, characters you've played before and bits and pieces from life." He had never worked with Mark Williams before but noted that "everybody says good things about him across the business, and it's true, he's the nicest man."[50] Kemp found gangsters "fun to play." He confessed, "I'm a big believer that all of us inside have this little box called 'evil.' But we all tend to keep it closed up and the nice thing about ... playing a bad guy is you get to open it up, look at all the toys, throw 'em out, play with 'em for a little while then put the lid back on and go back home."[51]

5.5 "The Hand of Lucia"

Scarlett—"I hear you're a bit of an amateur sleuth, Father."

Father Brown—"I dabble."

Original Air Date: January 5, 2017
Writer: Lol Fletcher
Director: Paul Gibson
Erotica novelist Lucia Morell moves into Kembleford and confronts her former lover. When one of them is found dead, the suspects' stories don't add up. Instead, Father Brown finds clues in Lucia's own book.

Guest Stars:
  Hetty Baynes as Lucia Morell
  Sam Cox as Friar Victor Novak
  Claire Brown as Mildred Nook
  Kris Olsen as James Lansford
  Nicola Thorp as Scarlet Finch
  Carol Royle as Lady Ursula Lansford

- *Lulu and Lucia* was also mentioned in the episodes 3.8 "Lair of the Libertines" and 4.4 "The Crackpot of the Empire."
- Bunty remembered that, in the novel, Lucia had Runic symbols on her wrist revealing Lulu's identity and explaining why the killer removed her hand. Runes were magical signs used to transmit secret messages. As the runes of stone or wood are cast, the symbols may stand for travel, gifts, joy, protection, success, or other divination prophecies.

5.6 "The Eagle and the Daw"

> Father Brown—"I believe that only God should have the power to take a life."

Original Air Date: January 6, 2017
Writer: Kit Lambert
Director: Gary Williams
Father Brown's old nemesis Katherine Corven wants to confess before
    she's hanged, but her confession is not what the priest expects to hear.
Guest Stars:
  Grace Chilton as Rebecca Cooper
  Vicky Entwistle as Warden Frances Whittaker
  Kate O'Flynn as Katherine Corven
  Benjamin Fisher as Raymond Worrall
  Alan Williams as Blind 'Arry Slow

- Mrs. McCarthy declared that putting Father Brown in jail really "takes the biscuit." This is the British form of "takes the cake," meaning an utterly ridiculous notion.
- A "rag and bone man," also called a ragman or "bone-picker," collected rags, bits of metal, or other trash to sell for a few cents. He might carry his finds in a bag slung over the shoulder or in a wheelbarrow or cart.
- Mystery writer John Dickson Carr was very much influenced by Chesterton and, like several of those who belonged to the Detection Club, he had a list of "rules" that mystery writers should follow. His

protagonist, Gideon Fell, ruminates on ways in which the classic locked room mystery could be solved. One solution was that "a man shoots himself with a gun fastened on the end of an elastic—the gun, as he releases it, being carried up out of sight into the chimney."[52]

- Mallory wonders if Father Brown was corrupted by his exposure to murderers or is he good at catching criminals because of his own homicidal instinct. In Chesterton's story "The Hammer of God," Father Brown is asked how he knew the murderer. He replied to a similar query, "I am a man … and therefore have all devils in my heart."[53]
- Father Brown related the story of the eagle and the jackdaw, a small inquisitive crow:

"A jackdaw sees an eagle swoop down on a spring lamb, carrying it away to eat and the jackdaw believes himself to be as powerful. So he flies over and lands on the back of another lamb, grips it with his claws and flaps away with all his might. But he can't lift the lamb. The shepherd sees him, catches him, clips his wings, and gives him to his children as a pet in a cage. Vanity is very dangerous."

5.7 "The Smallest of Things"

Father Brown—"Murder's not endearing."

Original Air Date: January 9, 2017
Writer: Tahsin Guner
Director: Bob Tomson
The tiny murder room staged in a dollhouse is the scene Father Brown investigates to solve an old crime.
Guest Stars:
    Mariah Gale as Agnes Lesser
    Colin Mace as DCI Webb
    David Yelland as Wilber Lesser
    Chloe Howman as Lucy Lesser
    Jude Owusu as Daniel Abeson
    Sonia Saville as Florence Lesser

- Frances Glessner Lee created *Nutshell Studies of Unexplained Death* that were miniature homicide scenes used to train investigators. As the first female American police captain, Lee began creating scenes in the 1940s after seeing a need for educating detectives in what to look for and how to handle evidence. Using crafting skills, her realistic blood splatters, tiny corpses, and teeny bullet holes taught observation and deduction by displaying a murder scene "in a nutshell." The dioramas are still used and were displayed in the Renwick Gallery of the Smithsonian American Art Museum in 2017.

- Performing a lobotomy involved drilling into a patient's skull to cut the connections between the prefrontal cortex and the rest of the brain. The method was used in the early 1900s to treat behaviors such as schizophrenia, mania, and depression. Agnes may have suffered from a dissociative identity disorder, thereby distancing herself from traumatic deaths.
- G.K. Chesterton also created dioramas of theaters, complete with characters. Later, writing that "all the essential morals which modern men need to learn could be deduced from this toy.... Art does not consist in expanding things. Art consists of cutting things down." In a toy theater "by reducing the scale of events it can introduce much larger events." He believed, "You can only represent very big ideas in very small spaces."[54]

5.8 "The Crimson Feather"

Janek—"It is in God's hands now."

Father Brown—"Yes, why do you think He sent me?"

Original Air Date: January 10, 2017
Writer: Kit Lambert
Director: Paul Gibson
Shooting locations: Toddington Railway Station, Toddington, Gloucestershire; exterior Earle's Spit'n'Sawdust Gym, Banbury, Oxfordshire
Mrs. McCarthy's goddaughter has come to visit, but when she goes missing, Father Brown follows clues to a risqué men's club.
Guest Stars:
    Alex Sawyer as Oscar Bergeres
    Letty Butler as Verity Persby
    Peter Stark as Janek Lasocki
    William Travis as Maurice Cranage
    Emily Atack as Fifi Caviara
    Eva Feiler as Joselyn O'Donnell

- When Janek asked Father Brown to help him write a letter home, the priest confessed that his Polish is *straszny* (horrible).
- Mrs. McCarthy would hardly describe working in a burlesque club as *artistic*, as Joselyn claimed. But such dancers did combine theatrics, erotic moves, extravagant costuming, singing, and even comedy in their act.
- The Abortion Law Reform Association was established in 1936 in order to campaign for legalized abortions. By the 1950s, with the

women's movement and availability of birth control pills, abortion was still illegal. It wasn't until 1968 that legalized abortion under certain conditions was allowed.

5.9 "The Lepidopterist's Companion"

Mrs. McCarthy—"I never realized how stressful being a librarian could be."

Original Air Date: January 11, 2017
Writer: Kit Lambert
Director: Paul Gibson
Mrs. McCarthy volunteers to take over the mobile library for the injured librarian. Father Brown discovers a malevolent scheme hidden in one of the books.
Guest Stars:
  Thomas Pickles as Lewis Ward
  Alan Williams as Blind 'Arry Slow
  Andrew Greenough as Graham Cartwright
  Elizabeth Berrington as Margaret Cartwright
  Holly Bodimeade as Ada Rawlins

- A lepidopterist is someone who studies butterflies.
- Mrs. McCarthy accuses Father Brown of being the Great Kembleford Book Thief for not returning overdue library books. When he protests, she exclaims, "Codswallop!" meaning nonsense or rubbish. Later, Blind 'Arry saw Lewis having a "barny" with Ada; that is, they were squabbling. Lewis was "skint," slang for "broke."
- Graham Cartwright used a Kodak Duaflex camera to photograph the check donation event. The twin lens reflex camera, manufactured between 1947 and 1960, had a large, bright viewing lens with a hooded cover and required 620 format film. Though it came with a neck strap, better shots could be had with a steadying tripod.
- For developing film in the photography studio and in Father Brown's improvised darkroom, film, sensitive to blue and green light, could safely be developed under red light.
- The half-crown that Harry paid his library fines with would equal about 25 cents in American currency.

5.10 "The Alchemist's Secret"

Father Brown—"I'm going to shake the tree and see what falls out."

Original Air Date: January 12, 2017
Writer: Rob Kinsman
Director: Simon Gibney
Father Brown searches for answers to an ancient riddle hidden at the university in order to exonerate his friend, an elderly professor, of the charge of murder.
Guest Stars:
  Michael Vivian as the Architect
  Darren Strange as the Alchemist
  James Laurenson as Professor Hilary Ambrose
  Richard Southgate as Timothy Hargreaves
  Danny Webb as Principal Malcolm Pendle
  Steve Furst as Porter Stanley Crawford
  Emerald O'Hanrahan as Victoria Nicholson

• The germ-infested items were from the Bubonic plague or Black Death that was caused by fleas on rats and then passed on to humans. The disease struck Britain in 1665 and killed three-quarters of the people afflicted. This explained the disappearance of the entire village of Thorndike and how such germs could be used as a military weapon.
• Janus was the Roman god of beginning and endings, of doorways and gates, able to look forward to the future and back to the past. January is named after him.
• When Bunty picks up the snake, Mrs. McCarthy exclaims in Irish, "Buíochas le Dia" ("Thank God").
• Professor Ambrose's imaginary phantom resembled a plague doctor who, in the 17th century, wore a beaked bird-like mask, believing that it would protect him from air-borne germs.

5.11 "The Sins of Others"

> Father Brown—"If there's one thing I have ever taught you, I hope it's that violence is never the answer.... Sid, you're the closest thing I have ever had to a son."

Original Air Date: January 13, 2017
Writer: Tahsin Guner
Director: Diana Patrick
Lady Felicia's former chauffeur Sid is released from prison after a year and seeks revenge for the injustice done to him. Father Brown attempts to save Sid from a worse crime.
Guest Stars:
  Alex Price as Sid Carter

Simon Shepherd as Edward Reese
David Reed as Giles Foster
Alex Felton as Randolph Reese
Susie Trayling as Lydia Reese
Sophie Bleasdale as Judith Miles
James Sutherland as Panama Hat Man

- The papers Sid read indicated the date of the episode. The witness statement was taken June 25, 1952. The newspaper reports that the luncheon for Giles Foster was held on August 18, 1953.
- Sid's home, a "caravan" parked in an open field, resembles a small travel trailer or a tiny house.
- Mrs. McCarthy said her scarf did not cost £20 or come from Swan & Edgar, a famous London department store near Piccadilly Circus.

5.12 "The Theatre of the Invisible"

Father Brown—"Landladies, like priests, often know more than is good for them."

Original Air Date: January 16, 2017
Writer: David Semple
Director: Bob Tomson
Shooting Location: Cornbury house, Oxfordshire
A popular radio quiz show has come to be recorded in Kembleford and, when their local landlady is murdered, Father Brown investigates the cast.
Guest Stars:
Arthur Bostrom as Richie Queenan
John Henshaw as Barney Butterfield
Jessica Turner as Joyce Merriman
Jon Glover as Jacob Rothstein
Simon Bubb as Jeremy Mayhew-Bowman
Lynda Baron as Mrs. Rudge

- The title is apt, for radio is a dramatization by invisible (to the audience) performers. Invisible theater is a public performance in which bystanders often become involved in the action that is portrayed outside of a theatrical setting, such as on a street or sidewalk.
- Barney says he wouldn't go farther than Muswell Hill, the suburb of London. He later tells the Inspector that he and Joyce were on *Variety Bandbox* together, a BBC radio variety show. Joyce thinks Father

Brown's suggestion of pastoral care sounds "jolly dee," meaning very decent.

• After seeing the damage the blocked fireplace caused, Inspector Mallory announced that he and his wife recently converted to "the electric." Central heating did not become commonplace in Britain until the 1960s and 1970s.

• Richie Queenan named his teddy bear Lord Reith. John Reith founded the British Broadcasting Company in 1922 for public service broadcasts offering educational and entertaining programs.

5.13 "The Tanganyika Green"

Father Brown—"The Lord sets a hard road for those he entrusts with a talent, but a hard road is easier with a friend."

Original Air Date: January 17, 2017
Writer: Catherine Skinner
Director: Simon Gibney
Father Brown investigates the murder of an East African Postal
    Service worker who has come to Kembleford with his daughter.
Guest Stars:
    Pepter Lunkuse as Grace Kemp
    Richard Huw as Aldous Kemp
    Shaun Prendergast as George Murray
    Gary Oliver as Frank Hammond
    Bradley Hall as John Hammond
    Miles Jupp as Wynford Collins
    Steve Hunt as Gunsmith
    Martyn Mayger as Colonial Postal Worker

• Tanganyika was a protectorate of German East Africa until World War I. Britain captured the holdings and retained them until after World War II when it became a United Nations trust territory. Besides Africa, the Colonial Service administered most of Britain's overseas possessions, including those in India, Canada, and Australia where its large staff was employed in agriculture, medicine, and education.

• Perhaps Father Brown was thinking of Isaac Newton when he mentioned that Britain has a tradition of scientists inspired by apples. Newton, myth has it, discovered gravity as he sat under a tree in Cambridge.

• Upon seeing hunting photographs in the Hammonds' shop, Father Brown wonders how it can be called a sport when instead it is a cruel and needless killing.

5.14 "The Fire in the Sky"

Father Brown—"It's time to embrace the future."

Original Air Date: January 18, 2017
Writer: Kit Lambert
Director: Diana Patrick
Inspector Mallory enlists Father Brown's help when strange alien
    lights are seen over Kembleford and a resident is found dead.
Guest Stars:
    Allegra Marland as Charlotte Bayley
    Nick Dunning as William Bayley
    Yadav Ganatra as Nikhil Prasad
    Kiran Sonia Sawar as Alisha Prasad
    David Sturzaker as Dr. Joseph Ashley
    Sam Jackson as Sean Crimp

- Scornful of rumors about aliens, Inspector Mallory wondered if he should call Buck Rogers, a character in a space opera. Rogers was a character in Philip F. Nowlan's 1928 novella *Armageddon 2419 A.D.* and subsequently appeared in comic strips, radio, film, and television.
- Doctor Ashley ordered a Galli Mainini test for pregnancy in which the patient's urine is injected into a male toad. After a few hours, if the woman was pregnant, the frog's urine would contain sperm.
- William Bayley called 999 to report the emergency. The number compares to America's emergency number 911.
- At seeing the symbol in the field, Inspector Mallory exclaims, "Flaming Nora!" a mis-pronounced phrase for the slang "flamin' 'orror."[55]
- In February 1953, the *Manchester Guardian* reported that Winston Churchill announced an amnesty for deserters. During the war, more than 13,000 soldiers, airmen, and sailors fled without leave, many of whom remained unaccounted for. Protection certificates would be given to those applying for amnesty, and they would be transferred to reserves as though after a normal demobilization.
- Doctor Ashley left the army on June 13, 1944, at the Battle of Normandy.

5.15 "The Penitent Man"

Father Brown—"No one has the right to take a life."

Original Air Date: January 19, 2017
Writer: Tahsin Guner

Director: Paul Gibson

After Flambeau is jailed, tried, and convicted for murder, Father Brown, knowing his old friend well, suspects all is not as it seems.

Guest Stars:

Ian Reddington as Samuel Jacobs

John Light as Hercule Flambeau

Dylan Brown as Terry Mitchell

Daniel Adegboyega as Lenny Stamper

Emma Pallant as Peggy Hardwick

Mike Royce as Clerk

Eric Carte as Judge

Callum Dixon as Flynn Hardwick

Manoj Anand as a Prison Inmate

Dominic Barrow as Lenny's Henchman

Marc Esse as Prison Inmate

- St. Michael the Archangel is often portrayed in battle mode with sword and shield. Persevering against evil, he stands on the back of a beast believed to represent Satan.
- Mrs. M brought Hardwick's widow some Bakewell tarts, a traditional British pastry with raspberry jam and almond cream filling.
- Mark 16:16—"The man who believes will be saved; the man who refuses to believe will be condemned."
- This episode can be dated after August 17, 1953, the date Flambeau allegedly killed Flynn Hardwick.

Season 6

The new season began filming on April 24, 2017, in locations across the Midlands in central England from Redditch to Warwick, a distance of about 18 miles. Will Trotter's excitement for *Father Brown* had not waned, and he promised that fans too would not be disappointed. "This series really puts Father Brown to the test, battling old foes, using wit and guile to right some serious wrongs and all while tending to his parishioners in the quaint village of Kembleford."[56] Gloucester City Councilman Paul James was eager to welcome the cast's return to the area that was becoming popular for production companies. "We certainly try our best to make the process of setting up the location a relatively easy one, so it becomes a place that people want to come to film," he said.[57]

The popularity of last season's pre–Christmas episode no doubt led to the reprise of Season 6's first episode also being broadcast before Christmas 2017. But despite calls for a more preeminent time slot than mid-afternoon weekdays, the BBC continued to schedule *Father Brown* for that period. Mark Williams maintained that "the effort we all put in— from the actors and writers to the production crew—shows. We work to make it the best it can be, and we turn what is a budget daytime show into real quality." The *Daily Mail* reported that

> Williams feels the BBC would do well to back *Father Brown* and reward it with a prime-time slot. He is politic enough to do no more than sigh and say with a shrug, "It's an extremely successful show. We all love doing it. We've had more success worldwide than any other BBC drama series—but we don't make those decisions. We are merely the actors."[58]

Having been an actor for many years before taking the role of Father Brown, Williams knew how the business worked. His first film as an Oxford graduate was 1982's *Privileged*, after which he held jobs totally unrelated to acting, including working in a facility where cows were artificially inseminated. He gained experience acting with the Royal Shakespeare Company and worked in films and television shows with familiar titles like *Doctor Who*, the *Harry Potter* franchise, *Shakespeare in Love*, *101 Dalmatians*, and some perhaps not-so-familiar titles, such as *Out of Order*, *Bunch of Five*, *Hunting Venus*, and *Golden Years*. Looking at his mirrored reflection, he realized he was never going to be a handsome leading man and considered that "if I'd been gorgeous I'd have risen much faster.... I was always going to be a character actor."[59]

After five previous seasons as the compassionate clerical mystery solver, he could take pride in one reviewer's assessment: "Murder has never been more delightful than on Father Brown."[60]

6.1 "The Tree of Truth"

> Father Brown—"God forgives everyone who confesses their sins and tells the truth."

Original Air Date: December 18, 2017
Writer: Jude Tindall
Director: Paul Gibson
During a Christmas pantomime, Father Brown solves a cold case making a happy holiday for a local family.
Guest Stars:
    Alex Price as Sid Carter
    Harry Long as Douglas Bovary
    Orlando Wells as Dr. Eugene Cornelius
    Lucy Briers as Prudence Bovary
    Charlotte Lucas as Rose Marie Sturgess
    Robert Ewens as Benny Clough

Laura Pitt-Pulford as Scarlett Dreyfuss
John Bowler as Bob Sturgess
Stephanie Fayerman as Ada Clough

- Father Brown's audition scene—"The lights turn blue, it is dead midnight"—comes from Shakespeare's play *Richard III*, act 5, scene 3.
- Sergeant Goodfellow urged Inspector Mallory to consider the German and British forces playing football on France's Somme on Christmas. Afterward, they went back to "beating the seven bells" out of the other, a nautical term meaning to beat someone severely. The police and Father Brown were on different sides as the armies had been but working toward the same result.
- Strangely, when Father Brown says that lying is the ninth commandment, he is using the Protestant version. In the Catholic view, forbidding to bear false witness is the eighth commandment.
- Ironically, in a previous play, Father Brown played the role of Pontius Pilate, the Roman prefect who sentenced Jesus to death.
- Douglas had been engaged to a WAAF (of the Women's Auxiliary Air Force).
- Mallory observed that Mr. Sturgess acts fishier than Billingsgate, a London fish market infamous for its vulgar language.
- Dr. Cornelius practices psychodynamic therapy. In doing so, he would help patients recognize negative emotions and realize how any repression of them affects daily behavior and relationships.

6.2 "The Jackdaw's Revenge"

Father Brown—"God is watching you every moment."

Original Air Date: January 2, 2018
Writer: Kit Lambert
Director: Gary Williams
When an old antagonist is released from prison, Father Brown acts to protect his friends from the prisoner's revenge.
Guest Stars:
Kate O'Flynn as Katherine Corven
Katie Buchholz as Edwina "Eddie" Hamsley
Paul Cawley as Robin Gladwell
Karen Meagher as Mother Winifred
Alan Williams as Blind 'Arry Slow

- In a rare continuing storyline, Katherine Corven had previously appeared in episode 5.6 "The Eagle and the Daw."

- Possibly old Mrs. Hubb went "doolally." Deolali was a Bombay sanitarium where British soldiers went to await a troopship home. Intense boredom produced peculiar behavior, coining the expression "Deolali fever."
- Katherine quotes the Book of Ruth 1:16 when Mother Winifred asks if she truly wants to enter the convent.
- Awakened by the police and Father Brown, 1950s nuns would at least be wearing night caps over their shorn hair.
- When Mallory observed that Father Brown would be "cock-a-hoop" to see Katherine again behind bars, his slang meant that the priest would be elated.

6.3 "The Kembleford Dragon"

Father Brown—"Sometimes the path of truth is the most difficult path."

Original Air Date: January 3, 2018
Writer: David Semple
Director: Christiana Ebohon-Green
After the local railroad stationmaster is killed, Father Brown must act quickly to prevent the station from being closed permanently.
Guest Stars:
    Sophie Duval as Julia Webb
    Neal Barry as Ben Webb
    Amerjit Deu as Deepak Chatterjee
    Jessie Cave as Pandora Pott
    Martyn Ellis as Buddy Arnold
    Doreen Mantle as Miss Tibby

- The characters used several distinctly British words: Buddy had a fleet of charabancs; that is, fleet buses. Ben wanted nothing to do with Pandora's "sprog," her baby. Mallory wondered why Buddy wasn't at the "gee-gees" on the holiday. Horse riders use the term "Gee!" to urge a horse on; "gee-gee" was invented by children to refer to a horse, so Mallory was inquiring why Buddy wasn't at the horse races.
- On a Bank Holiday most British businesses were closed. There are about eight such holidays celebrated throughout the year.
- Racism rears its ugly head when Mallory questions Deepak Chatterjee, "an unusual name for someone working for the *British* railway." Chatterjee asserts his knowledge by informing Mallory that he had worked for the India Railway and was responsible for thousands of miles of track.

- Mallory thought the bus company owner was richer than Rockefeller, a reference to John D. Rockefeller, considered the richest man in America. When Buddy bribes Mallory with a free excursion, Mallory retorts that not even a fortnight in Frinton would get him out of trouble. Frinton is a seaside resort.

6.4 "The Angel of Mercy"

Father Brown—"An unquenchable human spirit is one of God's greatest gifts."

Original Air Date: January 4, 2018
Writer: Dan Muirden
Director: Niall Fraser
Three deaths occur in this dark episode, but are they mercy killings, suicide, or just plain murder? Father Brown determines the answers as Mrs. McCarthy deals with a new not-so-helpful helper.
Guest Stars:
Janet Dale as Freda Knight
Roisin O'Neill as Caitlin O'Casey
Badria Timimi as Matron Sophia
Paul Greenwood as Charlie Coulter
Wanda Ventham as Ellen Jennings
Daniel Hawksford as Seth Knight

- Mrs. McCarthy has brought Freda a Battenberg cake which is traditionally a checkerboard-patterned sponge cake in pink and yellow. Its layers, covered with marzipan, are held together with apricot jam.
- Caitlin quoted 1 Peter 4:13—"Rejoice insofar as you are sharing Christ's sufferings, so that you may also be glad and shout for joy when His glory is revealed."
- Father Brown explained that the Epictetus' quote in Caitlin's journal on June 4, 1953, is wrong. The Greek stoic philosopher actually wrote, "Is freedom anything else than the right to live as we wish? Nothing else."
- Seth had a job in Swindon at Vickers, an airline manufacturing plant. Many of the planes there were built as attackers for the war effort, including one that set a world speed record.
- A white feather was the World War I symbol of cowardice meant to encourage men to enlist in the military. The term came from the white fluff on the tail of a game bird that indicated poor breeding.
- Caitlin leaves St. Mary's to be with her true love. Lesbianism was still considered illegal in 1953. Not until 1966 did Britain end criminal penalties for homosexual acts between consenting adults.

6.5 "The Face of the Enemy"

Father Brown—"If we see things only through the clouded lens of our own perspective then we are doomed."

Original Air Date: January 5, 2018
Writer: Tahsin Guner
Director: Christiana Ebohon-Green
Father Brown's involvement in a spy thriller is in keeping with the time of the Cold War. He intervenes when Lady Felicia is blackmailed to work a dangerous mission for MI5.
Guest Stars:
Alex Price as Sid Carter
Nancy Carroll as Lady Felicia
Richard Harrington as Benedict Northam
Daniel Flynn as Daniel Whittaker
Mary Antony as Lara Winslow
Richard Cunningham as Alfred Lane
Chris Wilson as the Mayor of Kembleford

- Britain's Official Secrets Act was introduced in 1911 to ensure that anyone who attempted to transmit secret military intelligence to a foreign state had to prove his innocence. After World War II, a Cold War—a political hostility that stopped short of actual war—existed between Russia and Western powers consisting of the United States and Britain until 1990 with the collapse of the Soviet Union.
- MI5 identifies its name as coming from "the fifth branch of the Directorate of Military Intelligence of the War Office." Its mission is to maintain the security of Britain against threats of terrorism and espionage. Steve Hewitt, PhD, served as intelligence advisor on the episode. His credentials include work in state surveillance and counterterrorism.
- Mrs. M observed that the romance between Felicia and Benedict was like that of Humphrey Bogart and Lauren Bacall who had met on a film set, fell in love, and married in May 1945.
- Lady Felicia tells Northam that he's her path not taken, a reference to the 1915 poem by Robert Frost, "The Road Not Taken." The final lines are its most quoted:

> "Two roads diverged in a wood, and I—
> I took the one less traveled by,
> And that has made all the difference."

6.6 "The Devil You Know"

Father Brown—"There is no mercy for those who reject His grace."

Original Air Date: January 8, 2018
Writer: Jude Tindall
Director: Niall Fraser
Father Brown helps Inspector Mallory search for the murderer of a VIP Kembleford visitor, leading him to Nazi war crimes.
Guest Stars:
    Sam Callis as Alec Frobisher
    Eva Magyar as Christina Worcester
    Adam Kotz as Eric Worcester
    Jacqueline Defferary as Shirley Krieger
    Chris Larkin as Roger Frobisher
    Clive Wood as Inspector George Ironside

- Roger claimed he and Alec were more like Cain and Abel than Romulus and Remus. Cain killed his brother Abel in Genesis 4:1–16; twins Romulus and Remus founded the city of Rome.
- Christina said Eric was more English than "John Bull," an imaginary character similar to America's Uncle Sam. Inspector Ironside referred to Father Brown as "Miss Marple," Agatha Christie's fictional village detective. Mallory renounced Ironside as "Wile E Coyote," the cartoon character forever chasing the roadrunner. When Mallory lamented that the police had "sweet Fanny Arkwright," he meant he had no clues at all.
- During the German occupation of Poland after 1939, millions of Polish Jews were killed in death camps. Polish resistance forces fought back and, when they resettled in Britain, they fought for the Allies. In 1947, Britain's Parliament offered citizenship to those who had fought the Nazis.
- Shirley enticed Roger to a new Arthur Miller play, possibly *The Crucible* premiering in London in November 1954 or *View from the Bridge*. The American playwright's latter drama debuted in London October 1956.
- As Mallory was volunteered to lead the boys' group, Bunty and Father Brown urge him to "Dyb, dyb, dyb" ("Do your best").

6.7 "The Dance of Death"

Father Brown—"Repent and the Lord will forgive you."

Original Air Date: January 9, 2018
Writer: Rob Kinsman

Director: Piotr Szkopiak
Father Brown is a poor dancer but an excellent detective who ferrets
out the murderer of a dance contestant and the reason for it.
Guest Stars:
  Jarrad Ellis-Thomas as Alexander Walgrave
  Holly Weston as Lucy Dawes
  Seb Carrington as Oliver Dewitt
  Diana Kent as Lady Rose
  Rosie Holden as Merryn Tyrell
  Justin Pearson as Ballroom Musician
  Andy Marshall as Ballroom Musician
  Karen Street as Ballroom Musician
  Rita Manning as Ballroom Musician

- Oliver remarked that Lucy and Merryn were "in a strop," meaning
  bad-tempered. Merryn claims that her father going bankrupt was a
  "jolly wheeze" to those who caused it, meaning a very bad scheme.
- To earn money, Merryn will be teaching "Second Form." These are
  children ages 12–13 in middle school.
- Mallory asked if Father Brown came to the station to learn *pas de
  deux* from Goodfellow. The dance duet is usually done by a man and
  woman couple. He also orders Goodfellow to bring him tea and a
  Garibaldi, a hard rectangular cookie.

6.8 "The Cat of Mastigatus"

> Father Brown—"Violence toward the weak shows no honor
> or courage, it is merely bullying."

Original Air Date: January 10, 2018
Writer: Mark Hiser and Bridget Colgan
Director: Piotr Szkopiak
Schoolgirl May Lewis is found injured in the boiler room of an
exclusive boys' school during an end of term fete. Is the black cat of
the title an important clue or a red herring?
Guest Stars:
  Robert Vernon as Jack Coll
  James Wilby as Sefton Scott
  Milo Twomey as Philip Hart
  Sammy Moore as Daniel Gates
  Toto Bruin as May Lewis
  Alicia Charles as Sheila Barnett

- Father Brown carried his umbrella in every episode but rarely gets a chance to use it for its intended purpose. It appeared that it really was raining on the set when the episode was filmed. Even Mallory's coat and hat are wet as are the school grounds.
- Bunty asks Mrs. M if she's found Narnia as she searches the closet. In *The Chronicles of Narnia* by C.S. Lewis, the wardrobe is a portal between worlds.
- When the headmaster threatens Jack, the gardener, Jack wonders if he'll give him "six of the best," meaning six strikes with a paddle.
- Father Brown counseled Daniel to keep the faith and be like the biblical Daniel who, during his stay in Babylon, was thrown into a den of lions for praying to his God instead of asking the king for favors. The next day, he was released when found unscathed.
- Philip defines the Cat of Mastigatus as a modified tawse, or thong, with slitted ends. Named after the cat-o'-nine tails, Father Brown identifies it as Latin for punishment.

6.9 "The Flower of the Fairway"

Father Brown—"I think that golf is a good walk spoiled."

Original Air Date: January 11, 2018
Writer: Rachel Flowerday
Director: Gary Williams
When American millionaire Raylan Reeve opens a prestigious golf course outside Kembleford and a dead body is discovered, Father Brown becomes embroiled in a family secret.
Guest Stars:
Guy Paul as Raylan Reeve
Jane Hazlegrove as Hermione Harvey
Ty Glaser as Tamara Reeve
Marcus Griffiths as Michael Nelson
Amy Lawrence as Morgana Reeve

- When Inspector Mallory insulted Hermione, Mrs. McCarthy commented on his "cheek," i.e., his rudeness. Sergeant Goodfellow says he knows about fertilizer "to his cost," meaning he had an unpleasant experience with it.
- Reeve charged visitors two shillings to watch the golf tournament, the equivalent of $15 in 1950.
- Father Brown was surprised to find bananas at Reeve's manor. In 1940, a ban was placed on the import of bananas because the fruit had to be transported in refrigerated ships needed during the war.

Housewives made mock bananas with parsnips without much success. The first real bananas were brought in 1945 meant as a treat for children.[61]

6.10 "The Two Deaths of Hercule Flambeau"

Father Brown—"As for your judgment, God will take care of that."

Original Air Date: January 12, 2018
Writer: Kit Lambert
Director: Paul Gibson
The Daily Telegraph announces that the "Infamous Art Thief" Hercule Flambeau was killed in Italy. However, Father Brown is convinced he is still alive and intends to steal the nail from Christ's crown of thorns.
Guest Stars:
  Roger May as Canon Damien Fox
  Sara Martins as Lisandra Flambeau
  Oliver Ford Davies as Bishop Golding
  John Light as Hercule Flambeau

- The gold Crown of Lombardy was crafted in the Middle Ages and became a Christian symbol when legend says it was fashioned to include a nail from Christ's crucifix given to Constantine by St. Helena, founder of the true cross. It is housed in the Cathedral of Monza, outside Milan, Italy.
- Flambeau's fake casket listed his birth and death dates as May 29, 1913–June 7, 1953.
- Lisandra claims her first husband was shot during the Italian occupation of Corsica in 1942. From November 1942 to September 1943, some 30,000 troops initially took over Corsica, a French island in the Mediterranean. Fighting raged among the local resistance, the Allies, the Germans, and French forces.
- Like Heinz Rühmann's German films, Canon Fox threatens that Father Brown will be sent to a remote island, far away from his present diocese.
- When Lisandra says she will avenge them, Father Brown quotes Roman emperor and philosopher Marcus Aurelius: "To refrain from imitation is the best revenge." It infers that the person who did the wrongful act will constantly be on alert for his victim to seek retribution and that will be more taxing than the wrong itself.

Season 7

Father Brown continues his crime-solving pursuit to bring criminals to justice in the eyes of the police and their souls back to communion with God on BBC daytime television. As Christopher Stevens of the *Daily Mail* reflects once again, "For aficionados, these neatly plotted murder mysteries, set in the Cotswolds during the early Fifties, are the perfect retort to anyone who claims that daytime telly is a waste of airtime."[62] But it wasn't only British fans that looked forward to new episodes featuring the clerical detective. Audiences from Australia to the Netherlands to Brazil delighted in Mark Williams' interpretation of *Father Brown*. While in America, the series reached 30 percent of all television households.

One of Father Brown's valued assistants, Alex Price as Sid Carter, continued to be missing from this season's episodes while he was in New York City playing Draco Malfoy in *Harry Potter and the Cursed Child*.

No doubt G.K. Chesterton would have been happy with the newest setting for the series based on his stories. The writer of his obituary in the *Yorkshire Post* in June 1936 noted that he was a staunch advocate for the preservation of the beautiful in England.[63] The Cotswolds with its ubiquitous and authentic caramel-colored stone buildings was becoming a popular vacation destination as well, however crime-ridden the village of Kembleford might appear to be. Suspension of disbelief is a necessary trait in vacationers and particularly crime-show viewers. John Nettles, who starred as DCI (Detective Chief Inspector) Barnaby in *Midsomer Murders*, commented tongue-in-cheek that

> there's a surprising amount of petty viciousness, rancour, ill-humour, lunacy and murderous intent lurking in the quiet villages of the Home Counties…. [Y]ou can't pass a cottage without there being a psychopathic spinster behind the lace curtains. Every church contains a homosexual vicar. No wife has married well, and therefore must indulge in affairs with at least six men.[64]

Williams agrees: "The classic English whodunnit is one of our very peculiar contributions to world literature, and at its heart, it's about the stress beneath the calm. And for that reason, the perfect place to set it is in a village. You've got these people who seem very nice on the surface stabbing and murdering each other. It's a great metaphor for seething repression."

Numerous guest stars populate the village to either become the unfortunate victims or the perpetrators of horrid crimes. Williams found himself impressed with many of the marvelous actors appearing on *Father Brown* and, despite being a professional actor himself, confessed that he still learns from them. "Sometimes it's just something intangible like stance or style or the way people behave on set to other people. That's always been a big influence to me."[65]

Continuing to keep things authentic and secure, Rev. Paul Keane joined the team as priest advisor and Jackie Cobner, who had previously worked with the BBC Drama Department, as safety advisor.

7.1 "The Great Train Robbery"

Father Brown—"For Christian ladies, you are very adept at lying."

Original Air Date: January 7, 2019
Writer: Jude Tindall
Director: Paul Gibson
When Lady Felicia and Mrs. McCarthy are taken hostages during a train robbery, they try to make the best of the bad situation by taking things into their own hands. Meanwhile Father Brown ensures that Inspector Mallory arrests the guilty parties and spares the semi-guilty.
Guest Stars:
    Nancy Carroll as Lady Felicia Montague
    Andrew Turner as Daryl Cudlip
    Darryl Clark as Lenny Cudlip
    Cecilia Noble as Dame Bianca Norman
    Olivia Hallinan as Barbara Norman
    Chris Lew Kum Hoi as Tony Norman
    Matt Rawle as Piers Huntington
    Jack Carroll as Tim Cudlip
    Jonathan Rigby as Radio Announcer

- A "behind the scenes" clip hinted at how this episode was made. Cusack, as Mrs. McCarthy, thought that the stooges who do the kidnapping really have hearts of gold and, since she and Lady Felicia got to boss them around, "it's got a great warmth and it's good fun." Doubtless part of the fun came in the dialogue reminiscent of a Laurel and Hardy sketch as well as the bumbling Keystone Cops behavior of the kidnappers.
- While the actors were inside of the train car which, in reality, sat in a shed, two men outside rocked the car to make it appear to be moving. Blinking lights gave the illusion of the train passing a series of stations.
- Bianca Norman preferred listening to Italian composer Gioacchino Rossini's opera *Stabat Mater*, which was based on a hymn honoring Mary's suffering at her son's crucifixion.

- Inspector Mallory reported, "All quiet in Dodge," possibly a take-off on the film *All Quiet on the Western Front*, with a reference to Dodge City, a notorious Kansas town in the Old West.
- To illuminate the nighttime landscape, Chris Preston, director of photography, filled a huge helium balloon with lights and sent it upward on fine wires, creating a moonlight effect.[66]
- In 1855, the "Great Train Robbery" was an actual event when four men stole gold and coins from a train between London Bridge station and Folkestone in southeast England. It was recreated with the American West as the backdrop in 1903 by Edwin Porter for the Edison company. In 1978 Sean Connery starred as the main character in the film based on Michael Crichton's book. Another "great train robbery" occurred in August 1963 when a Royal Mail train from Glasgow to London was stopped and robbed of two and a half tons of money, equaling about $73 million U.S. dollars today.

7.2 "The Passing Bell"

Father Brown—"Our bells have been here 500 years having a conversation with God."

Original Air Date: January 8, 2019
Writer: David Semple
Director: Ian Barber
Father Brown investigates when the hiring of a new musical director for the St. Mary's bellringers leads to disharmony and murder.
Guest Stars:
  Selma Griffiths as Ruth Thundersby
  Rupert Holliday Evans as Mervyn Glossop
  Abdul Salis as Enoch Rowe
  Laura Pyper as Phoebe Sims
  Jordan Metcalfe as Jamie Cheeseman

- Mrs. McCarthy was delighted with the songs and handbell-ringing, claiming it was like having Paul Robeson in your own living room. Robeson was an American actor and singer, athlete, and Black activist.
- Enoch Rowe probably migrated from Trinidad in the West Indies to Britain during a major migration period from 1948 forward. Besides being enticed as workers by the British Rail or National Health Service to help rebuild the country after World War II, they were also recruited to join the armed forces or to work in the munitions industry.[67]

- Phoebe opined that bell ringing must be a "doddle" for Bunty after all the other things she's done. Doddle means something very easy.
- Ruth admits she is an "invert" of Radclyffe Hall persuasion. Marguerite Radclyffe Hall, an English poet, was a lesbian who thought of herself as a "congenital invert." Ruth also called herself a sister of Sappho, a lyric poet born 500 years before Christ who was also thought to be a lesbian.

7.3 "The Whistle in the Dark"

Lilith—"A sleuthing priest. Strangest thing I've seen all night."

Original Air Date: January 9, 2019
Writer: Tahsin Guner
Director: Ian Barber
Father Brown wheedles himself into a "party" of psychics and discovers that a murdering spirit is around.
Guest Stars:
  Jeff Rawle as Professor Robert Wiseman
  Hayley Considine as Violet
  Mark Aiken as Major Basil Winthrop
  Maggie Steed as Dorothy Parnell
  Jonathan Broadbent as Archie Parnell
  Jemima Rooper as Lilith Crowe

- M.R. James, a popular English supernatural story writer, wrote "Oh, Whistle, and I'll Come to You, My Lad" (1904). *The Fourth Book of Occult Philosophy*, a treatise on Western magic, was written by Heinrich Cornelius Agrippa in 1559.
- Father Brown returned the book *Why I Am Not a Christian* to Wiseman. In it, Bertrand Russell argued against the existence of God, Christ's teachings, and the value of religion, but Father Brown was not persuaded to relinquish his cassock.
- Father Brown admitted that the Catholic Church has much to be ashamed of regarding people who claimed to have supernatural powers. For example, during the Inquisition, authorities sought out witches and condemned them to torture and death by burning.
- Inspector Mallory exclaimed, "Gordon Bennett!" The phrase expresses surprise or incredulity. While mainly British slang, it probably originated with James Gordon Bennett, American publisher of the *New York Herald*, and his disgraceful behavior as a wealthy playboy.

7.4 "The Demise of the Debutante"

Father Brown—"God is merciful. He will not turn his back
on you in your hour of need."

Original Air Date: January 10, 2019
Writer: Lol Fletcher
Director: Paul Gibson
A finishing school for young ladies is home to a headmistress,
an abortionist, a lecherous reverend, an unwed mother, and a
vengeful student. Father Brown promises to learn the identity of
the murderer when two of the individuals are killed.
Guest Stars:
Lucy Pearson as Nell Winford
Lauren O'Neil as Maude Riley
Forbes Masson as Reverend Willard
James Cartwright as Jimbo Riley
Cassie Layton as Cecelia Orchid-Squires
Amanda Drew as Miss Cynthia Rosewood

- The reverend, in scrounging through Cecilia's room, has found the
"disgusting, ungodly novel" of *Lulu and Lucia*, also mentioned in
three other episodes: 3.8, 4.4, and 5.6.
- Inspector Mallory told Father Brown to "sling your cassock,"
implying he should go away. The writer Lol Fletcher also gave that
line to Mallory in episode 5.5. It is borrowed from a nautical term
"sling your hook," meaning to put the ship's anchor away.
- Ruta Graveolens, a blue-green herbal shrub, can trigger contact
dermatitis, much like poison ivy. If large amounts are ingested, it can
cause stomach irritation, poisoning, and even death.
- Young ladies of the Rosewood school danced around a Maypole
singing from Shakespeare's *As You Like It*, act 4, scene 2. "What shall
he have that killed the deer? His leather skin and horns to wear. Then
sing him home. Take thou no scorn to wear the horn. It was a crest
ere thou wast born. Thy father's father wore it, and thy father bore it.
The horn, the horn, the lusty horn is not a thing to laugh to scorn." In
Shakespeare's play, it was sung in a round by foresters after they had
killed a deer.
- Men from Trundell's Gentlemen's College arrive at Rosewood
school to perform a Morris dance, a traditional English folk dance.
Bells attached to their white costumes are alleged to bring luck.
Reverend Willard, as the animal-man, encouraged the dancers to
their best.

7.5 "The Darkest Noon"

Father Brown—"Our only choice is to wait and have faith that God will deliver us."

Original Air Date: January 11, 2019
Writer: Kit Lambert
Director: Christiana Ebohon-Green
Father Brown and Inspector Mallory almost reconcile their differences when they are imprisoned together hoping the gang will save them.
Guest Stars:
    Alan Williams as Blind 'Arry Slow
    Billy Postlethwaite as Edmund Noon
    Asmara Gabrielle as Jasmin Haggard
    Emily Woodward as Patricia Wintham
    Nigel Hastings as George Haggard

- The police report and newspaper set the episode in 1953. The Haggards died in 1951 according to their gravestone, and Edmund has been on the run for two years.
- Father Brown likes humbugs, a sweet, minty-flavored candy with brown and white stripes.
- When Mrs. McCarthy asked Blind 'Arry to watch for Father Brown, Harry said, "Some blighter's got to do it." Blighter is a slang word for a contemptible pest, a person of low character, one who would cause a blight on society.
- Father Brown quotes Isaiah 42:16, "And I will lead the blind in the ways which they know not...." The chapter continues in verse 22: "This is a people ... trapped in holes, hidden away in prisons. They are taken as booty, with no one to rescue them."
- Also, Blind 'Arry promised Mrs. McCarthy that even undertaking the Labors of Hercules would not be too great a task for him to do for her. According to the Greek legend, in a bout of insanity, Hercules killed his wife and children. To atone for the crimes, he had to perform 12 nearly impossible tasks, like killing the nine-headed Lernean Hydra or bringing to the king the man-eating horses of Diomedes.

7.6 "The Sacrifice of Tantalus"

Father Brown—"God will forgive you ... if you truly repent, but you cannot let another man take the blame for what you've done."

Original Air Date: January 14, 2019
Writer: Kit Lambert
Director: Dominic Keavey
A familiar face returns to Kembleford to take over the case when
   Inspector Mallory bungles the pursuit of a fugitive.
Guest Stars:
   Samuel Anderson as Alan Tylett
   Reis Bruce as Colin Blaisen
   Sean Gallagher as Divisional Chief Superintendent Len Blaisen
   Ami Metcalf as Alice Bonham
   Tom Chambers as Inspector Sullivan

- In Greek mythology, Tantalus was a rich king who killed his son, then
  served him to the gods to see if they truly were all-knowing. Zeus
  punished him by having him stand in chin-deep water that receded
  when he tried to drink. He was also unable to eat because nearby
  hanging fruit was just out of his reach.
- Tylett, dubbed by the press "the Butcher of Bordesley Green" (an area
  in the city of Birmingham), was spotted by the "spinnery," a factory
  where wool was spun into fabrics.
- Sullivan said undercover police used the alias "Inspector Trueman"
  to honor a fallen colleague. Another Inspector Trueman appeared in
  "The Owl of Minerva," episode 3.15.
- Though Father Brown's first name is not known, this episode revealed
  that the sergeant is Daniel Goodfellow, and the inspector is Gerry
  Mallory.
- Tylett said he tried to "scarper," meaning to run away. Superintendent
  Blaisen threatened that his son could kiss the wedding to his
  "strumpet" goodbye; a strumpet was a loose woman or prostitute.

7.7 "The House of God"

> Father Brown—"Cheer up, Mrs. M. Not every man you're
> keen on will turn out to be a bigamist."

Original Air Date: January 15, 2019
Writer: Dan Muirden
Director: Paul Gibson
Father Brown uncovers a family's strange secrets when he solves the
   murder of a gardener.
Guest Stars:
   Sean Campion as Patrick O'Leary
   Amy Robbins as Angelica Evans

Ian Peck as Eddie Trist
Abigail Davies as Francesca Chase
Jack Wolfe as George Chase
Seline Hizli as Maria Hardy

- For Father Brown's lunch, Mrs. McCarthy made a shepherd's pie with ground meat and a crust or mashed potato topping.
- Father Brown greeted parishioners outside the church in a long-sleeved, floor-length white garment called an alb. A tie or cincture might be worn around the waist and, for Mass, a chasuble or colored vestment would go over the top.
- Before she collapsed, Angelica was about to quote from 1 Corinthians 14:34, an epistle written by St. Paul who believed that women should keep silent in gatherings of believers, calling it a "disgrace" when she does not. Father Brown quotes from the same epistle chapter 13, verse 4–8: "Love is patient, love is kind…. Love never fails."
- Sergeant Goodfellow quoted American comedian Bob Hope who joked that "bigamy is the only crime where two rites make a wrong."
- Bunty compared the O'Leary home to Sodom and Gomorrah, two cities full of sinful people mentioned in the Bible that were destroyed by God (Genesis 18:20–19:29).

7.8 "The Blood of the Anarchists"

Father Brown—"You don't have to be like the people you hate. There is another way…. Take responsibility for the pain and mayhem you've caused."

Original Air Date: January 16, 2019
Writer: Lol Fletcher
Director: Dominic Keavey
Father Brown investigates the murders of two performers from a troupe of traveling anarchists.
Guest Stars:
Kevin Mains as Angus Boyde
Lottie Tolhurst as Magdalena Stark
Jennifer Hennessy as Sally Clegg
Edward Dogliani as Titan Stark
Rogers Evans as Daffyd Clegg
Hugh Curtis as Lionel

- The Merriam-Webster dictionary defines anarchy as the absence of government, creating a state of lawlessness or political disorder. Anarchists believe in complete freedom without the control of government.

- The anarchists' play begins by listing characters from other controversial dramas like *Oedipus Rex* who married his own mother; *Ubu Roi* who killed the Polish king and then commits other obscenities; and *Woyzeck*, a military barber who jealously kills his common-law wife.
- Father Brown is called "the epitome of outdated values" and "a puppet of the Vatican" by Titan whose philosophy values anarchy as a religion over any church. Father Brown is not Dick Tracy as Inspector Mallory feels the need to remind him. Tracy was a hardened police detective in an American comic strip by Chester Gould.
- Father Brown approves of Bunty's poem:

> "Anarchy!
> Destroy the day. Destroy the night.
> Mutiny and revolt, rebel and fight!
> Anarchy for you. Anarchy for me
> Until there is nothing. Nothing but darkness.
> Until there is nothing.
> Nothing but nothing.
> From thus comes light,
> Glorious light!"

7.9 "The Skylark Scandal"

Father Brown—"It can be hard to accept that someone we love can be capable of hurting others, but every human being, beyond doubt, is worth more than the worst of their actions."

Original Air Date: January 17, 2019
Writer: Rachel Smith
Director: Christiana Ebohon-Green
The Kembleford Ramblers and Twitchers take a shortcut through the local lord's estate. When someone is murdered in the night on the estate, Father Brown uncovers a blackmail scheme dating from events 15 years previously and an odd murder weapon.
Guest Stars:
Miranda Hennessy as Henrietta "Hetty" Hollingworth
Jasper Jacob as Lord Henry Hollingworth
Mark Rice-Oxley as Norman Fawlter
Kelly Harrison as Cathy Fawlter
Callum Woodhouse as Randall Jones
Maggie O'Neill as Mrs. Kendall

- Father Brown refers to Percy Bysshe Shelley's poem *Ode to a Skylark*

which the poet wrote after hearing a bird on his evening's walk. Its song is so beautiful that Shelley called it a "blithe Spirit."
- Twitchers walk in the woods hoping to spot and identify as many birds as possible.
- Hetty remarks that the family has "been on our uppers," meaning poor or destitute. The phrase comes from people so poor they wore out the bottom of their shoes until all that was left was the upper part. This is also the reason Hetty was engaged to a "dull Duke," in hopes that his fortune would support the family.
- Mrs. Kendall reminds Mrs. McCarthy that the charabanc, meaning a tour bus, has arrived for them. It was originally a carriage for excursions pulled by horses.

7.10 "The Honourable Thief"

Father Brown—"In my opinion, there is no abyss, moral or physical, that cannot be overcome by a leap of faith."

Original Air Date: January 18, 2019
Writer: Kit Lambert
Director: Paul Gibson
When Lady Felicia's necklace is stolen, Father Brown enlists the aid of Flambeau to retrieve it.
Guest Stars:
    Nancy Carroll as Lady Felicia
    Mark Umbers as Nicholai Solovey
    Gil Kolirin as Yuri Galka
    Ben-Ryan Davies as Daniel Winks
    John Light as Hercule Flambeau

- Lady Felicia's necklace was the creation of the Finnish Henrik Wigström, chief workmaster for beautiful, jeweled Faberge Easter eggs. Solovey claimed it was stolen from his family by Bolsheviks, that is, members of the Russian Social Democratic Party, later known as Communists. The antikvariat were tasked with selling Russian art to raise money for the Communist party.
- The only item suspected stolen was the necklace, so why didn't the thief "chance his arm" or try his luck and steal the other valuables?
- Solovey's safe was built by the Mosler company that was founded in 1874 in Cincinnati, Ohio. Known for its strength, one Mosler safe survived the atom bomb attack on Hiroshima in 1945.
- Father Brown calls on Saint Martin de Porres to help Flambeau open the safe. Born in Peru, Martin spent his life nursing the sick no matter

their race or status and, in that position, he was able to magically traverse barred doors. He was canonized in May 1962.
- Father Brown jokes that the clergy learned to play cards during the Reformation when they were hiding from the Protestants. Martin Luther began the division in 1517 that saw the creation of other religions separate from the Roman Catholic Church.
- Father Brown's baccarat winnings will go to fix the clerestory, the upper part of the nave.

Season 8

Little did fans of *Father Brown* realize that this would be the last season for a while. Covid-19, the coronavirus that afflicted the entire world beginning in March 2020, was responsible for cancelling the filming of many productions for the entire year. Concessions needed to be made in all areas of entertainment. Masks were encouraged to avoid transmitting virus droplets, large gatherings were proven to be hotspots of virus transmission, and the real possibility that one asymptomatic person could sicken hundreds of others made it impossible for actors and production teams to work together in any kind of normal situation calling for close contact. Thus, the 2021 season was postponed. Fans would have to wait and watch reruns.

Blissfully unaware of how life would change in the coming months, the BBC Media Centre announced in September 2019 that the cast of *Father Brown* had wrapped up filming for Season 8 and that Season 9 had been given the go-ahead by Dan McGolpin for BBC One Daytime. He had happily announced that 20 more episodes of Father Brown would be forthcoming for 2021 and 2022.[68]

When asked in an interview for the BBC Media Centre about why *Father Brown* was so popular, producer Peter Bullock thought it was the "gloriously nostalgic" ambience. "It's a cosy crime," he said, "the whole family can watch, it's not offensive." Mark Williams agreed. He told one interviewer that people told him they like the program because it's "gentle." He laughed at that because there is always a murder. But "what's gentle is the way that the story is told. It's not an aggressive way of telling a television story by using lots of different effects and explosions and camera techniques and aggressive acting. It's much more storytelling. And there's no zombies, no dragons."[69]

Bullock went on to praise Williams for, even after doing so many episodes, remaining careful not to let the character become a parody of a 1950s priest. Williams granted that he worked hard not to become a cliché. "It's important to me that he's surprised by what happens around him...."

I don't want him to become blasé." Williams compared Father Brown to Agatha Christie's disarming spinster Miss Marple. "It is the unimportant which is important, which G.K. Chesterton said himself and I think possibly Agatha Christie took to heart." One secret to its success, Williams believed, is the good storytelling. "You are being told a story every episode—and that's what people love," he said. "It's like reading a comfortable novel." He lauded the cast for doing a good job and singled out costume designer Claire Collins for her talent in capturing the 1950s look.[70]

Collins, having had training on costuming for Victorian period dramas, realized the importance of her role in using costume to "set the world and tell the story." She reported that she and her team scoured vintage shops as well as London costume houses for the 1,700 outfits needed for the whole cast over the entire series. The challenge for her included making the background characters fulfill their role properly—either to blend into the scenery or to set the scene through costume which, in the 1950s included hip cushioning, shoulder pads, high-waisted pants, and hats. Even necklines, hemlines, and hair style had to be carefully considered to be period perfect. In the end, though, "I would say the fifties is all about underwear. ... All the structure and shaping of an outfit is underneath, and we can tweak what goes over the top."[71]

8.1 "The Celestial Choir"

> Father Brown—"You are engaged to be married. How can you give yourself to him before God unless you are willing to open your heart?"

Original Air Date: January 6, 2020
Writer: Kit Lambert
Director: Paul Gibson
Location: The Anglican Worcester Cathedral, Worcester
The Kembleford Choir runs into nothing but trouble on their way to Worcester to sing in the annual Choir Competition.
Guest Stars:
   Ashley Campbell as Wesley Summerton
   Sarah Ingram as Barbara Curtley
   Daisy Maywood as Audrey Belchant
   Joseph Prowen as Nicholas Curtley
   Hugh Sachs as Lawrence Ashton
   Roger May as Canon Fox
   Eloise Little as Janet Mallory
   Nancy Carroll as Lady Felicia Montague

- Mrs. McCarthy announces that the winning choir will perform at the London Coliseum in front of Queen Elizabeth. Her coronation had been June 2, 1953.
- The Kembleford choir sang the Catholic hymn "Faith of Our Fathers" by Frederick William Faber as they head to the train. They won with Franz Schubert's hymn "Ave Maria."
- Wesley quoted Exodus 14:6: "So he made ready his chariot and took all his people with him!" When the ticket seller is too deaf to hear their inquiries, Mrs. McCarthy wondered, "Why hast thou forsaken me," a Biblical quote from Matthew 27:26.
- Audrey reported that she "needs to spend a penny," which means to go to the bathroom. Public restrooms were little cabinets that were often kept locked and could only be unlocked with the insertion of a coin. It used to be a penny, but now the cost has risen.
- In a behind the scenes interview, John Burton (Sergeant Goodfellow) commented that there is usually not a lot of waiting around on the set. But on one particular day, they had to stop filming because of a burglar alarm going off that would have been picked up by the microphones.[72] Producer Peter Bullock, too, had mentioned that the production crew had to sometimes get creative in masking 21st-century items, like satellite dishes or immoveable contemporary vehicles, while setting up a scene. One thing that could not be controlled was the weather, so the production suffered and worked through high temperatures or torrents of rain.[73]
- To make it appear that the cathedral was filled, 50 people were photographed sitting in pews on the left front side of the church. Then they changed seats and were filmed sitting on the right front side; they were mixed up again and filmed sitting farther back. Then the director basically cut and pasted the photographs together for the final "full church" scene.[74]
- "It's like herding cats," observed director Paul Gibson when 51 people needed to get changed into choir robes in 15 minutes.

8.2 "The Queen Bee"

Father Brown—"On a given day, the female bees all rise up against their useless male drones and slaughter them without mercy."

Mrs. McCarthy—"We could learn a lot from bees."

Original Air Date: January 7, 2020
Writer: David Semple

Director: Dominic Keavey
When a loathsome beekeeper is found dead of asphyxiation, there are
plenty of suspects who would have wanted her gone.
Guest Stars:
    Annabelle Apsion as Beattie May
    Reece Bahia as Shambu Maier
    Pippa Haywood as Eileen Slither
    Grace Molony as Hannah Baxley
    Nigel Planer as Ronnie Grunion

- Bunty said she's "fagged," meaning exhausted, after working in the garden.
- By 1953, laws regarding World War II rationing of sweets, eggs, cream, butter, and cheese were finally coming off the ration books after nine years.
- Miss Slither claimed that she and Beattie had a "ding dong." The slang phrase means a heated argument.
- Beattie dumped a bucket of white feathers on the gardener, symbols of cowardice.[75]
- Bees are also a feature of Chesterton's story "The Man with Two Beards." Hannah stated accurately that "bees are what keep the world going." In their role as pollinators, they are an important species as one third of the global food supply depends on bee pollination. If bees become extinct, plants that they pollinate may be lost as well as the animals that eat the plants. John Burton (Sergeant Goodfellow) revealed in a behind-the-scenes interview that, since bees cannot be trained, all the bees in the episode were computer generated by the editing department. "No bees were harmed in the making of this episode," he reported.[76]

8.3 "The Scales of Justice"

Father Brown—"I believe in a lot of things ... but coinci-
dence isn't one of them."

Original Air Date: January 8, 2020
Writer: Dominique Moloney
Director: Darcia Martin
Bunty finds herself on trial for murder after a playboy's party. Father
Brown tries to prove her blameless.
Guest Stars:
    Julian Forsyth as Judge Gordon Pickering
    Alice Bailey Johnson as Margot Neville-Crowley
    Rob Callender as Max Neville-Crowley

Ziggy Heath as Teddy Neville-Crowley
Aki Omoshaybi as Charlie Reid
Robert Portal as Bertie Quinton QC (Queen's Counsel)
Nick Fletcher as Roger Sharpe QC
Jacob Shephard as Andrew Grimes

- Episode writer Dominique Moloney wanted to write about the 1950s because "there was so much sexism and racism and homophobia at that time, but I feel like it really chimes with what's going on today." Emer Kenny also felt excited about the episode because of the unusually grim moments for Bunty who usually is fun to play.[77]
- Sexual harassment or coerced sexual relations of women by men is centuries old. Wealthy or influential men preying on women, often their subordinates, has led to the fight for women's rights, including the most recent MeToo movement.[78]
- Teddy proclaimed that the party venue was Gatsby's mansion, a reference to the fictional millionaire of *The Great Gatsby*, F. Scott Fitzgerald's 1925 book. The jazz music and costumes of the guests were reflective of the 1920s.
- Inspector Mallory asked Father Brown what he was wittering about, meaning he thought Father Brown was going on about trivialities. Bunty's lawyer told her to "stiffen your sinews," encouraging her to feel positive about her case's outcome. After Father Brown visited Charlie in Bristol, Mrs. McCarthy asked him, "Still no joy from Bristol?" To have luck brought joy; no luck, no joy.
- Bunty's lawyer said he required Dutch courage, i.e., self-confidence gained from drinking alcohol.

8.4 "The Wisdom of the Fool"

Father Brown—"You do not have the right to judge another and take a life."

Original Air Date: January 9, 2020
Writer: Lol Fletcher
Director: Paul Gibson
At a Convention of Merriment staged by a traveling troupe of jesters, there is nothing merry about the events when Father Brown investigates a murder.
Guest Stars:
Annabel Cleare as Dr. Belmont
Neil Pearson as Sir Toby Dobson
Alexander Morris as Fred Dobson

Paul Copley as Mr. Feste
Natey Jones as Doodle
Emily Joyce as Edith Dobson
Nick Owenford as Villager/Jester
Richard Price as Villager

- Mr. Feste told Mrs. McCarthy that he was not a "chancer," he did not take risks.
- Sergeant Goodfellow's fear of clowns is known as coulrophobia. Perhaps he had a bad experience with a clown as a child or was influenced by media representations of some clowns as evil. It can be frightening to be confronted by someone in a mask or grotesque makeup that negates that individual's personal identification.
- Bunty had parked under a damson tree which dropped purple splotches onto her car. Those were most likely the juice from the damson, a purplish fruit like a plum.
- A scene at the beginning of the episode shows a pie-throwing contest. While the pies may look delicious, the meringue is really shaving cream. The prop department used Gillette sensitive shaving foam because it keeps its form for several hours.[79]

8.5 "The Folly of Jephthah"

Father Brown—"Eventually, we will all have to face the final judgment and ruthlessness cannot save you then."

Original Air Date: January 10, 2020
Writer: Kit Lambert
Director: Darcia Martin
Hercule Flambeau and his daughter Marianne meet again in a contest over who is the better thief. Father Brown sets the ground rules in a complicated challenge to victory.
Guest Stars:
Hannah Morrish as Pippa Thubron
John Light as Hercule Flambeau
Gina Bramhill as Marianne Delacroix
Simon Schatzberger as Alan Filchett
Vincenzo Nicoli as Vincenzo Murgida
Jonathan Rigby as Radio Newsreader
Josh Catalano as Vincenzo's Right Hand Man
Lee Simmons as Mafia Henchman

- Jephthah was a Biblical judge (Judges 11–12:7).
- The "mug" (gullible fool) in the museum claimed the ring was "a poxy,"

meaning of little value. "AR" (Alexander Romanici) had told him that he'd "grass him up" if he didn't do what he was told. The phrase comes from Cockney slang meaning to inform to the police on someone.

- Father Brown was to judge the contest with his "singular understanding of the criminal mind," a reference to both Chesterton's Father Brown and Chesterton's mentor, Father O'Connor, who gained his knowledge from hearing confessions, a throwback to one of the first scenes in the episode as well.
- Mrs. McCarthy worried about carrying the handbag, but Bunty assured her it will be "tickety-boo," an outdated phrase meaning hunky-dory or all right.
- Father Brown would know, as Marianne did, that hiding something in the altar table, the "mensa," would negate its consecration if the table were to be moved.

8.6 "The Numbers of the Beast"

> Father Brown—"The path to redemption remains open if you choose honesty and confess your crimes."

Original Air Date: January 13, 2020
Writer: Dan Muirden
Director: Paul Gibson
Mrs. McCarthy wins at bingo with help from a fortune teller, but her winnings might not be legitimate.
Guest Stars:
    Niamh Cusack as Roisin Crayford
    Grant Masters as Trafalgar Devlin
    Nigel Betts as Samuel Hinds
    Graeme Hawley as Peter Bailey
    Alison Pargeter as Anna Bailey
    Jonathan Rigby as Radio Commentator

- Niamh Cusack played Roisin, Mrs. McCarthy's sister. They are also sisters in real life.
- The bingo prize jackpot of £730, or approximately £19,272 ($26,900) in today's currency, is quite a large prize! The estimate to fix the church roof was £1200 or £31,680 ($44,180) today; it might have been wiser for the Hambleston pastor to use the prize money as down payment. Had she won, Sergeant Goodfellow's wife would have bought a Baby Belling Cooker—a stove—for a mere £32 in 1955.
- Bunty asks Father Brown to join them for a "flutter," meaning a small bet, at the church bingo.

- Several Biblical passages are quoted in this episode: "Your old men shall dream dreams and. your young men shall see visions" (Acts 2:17); "He that speaketh lies shall perish" (Proverbs 19:9); "The love of money is the root of all evil" (1 Timothy 6:10); "Now indeed you will feel sorry, but I will see you again and your heart will rejoice" (John 16:22).
- Inspector Mallory expresses surprise at his prisoner's escape with the phrase "Oh, my giddy aunt."
- Stunt coordinator Tony Smart and art director Wyn Jenkins tricked out the tree branch so it would move when Will Willoughby, Trafalgar Devlin's stunt double, hit it as he was riding away on the horse. Willoughby was also to double Father Brown in that scene, but Mark Williams was confident he could ride downhill on his bicycle.[80]
- UK and U.S. Bingo cards differ in that American cards feature 25 squares in five columns and five rows across. The word BINGO is written across the top, one letter for each column. Numbers are called according to columns, as in B-6 or G-54. In Mrs. McCarthy's bingo card, there were nine squares across in three rows. Fifteen of the squares contained a number; the rest were blank.

8.7 "The River Corrupted"

> Sid—"This is Father Brown.... He's gonna find the real killer in no time, trust me."

Original Air Date: January 14, 2020
Writer: Kit Lambert
Director: Jennie Paddon
Shooting location: Cropredy, Oxfordshire
When a canal boatman is found murdered, newly returned Sid trusts that Father Brown can find out who killed him.
Guest Stars:
    Gabrielle Creevy as Polly Beavington
    Ian Puleston-Davies as Pat Lochlin
    Andrew Whipp as Roger Barford
    Bronte Terrell as Maeve Lochlin
    Alex Price as Sid Carter
    Alan Williams as Harold Blind 'Arry Slow
    Hannah Yelland as Georgia Barford

- Narrowboats, at just under seven feet wide, were specifically built to navigate the UK's narrow canal and lock system.
- A "priest" is a tool used to kill fish after they are caught, so named because they administer the last rites to the fish.

- Lochlin "had a kip," meaning he slept.
- G.K. Chesterton once wrote, "The true soldier fights not because he hates what is in front of him, but because he loves what is behind him."[81] Both Blind 'Arry and Father Brown had been to war and had "watched life fade from another man's face." The experience changed them, causing 'Arry to turn to drink and Father Brown to turn to God and the priesthood. Chesterton could relate to the sorrow. When his brother Cecil was wounded during a battle in France in World War I, then collapsed after a 12-mile march and died, Chesterton was devastated. He had temporarily taken over Cecil's role as editor of *The New Witness*, a political and cultural journal, and continued it after Cecil's death. It later became known as *G.K.'s Weekly*.
- Alex Price, who reprised his role as Sid Carter in this episode, recounted being in America for a year and a half and being amazed at "what an unbelievably huge deal [Father Brown] is out there." But he was happy to return to the series, observing, "There aren't many jobs that are like this, there aren't any jobs that are like this 'cause it's such a small well-oiled crew that are just so good. I love being part of it."[82]

8.8 "The Curse of the Aesthetic"

Bunty—"You should never let a man define who you are."

Original Air Date: January 15, 2020
Writer: Lol Fletcher
Director: Paul Gibson
Sculptor Benjamin Milton is devastated when his muse and model commits suicide. When other injuries and deaths occur, Father Brown finds inspiration and the solution in a suicide note.
Guest Stars:
  Grainne O'Mahony as Isabella Peroux
  George Webster as Benjamin Milton
  Danielle Phillips as Rose Vickers
  Harriet Thorpe as Nanny Ribble
  Rhiannon Neads as Katie Milton
  Justin Avoth as Conrad French

- Inspector Mallory observes that Conrad French would have lit up "like Blackpool Tower" from the electrified door handle. Built in May 1894, Lancashire's unique landmark, inspired by the Eiffel Tower, stands more than 500 feet high with 360-degree views at the top. It is now lit with 25,000 LED lights.[83]

- Oprah Winfrey exactly repeated Bunty's advice in a 2013 article, "Never Let a Man Define Who You Are."[84]
- Benjamin wanted Bunty to dress and pose as a Jacobean strumpet, that is, a female adulterer. The early 1600s Jacobean era was named after King James I (Jacobus is Latin for James). In the 1613 play "A Chaste Maid in Cheapside," the marriage of maid Moll Yellowhammer is at the center of a multitude of affairs and liaisons carried on by unscrupulous characters. At the end, Moll appears to faint and die but later is revealed to be alive.
- Mark Williams liked this episode for being a "classic whodunit in the sense that it's in a very contained environment which is a country house with quite refined people and people who are not quite so refined. There's lots of false clues and some clues that don't look important and to-ing and fro-ing. Father Brown gets a bit confused with the amount of information. Well, I like that. I like it when he has to struggle a bit."[85]

8.9 "The Fall of the House of St Gardner"

Father Brown—"If only we could see into other people's souls, but that is God's prerogative."

Original Air Date: January 15, 2020
Writer: Rachel Smith
Director: Jennie Paddon
A bitter and insufferable journalist reports on the scandals of a fashion house and, when she refuses to stop, is murdered. Father Brown follows the clues to find out whodunit.
Guest Stars:
  Rosalie Craig as Lady Vivien St. Gardner-Verde
  Nick Waring as Sir Ralph Verde
  Ingvild Lakou as Camille Hogan
  Amanda Lawrence as Barbara Farrell
  Ben Lamb as Harvey St. Gardner
  Colin Deaney as Hornby

- The date on Harvey's check indicates the episode takes place around June 18, 1953.
- Bunty claims she is hardly a "convent girl," one who had gone to a school taught by nuns.[86]
- According to streetlist.co.uk, there are at least 30 Keats Streets in London.
- Sergeant Goodfellow contacted an "old mucker from the Met." In

other words, he spoke with a friend from the Metropolitan Police. Scotland Yard is headquarters of the Met, which was created in 1829 to replace individual watchmen or neighborhood police. The London Metropolitan Police supervise all Greater London but not the City of London itself which has its own force. The Met's jobs include crime detection and prevention.

- In a post-production interview, Emer Kenny (Bunty) observed that Claire Collins, the series' costume designer, "is a genius and [this episode] was a chance to flex her fashion muscles." Emer remembered the pajamas that Bunty wore in one scene. "I think it was written as a negligee.... We wanted to do something that was more intimate, more personal and we thought she'd be wearing some glamourous, comfortable pajamas, and they're my favorite because they were so comfortable."[87]

8.10 "The Tower of Lost Souls"

Chief Inspector Valentine—"If there's one thing I learned in Kembleford, nothing is ever plain and simple."

Original Air Date: January 17, 2020
Writer: Tahsin Guner
Director: Dominic Keavey
Three police inspectors and three Kembleford civilians work together (more or less) to solve three deaths involving a tower owned by a Member of Parliament.
Guest Stars:
Cal MacAninch as George Oakley
Gyuri Sarossy as Alistair Helmsley
Hugo Speer as Chief Inspector Valentine
Susannah Wise as Emily Helmsley
James Anderson as William Helmsley
Tom Chambers as Chief Inspector Sullivan

- G.K. Chesterton's Father Brown also suffered from acrophobia, a fear of heights. In the story "The Hammer of God," he says, "I think there is something rather dangerous about standing on these high places even to pray.... Heights were made to be looked at, not to be looked from."[88]
- Founded by Sir Oswald Mosley, the British Union of Fascists emulated Mussolini and Hitler and paraded in blackshirt uniforms. Their beliefs included anti–Semitism which they enforced through bullying and other violent tactics.[89]

- Stunt coordinator Bill Davey and Jackie Cobner, the BBC's safety advisor, certainly had their hands full, keeping cast and crew safe during the filming at the 65-foot-high Helmsley tower, which was actually Broadway tower in Worcestershire.
- In a behind-the-scenes interview, Tahsin Guner disclosed that he came up with the episode because they wanted Hugo Speer (Inspector Valentine) to come back. When Speer was asked by his agent if he'd be interested in reprising his role, he replied, "In a heartbeat ... because I absolutely adore this job." Tom Chambers too (Inspector Sullivan) admitted he was green with envy and asked the writers, "Can you somehow get rid of Mallory so that Sullivan can come back for good because I want to be here all season. Coming back to Father Brown is a bit like Christmas day because I miss it every time I'm not doing it." Jack Deam (Inspector Mallory) wasn't really put out at the others' return. "When you've got great scripts, great characters to play with, and a brilliant cast ... it's just great."[90]

Season 9

The long-awaited Season 9 was to be an exciting one for cast and viewers with the production of the milestone 100th episode. Few series could claim that distinction, giving credence to the popularity and international commercial value of *Father Brown*. No one needed to tell its countless viewers that the series rated as one of the most highly successful programs the BBC had broadcast. During the show's yearlong unforeseen hiatus due to the Coronavirus pandemic, fans spent the wait watching previous episodes once, twice, or multiple times. Several enthusiasts on fan blogs and websites, such as Facebook's "Father Brown World Fans Page" remarked that it helped them make it through the mandated isolation and resultant loneliness of the pandemic.

Despite the universal relief on the part of the cast, crew, and BBC team to bring another season to fruition, continued trepidation about the pandemic could not be ignored. TV production activity was not required to stop, but all aspects of television and film industries were governed by mandated guidelines as to what they could and could not do to protect everyone from contracting and transmitting the virus. Two separate documents advising and regulating television production were published: "Close Contact Cohorts and increased screening for COVID-19-protocol for TV production" and "TV Production Guidance: Managing the risk of Coronavirus (COVID-19) in production making." Specifically, before filming even began, scripts had to have been evaluated to take into account social distancing, and sets might have to be changed to allow for distance between actors. Outdoor film sets were preferable but, if not possible, then larger rooms with good ventilation were ideal. As in *Father Brown*, when familial homes were used as filming locations, a risk evaluation regarding the introduction of unfamiliar equipment and people into the location had to be undertaken. Plexiglass barriers might be used to separate the actors or, when close interaction could not be avoided, the actors should sit side by side rather than face to face.

Realizing that a resumption of production required interaction between actors and crew and the inability of those people to maintain social distancing while doing their jobs, the documents also recommended increased screening and routine antigen testing. They suggested that studios may consider additional PCR (polymerase chain reaction) testing as well as temperature checks before the actors arrived on set. When "cohorts" must be in proximity, it was advised that only a minimum number of people be present. When a guest star's role was complete, before they've left the set, an exit procedure should be in place to ensure that the regulars remained protected for a specified time afterward. Additional restrictions were placed on other social activity and, if any cohort displayed symptoms of the virus at any time, all members should self-isolate and be tested.

Privacy prevents the dissemination of information about the health of cast or crew members of *Father Brown*, but the audience might detect compliance with Covid guidelines. Perhaps the actors were given time off to minimize their interactions with others and were not afflicted with Covid. For instance, in the fifth episode of the season, Mrs. McCarthy wonders where Bunty is, and she did not appear on screen at all. In another, Mrs. McCarthy herself is absent, said to be off visiting her sister in Ireland (episode 9.7). Nancy Carroll's absence as Lady Felicia on *Father Brown* is explained with her being cast as Marine Bonnet in *Murder in Provence*. In yet another, Inspector Mallory is gone on annual leave (episode 9.8). With Mallory absent for several scenes, Sergeant Goodfellow took on an authoritative role. Hinting at a new, distinctive role for the sergeant, Father Brown told him that he's wasted in uniform and, after the solving of a case, applauds him with "Sergeant, I knew you'd be good at this."

Many of the *Father Brown* episodes have an over-abundance of outdoor scenes. In previous seasons, discussions might be held at the kitchen table in the presbytery, but for now Father Brown consults with Sid or Mrs. McCarthy at an outdoor café or outside the church's entrance. Exterior gardens play a large part in 9.2 "The Viper's Tongue," 9.3 "The Requiem for the Dead," and 9.4 "The Children of Kalon" as does the holiday camp in 9.7 "The Island of Dreams" and the outdoor spa in 9.9 "The Enigma of Antigonish."

As far as celebrations, the cast was nearly as surprised as its audience to be so successful. In June 2021 while filming Season 9, Mark Williams commented, "We love telling our stories as much as the world loves watching them. A modest, warm daytime drama that achieves one hundred episodes and global success. Who'd have thought it?"[91] In considering that question, Williams later commented,

> [I]t's Father Brown's open-mindedness that keeps his followers wanting more. The main thing is that he's non-judgmental.... He looks at the things that other people don't. He also offers hope. Father Brown's something that people really need and want. They express their love for it a lot. That was especially true during the pandemic when it was on TV all the time. People love losing themselves in the stories, the characters, the nature and the beauty of the UK.[92]

The reporter for *The Sun* asked him what the hardest part of the role was after all this time. Learning the lines, Williams quickly replied. "It's six to eight pages of dialogue every day. You have to remember everybody's name and what they've done before they've appeared on set and go through the Cluedo thing about each character's motivation and location."[93] Williams' experience in films prior to his work on *Father Brown*— *Harry Potter*, *101 Dalmatians* and *Shakespeare in Love*—prepared him for just about anything. Producers, he knew, "want problem solvers not problem makers." At this stage in his career, he was happy and boasted about *Father Brown*, "It's the ninth series and our 100th episode. That's more than Columbo."[94]

As the season was drawing to a close, *Radio Times* published yet another interview with Williams and John Burton, who played Sergeant Goodfellow. Commenting on the program's global influence, Williams said, "[*Father Brown's*] presence is one of warmth and comfort for people." He reiterated his conviction that "it offers storytelling at a high level every week." But Burton disagreed that it was the stories that attracted the audiences. In his view, "it's more about the ingredients, if you like, that make up the perfect cake—the locations, the costumes, the great guest star artists, the music; all the other stuff that come into the mix." Burton continued with the fact that the show is "formulaic. There's a murder inevitably, the inept coppers turn up—that's me and Jack [Deam]—we get it wrong, and then Father Brown solves it, and you see how he solves it with flashbacks."[95]

The use of a flashback was a technique that executive producer Will Trotter found valuable. Talking about the first episode of *Sister Boniface Mysteries*, which he also produced, he said he wanted his script writers to "get straight on with it" with less set-up, especially in detective stories where there are only 45 minutes to tell the story. Occasionally, the murder occurs before the introductory title and credits allowing for the balance of the episode to focus on events leading up to the crime and its solution.[96]

With the production of 9.10 "The Red Death," viewers might be forgiven for wondering if it is Father Brown's farewell. Almost the entire series took place in 1953, so with the celebration of the new year of 1954, is it a new beginning or the end? In the final scenes, all the regular stars are present, the long-cultivated storyline of the Montagues' marriage is resolved, Flambeau has moved to America, and Sergeant Goodfellow will be advancing in his career. Eager fans will have to await further developments.

9.1 "The Menace of Mephistopheles"

Father Brown—"Something is afoot … and I mean to get to the bottom of it."[1]

Original Air Date: January 3, 2022
Writer: Dominique Moloney
Director: Isher Sahota
Father Brown works with Sergeant Goodfellow after the police officer observes his inspector plant evidence that puts blame on an innocent man.
Guest Stars:
Ralph Davis as Lawrence Darlington
Anna Munden as Arabella Darlington
Jude Monk McGowan as Charles Huxton/Damien Tarrow
Melissa James as Shelly McGowan
Craig Conway as Bill Devlin
Dotty as Crumpet

- The legend of the demon Mephistopheles appeared in Germany in the late 16th century. He is usually associated with the scholar Faust who would trade his soul for knowledge.
- Alex Price resumes a place in the introductory cast list but missing are Emer Kenny and Nancy Carroll. In 2020, Kenny was working on adapting and starring in the *Karen Pirie* detective show by Val McDermid for ITV.[97] Carroll continued filming *Murder in Provence* in southern France.
- Mallory threatens Sergeant Goodfellow with his having to work at Woolworth's—a five-and-10-cent store founded in 1879 in New York. In 1909, founder F.W. Woolworth opened a store in Liverpool and eventually added 800 stores throughout Britain. It closed in 1997.

9.2 "The Viper's Tongue"

Father Brown—"Don't pick a fight with a man holding a meat cleaver."

Original Air Date: January 4, 2022
Writer: Kit Lambert
Director: Steve M. Kelly
Mrs. McCarthy may be the next victim after two other people in Kembleford are murdered.
Guest Stars:
Sophie Colquhoun as Ruby Nellins
Marcus Onilude as Gideon Fredericks
Denise Black as Peggy Langdon
Robert Hands as Walter Penmark
Ossian Luke as Mick Bidley
Leon Ockenden as Richard Belcroft

- In 1939 when King George and Queen Elizabeth visited America, the president and Mrs. Roosevelt served hot dogs to them at a picnic.
- When Father Brown arrives after the fire, Mallory asks if he saw the smoke and thought they were announcing the next pope, a reference to the smoke from ballots burned when cardinals elect a new pope. Black smoke signifies there has been no decision; white smoke indicates there's a new pope.
- Sergeant Goodfellow has read the weekly *Modern Wonder* magazine with its articles on science. The magazine ran from 1937 to 1941.
- Mrs. McCarthy claims she never offended anyone in her life. At that, a cock crows, alluding to the cock that crowed when Peter lied about knowing Jesus (Matthew 26:74).
- Father Brown prays a funeral chant over one of the victims: "Subvenite, Sancti Dei, occurite angeli domini" ("Saints of God, come to her aid. Come to meet her, angels of the Lord").
- Ruby Nellins went to Sunday school, but Catholics usually learn about their religion in parish schools or in after-school classes for public school students.

9.3 "The Requiem for the Dead"

Father Brown—"You confessed to the police. What about God?"

Original Air Date: January 5, 2022
Writer: Michelle Lipton

Director: John Maidens
When a child killer returns to Kembleford after his prison release,
    Father Brown investigates when the man too is found murdered.
Guest Stars:
    Gerard McDermott as William Gracy
    Penny Layden as Nora Banks
    Michael Cooke as Ned Hannigan
    John Thomson as John Banks
    Tommy Garside as Daniel Banks
    John Cooke as Bryn Hannigan
    Alex Price as Sid Carter

• The wooden disk depicts the Gemini constellation. In Greek
  mythology, the identical twins Castor and Pollux were inseparable.
  When Castor was killed in battle, Pollux begged Zeus, god of the sky,
  to bring him back. Zeus agreed only if they spent half their time on
  earth, the other half amid the stars. In astrology, a person is a Gemini
  if he is born between May 21 and June 20.
• A requiem is the Catholic Mass said for the souls of the dead. During
  the Mass for Maggie Banks, Father Brown blessed her casket with
  holy water as a sign of her baptism, then with incense to signify
  prayers for her soul arising to heaven. The congregation sings "Abide
  with Me," a Christian hymn written by Henry Francis Lyte and based
  on Luke 24:29, when Jesus' disciples met Him on the road to Emmaus.

9.4 "The Children of Kalon"

> Father Brown—"As a priest, I find sometimes that a literal
> reading of a scripture can lead you away from the truth,
> not towards it."

Original Air Date: January 6, 2022
Writer: Tahsin Guner
Director: Jo Hallows
The Church of Apollo returns to Kembleford, and Father Brown gets
    involved when its former high priest Gerald/Kalon is released from
    the psychiatric hospital.
Guest Stars:
    Michael Maloney as Gerald Firth/Kalon
    Edward Wolstenholme as Dr. Bainbridge
    Jackie Clune as Thelma Bryce
    Jessica Jolleys as Clara Bryce
    Luke Matthews as Albert Timmins

Steven Elder as Tobias Faulkner
Tafline Steen as Celeste Shelton
Alex Price as Sidney Carter

- Writer Tahsin Guner resurrected Kalon from episode 1.5 "The Eye of Apollo," in which he was suspected in another locked room mystery.
- In calling Sid, Father Brown only dialed four numbers, indicating that there were more than a thousand lines using that telephone exchange.
- The photo of the astral temple shows a beautiful, pillared building at which Father Brown comments on its extravagance. He has forgotten the magnificent Catholic cathedrals.
- If the followers of the sun believed in modern medicine, the Phenytoin found in Thelma's pocket would have been prescribed to treat Clara's epilepsy.
- The Summer Solstice occurs on the equinox, June 21.
- While searching in Tobias's study, Father Brown came upon a secret drawer and called it a tabernacle. In the Catholic church, a tabernacle is a secure locked cabinet that sits on the altar and holds consecrated hosts. A lighted candle is always nearby to indicate the presence of the Eucharist.

9.5 "The Final Devotion"

Father Brown—"Better to believe a liar than to doubt an honest man."

Original Air Date: January 7, 2022
Writer: Kit Lambert
Director: Steve M. Kelly
After Cardinal Ratcliffe asks Father Brown to find a 13th-century tiara used for papal coronations, the priest enlists the help of Flambeau.
Guest Stars:
John Light as Hercule Flambeau
Nancy Carroll as Lady Felicia
Raffaello Degruttola as Ispettore Mario Angelini/Vincenzo Gavagna
Aneirin Hughes as Cardinal Ratcliffe
Diana Quick as Lady Cecily

- Father Brown's suggestion to Flambeau—"The road you are on is going down and down and one day you'll find yourself in a hole

from which, despite your cunning, you will be unable to escape"—is remarkably prescient.
- Lady Felicia says that Mrs. McCarthy is flapping about like grouse on August 12, a day that marks the start of 121 days of grouse hunting.
- The tiara of Saint Sylvester is a three-tiered crown, last used by Pope Paul VI in June 1963. For more information on the history of the tiara, see https://alchetron.com/Papal-tiara.
- Father Brown suggested they might find clues in the family's solar, a sunny room reserved for lords and ladies of the manor.
- The men find William Caxton's translation and printing of the Golden Legend, a popular collection of lives of the saints, originally by Jacobus de Voragine, 13th century.[98]
- Father Brown absolves Flambeau from his sins with the Latin words "Deinde ego te absolve a peccatis tuis in nominee Patris, et Filii, et Spiritus Sancti" ("Then I will absolve you from your sins in the name of the Father, and the Son, and the Holy Spirit").

9.6 "The New Order"

Father Brown—"God is testing me, but I have faith that the truth will out."

Original Air Date: January 10, 2022
Writer: Neil Irvine
Director: Jo Hallows
Father Brown is in danger of being excommunicated when an insufferable person moves into Kembleford and demands his obeisance.
Guest Stars:
Matthew Marsh as Lord Arthur Hawthorne
Luke Nunn as Gabe Hawthorne
Sara Stewart as Lady Margot Hawthorne
Zephyrn Taitte as Father Featherstone
Roger May as Canon Fox
Evan Milton as Stanley Buchanan

- Mrs. Hawthorne tells her son they will "draw a line under it," meaning they will talk no more about the distressing situation. Hawthorne had assured his wife his affair had been a "one off," i.e., something that happened only once.
- *The Enquirer* is a current British newspaper in print and digital formats. Hawthorne's son sets off for Fleet Street in London, home to many of the newspaper publishers in the UK.

- Curiously, in episode 9.2, Mrs. McCarthy advised Frances Penmark to make her unhappy marriage work. However, she hints that Lady Hawthorne should leave her husband. Remembering her own husband's adultery, Mrs. M speaks from experience.
- The "FL" monogrammed on the cufflink Father Brown found stands for "Footlights." Canon Fox hints at its meaning when he admits he liked to "tread the boards," meaning to act onstage. The Footlights at Cambridge University is a student comedy society which propelled many of its members to success in the entertainment industry.
- A strange scene occurs when Father Brown in his pajamas sits at the presbytery's kitchen table. Mrs. McCarthy enters, also in her night clothes, explaining that she saw the light on. Was she sleeping at the presbytery, or does she live close enough to see presbytery lights?
- Contrary to the prevailing attitude toward smoking in the 1950s, that it was "cool," Father Brown objects to Lord Hawthorne smoking. He had also asked Flambeau to not smoke when they shared a room in 9.5 "The Final Devotion."
- Father Featherstone is off to Swaziland, a small country in southeast Africa.

9.7 "The Island of Dreams"

> Father Brown to Sergeant Goodfellow—"I imagine that is a nightmare of the Inspector's—the downtrodden workers overthrowing their tyrannical bosses."

Original Air Date: January 11, 2022
Writer: David Semple
Director: Ruth Carney
Location: Chipping Norton Lido
Father Brown investigates a murder when a practical joker sets out to ruin a carnival-like holiday camp.
Guest Stars:
    Zita Sattar as Mavis Jug
    Lesley Nicol as Marjorie Chummy
    David Rees Talbot as Griff Grimshaw
    Will Hislop as Sandy Beauchamp
    Ted Robbins as Jock McCudgeon

- Mavis reports that another performer has a "gippy tummy." The phrase, meaning diarrhea, comes from "Egyptian tummy," an illness contracted in tropical countries.
- The Knobbly Knees contest was a staple of holiday camps. Everyone

from politicians to sports figures to everyday folks vied to have the "knobbliest."[99]

- In a skit, Griff wonders if he might be sick from eating Black Pudding, which is not a pudding at all, but a sausage made of pig's blood mixed with oats or barley and stuffed into a casing. Allegedly, it is rich in protein though highly caloric. Its sale is banned in America.
- Tannoy, named for the company that built it, refers to the public address, speaker, or amplifying system.
- Father Brown prays over the corpse, "Requiem aeternam dona ei, Domine, et lux perpetua luceat ei. Offerentes eam in conspectus Altissimi" ("Eternal rest grant to her, O Lord, and may perpetual light shine on her. We offer her in the sight of the Most High").

9.8 "The Wayward Girls"

> Father Brown—"I don't believe in lost causes, only lost souls…. And if you do not repent your crime, then I fear that it is you who is lost."

Original Air Date: January 12, 2022
Writer: Dominique Moloney
Director: Ruth Carney
After Sergeant Goodfellow tickets Bunty for speeding, Father Brown advises her to do a voluntary service at a borstal—an institution for juvenile delinquents.
Guest Stars:
  Emer Kenny as Bunty
  Catherine Russell as Cecilia Watson
  Paula Lane as Emily Harris
  Laura Rollins as Helen Delaney
  Alice Nokes as Kate Goodall
  Ruby May Martinwood as Brenda Palmer
  Makir Ahmed as Joe Randall
  Clare Lawrence-Moody as Deborah Webb

- Dr. Heather Shore advised the episode writer on the borstal, an institution which was established in 1902 to be a "halfway house between prison and the reformatory" for offenders of both sexes between the ages of 16 and 21. The borstal system was abolished in 1982.[100]
- Bunty's speeding fine is unknown, but before 2017, when fines were increased in hopes of minimizing the frequency of road accidents

in the UK, the minimum fine was £100 ($130 in 2022 U.S. dollars). In more serious situations, fines could have equaled an offender's weekly income which, because of Bunty's wealth, could have been considerable.[101]

9.9 "The Enigma of Antigonish"

Elsie—"Sometimes you may feel that you don't exist but it's not true…. Celebrate your existence and rejoice that you're alive."

Original Air Date: January 13, 2022
Writer: Lol Fletcher
Director: Isher Sahota
When an ex-employee of a health spa is found murdered in a field, Father Brown must sort through the remainder of the staff for the murderer.
Guest Stars:
    Jennifer Hyde as Lola Briggit
    Peter Singh as Captain Viktor Peters
    Robyn Addison as Elsie Peters
    Ryan Gage as Finbar Finch
    Camille Mallet De Chauny as Serge Duras

- When Inspector Mallory learns that a gun is kept behind the spa desk, he retorts that the place is hardly Fort Knox, a reference to a secure Kentucky depository where a large portion of America's gold reserves are stored. The shotgun used Langbridge Limited shells, invented by the gunsmith John Langbridge in the 1700s.
- Usually so careful at leaning his bicycle against a fence or building, in this episode Father Brown uncharacteristically tosses it down, not once but four times.
- Viktor had eaten apricot seeds ground up in a salad. Amygdalin found in apricot kernels converts to cyanide and can cause nausea and other illnesses.[102]
- Elsie confesses that thoughts of Finbar are inside her like "a virus," a curious comment in the 1950s but not so unusual at the time of the 2021 filming. She reads a comforting quote from Revelation 12:9, "That great dragon was cast out, that old serpent who is called the devil and Satan who seduceth the whole world and he was cast unto the earth, and his angels were thrown down with him."
- Searching Finbar's caravan, Father Brown finds the poem *Antigonish* written by Hughes Mearns in 1922 and reads the first stanza:

"Yesterday upon the stair,
I met a man who wasn't there
He wasn't there again today
I wish, I wish he'd go away."

Several lines of the poem were also quoted in Alec Guinness's *Father Brown* film by the wealthy socialite Mrs. Warren as Father Brown despairs of ever finding Flambeau.

- Finch tells Father Brown, "I'm a believer just like you." Another character in the Chesterton story, "The Dagger with Wings," likewise tells the priest, "It's your business to believe things." Father's reply, "I do believe some things, of course … and therefore, of course, I don't believe other things."[103]

9.10 "The Red Death"

Father Brown—"Sometimes we don't notice that which we see every day."

Original Air Date: January 14, 2022
Writer: Kit Lambert
Director: John Maidens
Lord "Monty" and Lady Felicia Montague throw a New Year's Eve masquerade ball that is overshadowed by the death of the Minister of Defense. To literally unmask the killer, Father Brown must eliminate family as well as invited guests.
Guest Stars:
    Alexander Hanson as Lord "Monty" Montague
    Richard Dillane as Sir Charles Hakeworth
    Gemma Page as Lady Agnes Hakeworth
    Caleb Frederick as Dr. Elliot Muthomi
    Nicholas Audsley as Robert Earl of Finchmore
    Cam Spence as Ruth Moulton
    John Light as Hercule Flambeau

- Lord Montague receives news from Special Branch, i.e., the British department of police concerned with political security.
- Researchers David Winfield and Harriet Duddy managed to tie in several political events and issues that Great Britain was dealing with at the end of 1953. Sir Anthony Eden was Winston Churchill's foreign secretary and was expected to succeed Churchill when he retired, which he did in 1955. However, Sir Eden fell ill in 1953 and never fully regained his health; hence, Hakeworth's assumption of succeeding Churchill himself.[104]

- Ruth Moulton visited Hakeworth to protest sending more troops to Kenya after the 1952 Mau Mau revolt that was instigated to gain independence from British rule. Instead, the British moved its army in to quell the insurgency resulting in the death of 11,000 rebels during the eight years of fighting.[105]
- Sergeant Goodfellow informed Mallory that he had been studying *Kerr's Guide to Forensic Medicine*. By Edinburgh police surgeon Douglas Kerr, it was first published in 1936 and was updated periodically.
- In 1842 Edgar Allan Poe published his very short story "The Masque of the Red Death." In medieval times, the land was ravaged by a plague, so Prince Prospero withdrew into his castle with 1,000 members of royalty and secured the windows and doors to escape the sickness. He then gave a masquerade ball, but at midnight the guests noticed a grotesque figure among them—the Red Death— and Prospero and his guests all die. In eerie similarity, shortly after the Covid pandemic began in March 2020, Rupert Neate in *The Guardian*, reported that wealthy people were secluding themselves in "disaster bunkers" in countries that did not have a great Covid outbreak.[106]
- After Father Brown gives out assignments, Bunty quotes, "Once more unto the breach," a line from Shakespeare's *Henry V* meaning to head out to battle again.
- Whatever Sid had drunk "knocked him six," meaning it quite thoroughly sickened him. Father Brown asks him if he had had "one over the eight?" also meaning one last drink that makes someone sick.[107]
- Mrs. McCarthy eschewed bringing her award-winning strawberry scones to the fancy event, instead bringing petit fours, bite-size cakes.

Season 10

If former BBC editorial director Roger Mosey had his way, *Father Brown* would be among the "lower-grade stuff that's schedule filler" and would be dumped in favor of programs that viewers would happily pay the BBC's £159 ($193 U.S. dollars) annual license fee to watch. Mosey's comments in January 2022 followed an announcement by Culture Secretary Nadine Dorries that government funds may soon run out if the license fee will be frozen for two years.[108]

Fortunately for fans, the popularity of *Father Brown* brings in much needed revenue from overseas markets. It's hard to argue with its value, given that it became the BBC's second longest-running daytime television series.

However, as soon as Season 9 ended with what seemed like a major finale, rumors began flying as to whether it really *was* a finale and whether there would be a Season 10. With several long-running threads wrapped up—one of the most important being Lady Felicia and her quasi-romance with Flambeau and then the appearance of her husband Lord Montague she had talked about but whose name viewers never got the chance to put a face to.

After Season 9 aired, *Radio Times* journalist Naomi Gordon asked Mark Williams what he would like to see next in Father Brown. He replied, "I'll tell you what we haven't done, we haven't done anything about where he was in the '30s.... I've got a backstory for him ... I think he was troubled in the trenches—that's exactly what the logic is of our timescale, is that he had an ecstatic revelation as a young man, as a teenager, and that reinforced or created his faith and then he trained to be a priest and he's back in Gloucestershire."[109]

When filming ended for Season 10, John Burton (Sergeant Goodfellow) revealed that it included cast changes, e.g., some familiar faces would be missing, but Inspector Sullivan, Lady Felicia, and Flambeau were returning. New characters included Claudie Blakley as Mrs. Isabelle Devine and Ruby-May Martinwood as Brenda Palmer from a Season 9 episode.[110] It remained to be seen how new dynamics would change the village of Kembleford.

10.1 "The Winds of Change"

Mrs. Burns—"This is the end of Kembleford."

Father Brown—"Who knows . . .. Having new people in the village might be a good idea."

Original Air Date: January 6, 2023
Writer: Dan Muirden
Director: John Maidens
Father Brown is kept busy not only interviewing a new parish
  secretary to replace Mrs. McCarthy but also in solving the murders
  of two Kembleford citizens.
Guest Stars:
  Mike Sengelow as Peter Mossop
  Clare-Louise English as Jennifer Mossop
  Lucas Hare as Joe Telford
  Witney White as Scarlett Streatham
  Ash Hunter as Brendan Streatham
  Elizabeth Bennett as Agnes Burns

- Father Brown has clearly found an ally in his sleuthing in the enthusiastic Isabelle Devine.
- Mrs. Burns claimed to know the entire Penny Catechism, a book of questions and answers covering the basics of the Catholic religion and originally costing one penny. American Catholics might have learned from the similar Baltimore catechism.
- The absence of familiar characters is explained by their having departed for distant places: Ireland (Mrs. McCarthy), Scotland (Inspector Mallory), and Africa (Bunty).
- Mrs. Devine sees the parish office as a sort of 221B Baker Street, the famous address of Sherlock Holmes.
- Kembleford in miniature is reminiscent of episode 5.7 in which model murder scenes are also featured.
- Mrs. Devine named her car Hercules for the Roman god known for his strength.

10.2 "The Company of Men "

Father Brown—"A crime of passion can be understood, if not easily forgiven."

Original Air Date: January 13, 2023
Writer: Dominique Moloney
Director: Paul Riordan
Father Brown encounters an acquaintance working at a men's-only club and, with the help of some strong women, clears her of a crime.
Guest Stars:
  Nancy Carroll as Lady Felicia Montague
  Ruby-May Martinwood as Brenda Palmer
  Roger Barclay as Jasper Granford
  Emma Davies as Charlotte Granford
  Joseph Potter as Albert "Bertie" Granford
  David Webber as John Harrow
  Lu Corfield as Moira Barns/Colonel Partridge
- Gentlemen-only clubs originated in West London in the 19th century as a sort of home away from home for their members.
- Unlike Mrs. McCarthy, Mrs. Devine serves only as parish secretary, so the role of housekeeper is taken by Brenda Palmer.
- The episode revels in strong women unafraid to have opinions of their own, to protest to get what they want, and to "take care of" men who have done them wrong.

- Once again, theatrics referenced by the makeup and costume worn by Moira is a throwback to Chesterton's love of the theater.
- Mrs. Devine claims that maybe it's a case of Occam's Razor, which theorizes that the simplest solution is probably the correct one.

10.3 "The Gardeners of Eden"

Father Brown—"I've searched for the truth my whole life, and it is never simple."

Original Air Date: January 20, 2023
Writer: David Semple
Director: Michael Lacey
Father Brown participates in galas involving a famous florist's return to Kembleford and finds the reason for one resident's murder.
Guest Stars:
    Jonathan Rigby as Edward Appleby
    Elaine Page as Octavia Eden
    Jasmine Hyde as Lizzy Eden
    Kaye Wragg as Noele Schama
    Philip Martin Brown as John Mulch
    Rosanna Maren as Marjorie Mulch

- At garden parties, Father Brown wears a biretta, a three- or four-ridged hat, unlike his usual soup bowl hat. He also wears a pelegrina, a cape-like garment, over his shoulders.
- Many of the women are costumed in flowery dresses including Mrs. Devine and Lizzy Eden. If not florals, they are dressed in green.
- The toxic plant was from the Aconitum family; ingestion or injection can cause death within hours.
- Another miniature building is featured when Lizzy and Noele re-created Octavia's first flower shop.

10.4 "The Beast of Wedlock"

Brenda Palmer—"You'd make a great thief, Father."

Original Air Date: January 27, 2023
Writer: Lol Fletcher
Director: John Maidens
The legend of a vicious white tiger is perpetuated with the death of two Wedlock citizens. Father Brown determines the real cause of death.
Guest Stars:
    Anna Wilson-Jones as the Duchess

Celine Arden as Sylvia Garcia
Clifford Barry as Sam Wadey
Paul Forman as Gabriel Wadey
Scott Handy as Reverend Duncan
Alex Waldmann as Professor Garcia

- To some extent, Mark Williams got his wish for a backstory regarding his war service when he encounters Sam Wadey who saved his life in the trenches. Their conversation is similar to reminiscences Father Brown had with Blind 'Arry in a previous episode.
- Brenda observes the looks and unspoken words between Mrs. Devine and Inspector Sullivan that predicts a future revelation of a past they shared.
- The legend of Bakko, the white tiger allegedly terrorizing the village of Wedlock, can be traced to the mythological white tiger in the Chinese constellation.
- Numbers on the Duchess's painting indicate the date of the episode as June 5, 1954.
- Father Brown finds Gabriel under the mausoleum in an area known as catacombs.

10.5 "The Hidden Man"

Father Brown—"Flambeau may deserve a prison sentence, but I still believe there's a good man in there."

Original Air Date: February 3, 2023
Writer: Tahsin Guner
Director: Michael Lacey
Flambeau returns to Kembleford seeking revenge on a man who is retaliating for Flambeau's previous thefts.
Guest Stars:
John Light as Hercule Flambeau
Jolyon Coy as Sebastien Fleming/Edwin Blythe
Geoffrey Newland as Lester Garrick
Eddie Eyre as Joe Loom
Cora Kirk as Lila Tate

- Saint Nicholas, a third-century bishop of Myra, is said to have miraculously restored to life three children who were cut up and buried in a vat of brine. In Holland, he became known as Sinterklaas, the inspiration for Santa Claus. His feast day is celebrated on December 6.
- Flambeau appears unnaturally tanned and with much longer hair than in all previous seasons.
- Father Brown, Mrs. Devine, and Brenda look at old newspapers

on microform. Invented a hundred years previously, it was (and is) utilized by libraries as a compact storage system for newspapers and some books.
- It is ironic that Inspector Sullivan so wishes to leave Kembleford, but Tom Chambers as Sullivan begged the BBC to bring him back to the series.[111]

10.6 "The Royal Visit"

Brenda Palmer—"[Royalty] they're just people at the end of the day."

Original Air Date: February 10, 2023
Writer: Mark Brotherhood
Director: Paul Riordan
Princess Margaret's visit to Kembleford may be cancelled if Father Brown can't determine who killed the school janitor beforehand.
Guest Stars:
    Sarah Smart as Amanda Clement
    Tristan Gemmill as Inspector Neil Beckett
    Kara Tointon as Elizabeth Barnes
    Gary Lilburn as Raymond Harrison
    Howard Ward as Mayor Anthony Wood
    Olivia Benjamin as Princess Margaret
- Brenda was feeling "a bit of a gooseberry," meaning a third party watching others in a romantic relationship; she also referred to the goings-on in the Red Lion as "a bit Mills & Boon in there." Mills & Boon is a publisher of romance novels, similar to Harlequin.
- The new Saint Arilda's library was named for a Gloucestershire martyr who was killed defending her chastity. Princess Margaret was the only sibling of Queen Elizabeth II.
- The brass band plays "God Save the Queen." Americans would recognize the familiar tune as that of "My Country, 'Tis of Thee."

10.7 "The Show Must Go On"

Charlotte Maidland—"Even the shortest life has a purpose."

Original Air Date: February 17, 2023
Writer: Sarah-Louise Hawkins
Director: Miranda Howard-Williams
As the Kembleford Players rehearse for their next performance, a

murderer takes out one of the actors, leaving Father Brown to discover who it is.

Guest Stars:

Sam Phillips as Patrick Maidland

Mark Fleischmann as Jeremy Sandford

Sonita Henry as Charlotte "Charlie" Maidland

Elizabeth Roberts as Millie Tucker

Jack Loxton as Thomas Church

Helena Barlow as Penny Briggs

- In Shakespeare's comedy *Much Ado about Nothing,* Benedick and Beatrice swear off love and marriage but, after overhearing friends' conversations about them, realize that they really do love each other.
- Sergeant Goodfellow is happy not to have to wear a dress in this play. His line is a throwback to episode 6.1 when he and Inspector Mallory dressed as Cinderella's sisters for a Christmas pantomime.

10.8 "The Sands of Time"

Father Brown—"God hasn't given up on you, and neither have I."

Original Air Date: February 24, 2023

Writer: Neil Irvine

Director: Dominic Keavey

A clockmaker's secret affects the lives of others in his household and inadvertently causes a murder.

Guest Stars:

Jasmyn Banks as Betty Hartigan

Bob Barrett as Oswald Hartigan

Rowan Polonski as Jake Hunt/Jakub Horynski

Jesse Fox as Lord Quentin Hartigan

Stephen Kennedy as Stan Hoskens

- In Jake's drawer, Isabelle discovers *Lady Chatterley's Lover,* the book by D.H. Lawrence banned for obscenity in many countries.
- The Nightingale clock is another example of valuable items Nazis stole from the Polish people.

10.9 "The Wheels of Wrath"

Chief Inspector Sullivan—"One thing I've learned: never underestimate Father Brown."

Original Air Date: March 3, 2023

Writers: Matthew Cooke and Vincent Lund

Director: Dominic Keavey
When a gang of bikers, the Ton-Ups, arrive in Kembleford, death
  follows. Father Brown solves one biker's murder and, with Sergeant
  Goodfellow's help, one from the past as well.
Guest Stars:
  Dominic Jones as Lance South
  Jamie Bacon as Billy Turner
  Joshua Griffin as Roger Norton
  Amy Cudden as Agnes Morris
  Annie Cordoni as Lisa Morris
  Trevor Cooper as Denny Beaton
- "Life Could Be a Dream" aka "Sh-Boom" was first recorded by the
  Chords in 1943.
- See caferacertv.com/history/the-history-of-do-the-ton/ for the story
  of the real Ton-Up Boys.
- Father Brown admitted that he had doubts during his seminary days,
  "wondering whether I was worthy of my calling." He managed by
  focusing on why he was there—to help people and bring them closer
  to God.

10.10 "The Serpent Within"

Father Brown—"Why on earth would anyone want to leave
Kembleford?"

Original Air Date: March 10, 2023
Writer: Dan Muirden
Director: Miranda Howard-Williams
Inspector Sullivan's wish to return to London almost comes true
  with his arrest of a corrupt superior, Goodfellow gets his inspector
  exam results, and a joyous dinner is planned.
Guest Stars:
  Jay Taylor as George Kavanagh
  Ciarán Owens as Martin Jackson
  Megan Placito as Sergeant Francis
  Jonny Phillips as Detective Superintendent Alan Alford
  Christian Ballantyne as Harry Davenport
  Michael Akinsulire as Ricky "Crafty" Taylor
- The episode resolves continuing plotlines—Sullivan's proven
  evidence against Superintendent Alford, Sergeant Goodfellow's
  worries about taking the inspector exam, and the burgeoning love
  interest between Sullivan and Isabelle Devine.

5

Despite the Critics, Success!

> When Father Brown first stepped off an Atlantic liner on
> to American soil, he discovered as many other English-
> man has done, that he was a much more important person
> than he had ever supposed.... America has a genius for the
> encouragement of fame; and his appearance in one or two
> curious criminal problems ... had consolidated a reputa-
> tion in America out of what was little more than a rumour
> in England.[1]

The BBC's *Father Brown* is not G.K. Chesterton's Father Brown. The
trick is not expecting him to be. Chesterton's priest is short and stumpy,
Mark Williams is at least six feet tall, yet he is totally believable as being
unremarkable and unobtrusive as the original when the scene calls for it.
However, it is not only in appearance and manner where these two versions of the priest-detective diverge. Although any adaptation will never
please Chesterton purists, the success of the BBC version suggests that its
modifications have produced stories that continue to resonate with wider
audiences.

In any case, it's a rare adaptation that perfectly imitates a classic
original. If it does, then that might very well be a definitive case for pla-
giarism. Instead, each episode of the *Father Brown* series begins with
an acknowledgment that it is "*based on* [author's italics] the character
created by G.K. Chesterton." Likewise, previous incarnations of Chesterton's priest also acknowledged their origin. In Kenneth More's 1974
series, each episode began with the phrase "From the Father Brown Stories by G.K. Chesterton"; similarly, Alec Guinness's movie was "Based
on Father Brown stories by G.K. Chesterton." With a caveat like that,
the subsequent production is as likely to be a television program, a film,
an audio recording, a comic book, or a graphic novel. Mark Williams'
Father Brown is, as detailed in Chapter 2, only the latest in a long series

of characterizations of the sleuthing priest and, by all accounts, one of the most successful worldwide.

Since the advent of radio and silent film, producers have capitalized on the commercial potential for adaptations of classic literature ranging from the 1939 film version of L. Frank Baum's *The Wizard of Oz* to Louisa May Alcott's *Little Women* in 2019. According to Alexander Manshel, et al., *Publishers Marketplace* (a database of editors, agents, and publishing deals) reports that, since 2000, literary adaptations of books to television have been significantly increasing. Historical novels or, one might guess, short story collections such as Chesterton's tales, are particularly suited for adaptation. The reduced scope of a short story more easily facilitates a successful adaptation as there is of necessity some redaction or addition to the original text. The setting of a story in a bygone era builds a new world that takes the reader or audience out of his everyday life. The adaptability in exploring these brave new worlds epitomizes television's narrative form.[2]

Adaptations in general may originate from any other source as well: musicals, best-selling fiction, or histories. But many of those "originals" were not truly unprecedented: William Shakespeare, for example, whose works have frequently inspired adaptations, borrowed from Scottish legends and Roman and Greek histories on which to base his plays. The lives and tragedies of Kings John, Henry V, and Richard III provide the background for dramas of the same name. Charles Dickens's *A Christmas Carol*, coinciding with a flourishing preponderance of Victorian ghost and fairy stories, has undergone dozens of adaptations for both film and television, ranging from strict adherence to the original, as in the case of those starring George C. Scott or Alistair Sim, to the more modern take-offs of Bill Murray's *Scrooged* and *A Muppet Christmas Carol* starring Jim Henson's puppets with Michael Caine as Scrooge. Remakes, as such, could be justified as productions providing a fast and reliable opportunity for profit based on audience familiarity. Even G.K. Chesterton, it might be argued, could be said to have adapted his Father Brown character after stories told by his mentor, Father John O'Connor.

Because it is advantageous economically for producers to borrow from older, out of copyright works or literature in the public domain, mysteries such as those by M.R. James, Agatha Christie, and Arthur Conan Doyle have frequently been tailored to other media formats and are generally well received unless the original texts are changed in such a way as to contradict actual historical events.[3] Since Chesterton's stories were written over a period of 26 years which saw the anticipation, misery, and aftermath of a world war, his commentaries on social conditions and the foils of humanity still resonate universally. By setting the BBC series in the mid–1950s, producers could tap into the sentiments of the author who had lived through the first World War by dramatizing those same events 40 years later with characters who continue to deal with the effects of the second war.

Neil McCaw in his *Adapting Detective Fiction* refers to the new versions as "heritage," in that they "provided an opportunity for the modern nation to be re-imagined in a way that commemorated an earlier time in the national past, offering an appealing contrast to modernity."[4] Take, for example, the original Sherlock Holmes stories from 1887 to 1901, written in and very much representative of the Victorian era. Scientific experiments and increasing technological advances of the age belied his very Victorian standards of dress and speech. Contrast that to the recent Holmes as performed by Benedict Cumberbatch, a thoroughly modern reincarnation set in 21st-century London. The series *Sherlock* has given Holmes a contemporary twist, reimagining him embroiled in mysteries involving computers, cell phones, and SUVs. As David Bianculli of NPR's *Fresh Air* observed, "Even if you're not familiar with the old Sherlock Holmes adventures, you'll love this new Sherlock series. If you are familiar with them, chances are you'll love this new Sherlock even more."[5]

Consider another example of a "heritage" adaptation, Agatha Christie. The actor David Suchet who has played Hercule Poirot in adaptations of myriad Christie stories has *become* Poirot, embodying the iconic detective—his impeccable appearance, his ego, his accent, and references to his "little grey cells." His identification with Poirot is appealing because it is faithful to the original, but, of course, some revision is always essential. The episodes themselves vary in quality proving the difficulties of altering a story with too few or too many characters or a scarcity or overabundance of red herrings that require deliberation during the re-write, as well as tailoring the action to fit exactly into a 50-minute or hourlong time slot.

Ten years into the writing of Father Brown, Chesterton saw an advertisement for a dramatic version of Gaston Leroux's "The Mystery of the Yellow Room," a locked room detective tale. He wrote in his essay "Errors about Detective Stories" that he had heard the play was a great success, "though it by no means follows, from the nature of the problem, that a good mystery story will make a good play. Indeed, the two things in the abstract are almost antagonistic."[6] Chesterton's point, that locked-room mysteries depend as much on what is imagined as what is seen, highlights one of the key difficulties of adaptation: how to communicate a character's mystery-solving train of thought to viewing audiences. Because his Father Brown often follows the structure of solving mysteries after much contemplation and observation, the producers and writers of various versions or updates had to create additional storylines with supplementary characters and significantly more action to fill the allocated time and to communicate those cerebral processes visually.

Chesterton did not elaborate on the play itself nor on the playwright who transformed Leroux's words into a dramatic script. Had the theatrical rewrite been poorly done, playgoers might not have been aware of its faults unless they were also familiar with the 1907 book. As we shall see, this remains a point of contention with today's critics as well.

Depending on one's perspective, the success or failure of the BBC's adaptation of Chesterton's Father Brown is attributable to many factors. Mark Williams has repeatedly insisted that the series has benefited from the storytelling, which is a credit not only to Chesterton, but to the skilled writers employed by the BBC. As Professor Pamela Milne has pointed out, the original Father Brown was the product of Chesterton's perspective as an early 20th-century white male Englishman. To the BBC's credit, script writers of Williams' Father Brown stories varied: some were white males, many were women, a number were people of color, some were not native Britons.[7] Scriptwriter Jude Tindall, who wrote 14 of the one hundred episodes, won three Royal Television Society (RTS) Midlands awards for Best Drama for episodes 2.6 "The Daughters of Jerusalem," 4.1 "The Mask of the Demon," and 5.1 "The Star of Jacob." She is also the co-creator and associate producer of *Sister Boniface Mysteries*, a spin-off of *Father Brown*. Paul Matthew Thompson won Best Drama for a Fictional Program at the RTS awards for his rendering of episode 1.10 "The Blue Cross." Kit Lambert, Lol Fletcher, and Tahsin Guner, the co-creator of *Father Brown* who had confessed at the beginning that he had never read Chesterton or written a mystery, each had more than 10 scripts to their credit, with Lambert contributing 17. Throughout the series, their various scripts have referenced Catholic prayers, Biblical quotations, and numerous literary, mythical, or legendary persons and terms, such as Hermes, Bucephalus, Autolycus, Apollo, Amenhotep, Mastigatus, Tantalus, and Mephistopheles, enabling viewers of varying inclinations and intellectual abilities to appreciate the culture of the series. By bringing classical literature to the masses effectually, the masses are brought to literature, diluted or simplified as it may be.[8]

Acknowledgment must also go to advisors who kept the scripts as accurate as possible historically, politically, and religiously: Fathers Tony Nye, Gwilym Lloyd, and Paul Keane; historical advisors Bob Bushaway, Jonathan Reinarz, and Matthew Francis; police consultants John MacDonald and Dave Cross; Dr. Terry Quinn, M.D.; government intelligence advisor Steve Hewitt; and Jackie Cobner, safety advisor.[9]

Williams has also recognized the costumers, the cameramen, and the gifted guest stars who all contributed to the show's success.[10] He too must be lauded for his characterization of the sleuthing priest. He has given a lot of thought to the priest's history, how Father Brown's military service affected his vocation, how a priest would relate to his parishioners. When Father Brown hears the confession of an accused person, he sits next to the penitent, understanding that something heavy is weighing on this soul and indicating his desire to listen and help. They are both on the same side of the situation. "One of the things he does, is that he is still, which Chesterton gives an image of," says Williams, "but when he moves, he moves very quickly, because he has made a decision."[11] Frequent viewers will recognize Williams turning on his heel as an idea or solution presents itself, often much to the surprise of the person he was talking to, his cassock swirling around his ankles in his need to quicky act on an idea.

How well the cast, scripts, and production effects worked overall was evident after just one season. *The Guardian* reported that the BBC's new daytime lineup had led to increased audience numbers. Part of that achievement was due to the *Father Brown* series. But another part, controller Liam Keelan conceded, was the weather. In January 2013 during the two weeks when *Father Brown* premiered, the UK suffered through the most widespread and prolonged snowfall in three years. The inclement weather led to school closings, the disruption of train travel, and the cancellation of hundreds of flights at Heathrow airport. People stayed home and watched television, up to two million of them tuning in to *Father Brown* in the afternoon and liking what they saw and eventually becoming committed fans of the series.[12]

The numbers were verified by Parrot Analytics, a global company whose mission it is to analyze and predict media content that audiences will demand. They work with studios and networks to advise on content, distribution, and advertising. After Season 9, in February 2022 Parrot determined that Father Brown's "travelability" to the United States from the United Kingdom was 80 percent, meaning that, if 100 British people favored the series, 80 out of 100 Americans did. Curiously, more Germans approved of *Father Brown* than did the British. Equally high in audience ratings scores are the Netherlands and Russia. *Father Brown* also ranks extremely high in the United States in the drama genre with 96.1 percentile; that is, of all the dramatic programs in the U.S., the demand for *Father Brown* is higher than 96 percent of all others.[13]

Just seven months later, the program remains popular with a demand of 94 percent of Americans compared to its home country the United Kingdom with 100 percent. What is most surprising is Parrot's current statistics showing that the demand in Russia is 205 percent of the demand in the UK,[14] and coming at a time when Russia is fighting an unpopular war in Ukraine.

While not referring to *Father Brown* specifically, Neil McCaw would explain such numbers as American audiences especially "enjoy[ing] the experience of being voyeurs not only of an alien lifestyle in the past but in a foreign land, yet a land enough like the United States so as not to be threatening and inhabited by people who actually speak English."[15] Perhaps the Russian people are intrigued by the peaceful and ecumenical position of the mild-mannered priest.

Americans may be watching their British cousins engaging in a massive "nostalgiathon" for the days when the empire governed more than a fifth of the world's population and, to rephrase Robert Browning, "God was in his heaven, and all was right with the world." Considering the preponderance of adaptations of classic literature by the BBC and other British producers since 1980—*Brideshead Revisited* (1981), *Silas Marner* (1985), *The Mill on the Floss* (1997), *Pride and Prejudice* (1995), *Great Expectations* (2011), to name a few—it appears that the British are, according to one reporter, averting their eyes from the complications intrinsic to their legacy of imperialism and instead focusing on the good things that are part of their past. Americans can rest assured that when its "reckoning" comes, it too will be all right and, "if the national memory is selective enough, [they] can get away with living quite contentedly entirely in a past of one's choosing" also.[16]

Besides audience numbers, the success of the *Father Brown* series can also be measured in terms of longevity and awards. Five years after its premier, through a syndication deal with Public Broadcasting Stations (PBS), it was the only UK drama to reach more than 100 million homes in the United States in primetime.[17] At the Royal Television Society's award ceremonies, the series was presented with Best Fictional Television Programme for the years 2013, 2014, 2015, and 2016.[18] It was nominated for Best Daytime Programme, Broadcast Awards in 2014 and 2015; and the Best Daytime Programme, National Television Awards in 2014, 2015, and 2016. Mark Williams was recognized in the Best Acting in the Male category in 2015 and won the Best Acting Performance Award. In 2019, nominees at the RTS included Sorcha Cusack (as Mrs. McCarthy) for Acting Performance, Female; Jack Deam (as Inspector Mallory) for Acting Performance, Male; and Claire Collins (Costume supervisor) for Craft-Production, *Father Brown* for Single Television Drama or Drama Series.

Upon reaching the 100th episode, the BBC proudly acclaimed the global success of the series: It was shown in more than 235 world-wide territories, including primetime in the United States; it received the UK's top rating for any daytime drama of the last five years. The program ranked above average for viewership in Canada, the Netherlands, Germany, Sweden, and Finland and was a major hit in Australia; 2.8 million viewers tuned in to watch the first episode of Season 9, making it the biggest audience ever for *Father Brown*.[19]

The Internet Movie Database (IMDb) is a free online source for information about movies and television programs, including synopses, cast lists, reviews, and trivia. While it is valuable as a quick reference, when taken as an assessor of episode popularity, IMDb is much less reliable. The simple fact is that a very few percentage of viewers (the average for each episode being only 261 out of the millions) bothered to rate their satisfaction with any one particular *Father Brown* episode. Nevertheless, it is interesting to examine the numbers: The first episode broadcast—1.1 "The Hammer of God"—not surprisingly, received the largest number of votes (525) for a score of 7.2 out of 10. The fewest votes (91) went to episode 9.9 "The Enigma of Antigonish." United States voters almost unanimously ranked episodes equal to or higher than non–U.S. voters. Twenty-one episodes received a vote of 8/10 or above, with episode 8.10 "The Tower of Lost Souls" ranking highest of them all at 8.8/10 from 255 voters. One could guess that the return to Kembleford by the two previous police inspectors was the draw, but there is no way to know with any certainty.[20] The lowest ranking episode, "The Island of Dreams," from season 9 was only scored at 6.2. The few reviewers did not hold back their disdain, calling it "ludicrous," "really awful," and "utter crap." They suggested that the characters missing from the episode—Mrs. McCarthy, Sid, and Lady Felicia—purposefully gave it a pass which dubiously assumes that the actors have a choice in episodes in which they will perform.

Despite the enthusiasm for the show (aside from "The Island of Dreams") as generated by its millions of fans, sooner or later, critics began writing and talking about it, often as vitriolic assessments. The Internet and blogosphere provided the venue through which professional reviewers as well as those who simply had an opinion to offer could publicize their evaluation of the *Father Brown* series. Too often too many were unwilling to divorce Chesterton's stories from the BBC's adaptation without considering that excellence in the series did not depend on its faithfulness to the stories. McCaw, quoting film professor George Bluestone, has pointed out several issues involved in the adaptations of novels into films. The same holds true for short stories adapted to television. Because the story is linguistic and television is a visual medium,

> the "visual rhythms" of film are seen as especially unique: "the inter-cut, the parallel development, the extreme long shot, the fade-out, the fade-in, the dissolve, the flashback, all became common currency in editing techniques." Which all leads to the common sense acknowledgement that the filmed novel, in spite of certain resemblances, will inevitably become a different artistic entity from the novel on which it is based.[21]

"This recognition," continues McCaw, "of the inherent qualities of different forms is unarguable."[22] If one judges the *Father Brown* series only by its similarity in all aspects to Chesterton's originals, then flawed reasoning implies it must not be any good. Gil Steven suggests that "adaptation" or "remake" are terms interchangeable with "reboot." And "reboot" is exactly what the creators of the *Father Brown* the series intended. Using the Father Brown name and several identifying qualities led to a pilot that was followed by the first season and several thereafter. No less importantly, they re-introduced a classic author. It is noteworthy that very few critics who watched and harshly criticized the first season returned (or if they did, they didn't write or blog about it) to ascertain if their initial impression of the show had improved. Notwithstanding the global audience numbers, critics—primarily G.K. Chesterton aficionados—hastened to find opposition to this new Father Brown.

Chesterton himself was not immune to disapproval, observing,

> The function of criticism, if it has a legitimate function at all, can only be one function—that of dealing with the subconscious part of the author's mind which only the critic can express, and not with the conscious part of the author's mind, which the author himself can express. Either criticism is no good at all (a very defensible position) or else criticism means saying about an author the very things that would have made him jump out of his boots.[23]

Chesterton's disparagement of Inspector Valentin in "The Blue Cross" he might also have ascribed to his critics—"When he could not follow the train of the reasonable, he coldly and carefully followed the train of the unreasonable."[24] Some reviewers failed to grasp the concept of *adaptation* versus duplication, i.e., word-for-word dramatization of the original. As one series critic wrote, "it's not bad as a mystery, the real mystery is why one would want to change from the originals.... Chesterton's stories were masterpieces of the genre, why change them?"[25] The short answer, of course, is that they did not translate to the modern visual medium of television.

This particular criticism was nothing new. In 1954, the *Radio Times* critic, in a comment about Alec Guinness's portrayal of the priest, now seems prescient of future Father Brown adaptations, when he wondered if fans of Chesterton would be "a tad aggrieved by the slight shift of period and the marked reduction in religious undertones."[26] Taking the opposite view, only a few months before the first broadcast of Mark Williams' Father Brown, "TM" of London's *Time Out* (a guide to events and other happenings in the city) reviewed the Guinness film. For him (or her), one of its attractions was how director Robert Hamer had updated the story "to a contemporary setting without losing any of its quintessential period flavour."[27]

For the most part, reviewers who did not like the BBC's *Father Brown* after the first episode or first season were those who had anticipated not liking it at all, i.e., fans of Chesterton who would not tolerate the beloved priest-detective being sullied, tampered with, or interpreted in any other way than how Chesterton first created him more than one hundred years ago. Admirers of Chesterton suspected and feared as much as soon as the newest adaptation was announced. Dale Ahlquist, president of the American Chesterton Association, predicted, "I have a feeling it won't be based on anything G.K. Chesterton ever wrote." Upon hearing of the proposed BBC production, Kevin O'Brien, who once performed in a one-man show as "Father Brown—Detective," blogged that he learned the producers didn't seem to have faith in Chesterton, in the priest's character, or that Chesterton's plots would hold up to modern scrutiny. Therefore, he wondered, "how good could this BBC series possibly be?" During the first season, O'Brien commented again that he couldn't bring himself to watch *Father Brown*. "I'm told it's an insult to Chesterton, to Father Brown and to the Catholic Church."[28]

Calling the series "uninspired," the reviewer for *Cinema Sentries* was also familiar with the Chesterton stories. In those, Father Brown may care about souls not crimes, he pronounced, but the series does not. He wondered, then, who the series was for—not Chesterton readers who wouldn't recognize Father Brown; not fans of village mysteries, nor fans of murder mysteries who would be bored by the series.[29]

To wit, Chesterton's Father Brown was a simple parish priest, but acutely cognizant in the ways man sins. He was rather bumbling at times, dropping his packages, or losing his umbrella. While these quirks might be deemed cute or humorous once or twice, instead of an audience reacting with a "tut tut" or "tsk tsk" each time, it is more likely these traits could easily become annoying if episode after episode featured such bumbling and could cause viewers to urge him to get on with it already. No, Mark Williams' Father Brown's face may not exactly duplicate Chesterton's description. He is not as dull as a dumpling, nor are his eyes as empty as the sea. He also does not blink owlishly but does remove his spectacles occasionally in frustration with a situation or to visualize facts of the case introspectively. It is likewise ridiculous to suggest that this Father Brown does not care for souls. He frequently makes police officials wait while he prays over a deceased victim or encourages a sinner to repent and make his peace with God. One of his parishioners recognizes Father Brown's compassion in episode 8.8 "The Curse of the Aesthetic." An artist is exhibiting his works about people with a saintly quality. Turning to Father Brown he says, "not unlike your good self, Father."

Around the time of the publication of the first collection of Father Brown stories, several years after meeting Father O'Connor, Chesterton, in the introduction to his book on criticisms of Charles Dickens, wrote, "Nothing is important except the fate of the soul."[30] It is unknown how he arrived at this conclusion or if he was convinced of its reality by O'Connor, but the premise is evident in each of his stories about the priest-detective. Writers of the *Father Brown* series accepted this tenet and likewise instilled its faith-in-action into Mark Williams' Father Brown. For him, God is personal, not a vague Somebody out there somewhere, not an abstract concept.[31] He believes the Creator is an all-merciful God who forgives the sinner who truly repents. The priest knows God intimately enough to proclaim assuredly to Reverend Bohun, "God is not your scapegoat!"[32] Father Brown's parish, Kembleford in the BBC series, exemplifies simple village life with a range of homey characters including, in the first episode, an Anglican vicar, the village blacksmith, the Polish housekeeper, a gossipy secretary, the socialite, and a gay man. As the episodes progress, Father Brown tools around on his bicycle greeting his parishioners or introducing himself to newcomers, as audiences are treated to sights of the beautiful houses, the fences of honey-colored stone, and the vast fields of the surrounding countryside. The murder victim is usually easily deduced by being the most obnoxious guest star ever to come into the village, while the who, how, and why of the crime takes some ferreting out by Father Brown. Nearly always at odds with the police but aided by his faithful sidekicks, he does a neat job of tidying up each mystery so that at the end of each, audiences can once again agree with Robert Browning that "all's right with the world...."

That is, unless you're the reviewer from *Mystery File* who skewered the BBC series and found in it zero redeeming qualities. The Chesterton aficionado had also disliked "that awful television movie" with Barnard Hughes and the terrible miscasting of Walter Connolly, Kenneth More, and Alec Guinness in their characterizations of Father Brown. He accused Williams' Father Brown of never rising to the occasion, never blinking behind his spectacles, never simply standing and observing.[33]

His negativism can hardly match that found on the "At the Scene of the Crime" site wherein the blogger detested the first episode so intensely that he had to watch the entire season to assure himself that it never got any better. He rails that he was unable to write anything about the show, then publishes nearly 1,000 words on the topic to "discuss just how wrong the adaptation got the stories." After he praises Chesterton for having written "some of the finest short stories ever written," he admits that Chesterton is "such a polarizing figure because he was so adamant in proclaiming his beliefs were true, thereby implying that all others were false." The BBC did not allow its newest Father Brown to defend his faith, sticking instead to tried and true politically correct opinions.[34] One must wonder why he should have to defend his faith? Is not his vocation as a priest enough?

Finally, in an article titled "Definitely *not* Chesterton's Father Brown!"

another critic wonders if it matters that the BBC series is "merely another light entertainment, harmless in its way, and only remotely based on the original Father Brown?" He laments that, yes, it does matter because "it gives a wrong impression of the originals and is a lost opportunity to introduce the real Father Brown."[35] To counter this argument, numerous commentators in online blogs or television review websites have admitted to having never read Chesterton before but now plan to. As Manshel ascertained, "becoming a TV show increases a novel's popularity enormously. Adaptations can drive book sales.... TV doesn't just borrow highbrow status from the novel; it apparently sends some back."[36] Consequently, when critics argue that the BBC's adaptation has led potential enthusiasts away from G.K. Chesterton, the fact is that the opposite is true. This suggests the inquiry, if there had never been original Father Brown stories, would a series about a clerical detective become as successful as this one has been?

Several international versions, almost certainly also based on Chesterton's protagonist, if not his stories, suggest the broad appeal of a sleuthing priest. The Italian television program *Don Matteo* (*Father Matthew*) starring Terence Hill, previously of the 1970s comedy team with Bud Spencer, broadcast for 20 years beginning in 2000. Its popularity implies that the answer to that question also would be an unequivocal yes. *Don Matteo* features the mystery-solving Catholic priest of the small Italian village of Gubbio, which he navigates around on his bicycle. Sound familiar? Like *Father Brown*, the storylines are uncomplicated in order to fit into the fixed time slot, but the Catholic faith is integral to the plot development, proven again and again by Don Matteo's care for the souls of his parishioners. Helping in his investigations is his best friend Marshal Antonio Cecchini, a local policeman. As Don Matteo, Terence Hill won the award for Best Actor at the 2002 Monte Carlo Television Festival.

Based on *Don Matteo* and, yet again, certainly inspired by *Father Brown*, the Polish priest *Ojciec Mateusz* (*Father Matthew*) also serves in a small parish. Familiar characters include his loyal housekeeper, his bishop who fortunately turns a blind eye to Father Matthew's detective investigations, and the local police inspector who is never happy to see him at the scene of the crime. Starring Artur Żmijewski as Father Mateusz Żmigrodzki, the series was broadcast from 2008 to 2021 and won three Best Drama awards in 2010, 2016, and 2019 and the "Golden Telekamera" in 2020.[37]

The popularity of programs about priests is indeed of significance. Despite damaging news reports in which there is little to motivate anyone to the life of a cleric, inspiration may still be found in the Father Browns. Maybe there's more to them than a simple crime to be solved or a mystery to be unearthed.

A Final Word

A Mystery or Proselytizing?

Magdalena—"Do you ever question your faith, Father?"

Father Brown—"Don't tell the bishop, sometimes yes. Religion, like all belief, should be open to enquiry. It should evolve, embrace."[1]

With cassocks flapping, as Fathers Matteo, Mateusz, and Brown pedal their bicycles around their respective villages on their way to the scene of a murder, what are viewers to make of them? Does the sight of a grown man in a long black dress invoke a snigger or a giggle? Do his prayers over the victims foster a sense of relief that someone cares enough to stop and reflect on the deceased's immortal soul before accusing the one who caused the tragedy? Does his morality, belief in God, and genuine compassion toward those he encounters inspire similar feelings? The developers of these series have communicated something of their own beliefs to the viewing audience. The religion (or faith) of those audiences determines how the message will be received. "Those with pre-existing religious views can interpret the programmes as explicitly supporting religion, while the fictional form allows a distancing from faith elements and connection with the social realities explored for those without a faith-based perspective," argues Andrew Crome in his thesis "'Wonderful,' 'Hot,' 'Good' Priests: Clergy on Contemporary British TV and New Visibility of Religion."[2] With *Father Brown*, we see audiences responding to the series in both ways. One correspondent told this author that "the religious aspects add a whiff of 'other' or 'remoteness' to them. Because the nuances are new and/or unfamiliar to me, they not only pique my interest, they enhance my enjoyment. Sometimes, though, it can be hard to relate to characters who behave a certain way because of their devotion to their religion and in those instances, I just have to go with the flow."[3]

Notwithstanding *Father Brown*'s millions of viewers or the high rankings of the episodes, religion's television presence has not been accompanied by a revival of organized religion. During the decade the BBC's *Father Brown* series was originally broadcast, only just more than half of the UK population identified itself as Christian and increasing numbers were turning away from the Catholic church. It is to the credit of the series developers that the potentially controversial project was not only greenlighted, but produced, renewed season after season, and awarded with a worldwide fandom. After programs like the irreverent comedies of *Father Ted* and ITV's *Hell's Bells*, the risk of offending audiences with a truly spiritual representation of a priest was a gamble the BBC took. According to Richard Wolff, spiritual programs dealing with church leaders have not been as successful as those taking a more lighthearted approach.[4] Comedy and satire dressed in clerical robes claim more audience numbers than those dealing with matters of the spirit. Yet, given these statistics, the gamble that John Yorke took in suggesting a revival of Father Brown proved to be a well-conceived opportunity.

Professor Milne has blogged a thought-provoking article titled "The BBC's Father Brown Series: Moving Beyond Chesterton" that details her impression of the series she watched during the Covid-19 virus mandated isolation. She agrees with critics who note that "there is relatively little that connects it to Chesterton's stories" but maintains that disconnect is beside the point. Instead of regarding change from the original as a defect, Milne considers it an asset, an invitation to the viewer to compare our reaction to that of Father Brown's upon encountering a person who is hurting physically, mentally or emotionally. Almost every episode, she argues, "models in some way how we might treat each other in more humane ways." In that sense, "[t]his series is doing something much different … something much more important than did Chesterton."[5]

Stories such as the Father Browns could not have existed without the gospel. Culturally, they are Christian myths with savior heroes, existing within the framework of the gospel as a sort of parable, i.e., the moral of the story is presented as the solution to the episode's mystery.[6] Which was the priest's higher goal, to solve a crime as an intellectual problem much like finishing a crossword puzzle or was it to get at the truth and save the soul of the criminal? Was his purpose to counsel the suspect to repent of his sin, be it embezzlement, theft, idolatry, adultery, or murder? Of those, murder is particularly horrendous because it is a sin against God, claimed Chesterton scholar John Peterson. "The Ten Commandments are never far below the surface of the old detective stories."[7]

Chesterton might comment, "I wish we could sometimes love the characters in real life as we love the characters in romances. There are a great many human souls whom we should accept more kindly, and even appreciate more clearly, if we simply thought of them as people in a story."[8] Script writer Tahsin Guner followed a similar line of thinking when, in episode 9.4 "The Children of Kalon," he has the former priest Kalon wondering how Father Brown manages to "see the good even in the darkest of souls." Father Brown's reply is solely and simply, "Because it's there."

Having developed as a cultural storyteller, television often serves as religious instruction for millions of viewers. Martin Marty, writing about media and the Christian faith, states, "the compelling power of a story is never to be underestimated. Christianity has always made its way as a good story." He continues, "An account of the acts of God in the lives of men can insinuate itself into the consciousness of people in ways that proclamation and teaching cannot."[9] What viewers, particularly non–Catholic viewers, are seeing is a representation of the church and how well that church is fulfilling its role of living and disseminating the gospel message. But, as Williams' Father Brown says to Philip, a gay man in episode 1.1 "Hammer of God," "If you ever need to talk, I won't try and convert you." Philip's laconic comeback: "Likewise."

Twenty years ago, the Presbyterian clergyman who was head of the BBC's Religion and Ethics department resigned due to the denigration of religion on the part of those who thought God was "a nonsense" and that religion was outdated.[10] Religion, it was feared by some, had been reduced to mere entertainment. The problem, as one critic believes, "is not that television presents us with entertaining subject matter but that all subject matter is presented as entertaining."[11] Others saw religion in a context of contemporary culture and demonstrating it in practice proved that it remains important. Marty claims that "[w]hen people are shown something that confronts them in the context of the life which they now live, yet which represents a voice from beyond summoning for belief ... [for those intent on proselytizing] it provides the soil in which Christian seed can be sown."[12]

Therefore, it's fitting to wonder if *Father Brown* is really a mystery superimposed over obvious religious underpinnings or religious evangelizing couched in mystery terms? Is the faith and example of Mark Williams' Father Brown reflecting a hope that we all treat our neighbors with kindness? These are questions viewers must answer for themselves. As Jay Newman points out in *Religion vs. Television*, in a detective story "there is often plenty of moralizing going on." The good guys win. We are made aware of the sanctity of life, "the corruptive influence of ... vices and sin ... the availability of redemption."[13] So, whether subliminally proselytizing or only for good theater, by putting inspirational words into Father Brown's mouth and through his compassionate actions, the scriptwriters have endowed him with inspiring spiritual guidance that need not apply only to the sinner he confronts episode by episode. *Father Brown* can be viewed as amusing entertainment or, more keenly, as lessons on how we can get along with others in our world.

This, then, is the legacy of the BBC's *Father Brown*.

Appendices

A: *G.K. Chesterton's Father Brown Stories, Dates of First Publication, 1910–1936*

"The Blue Cross" (as "Valentin Follows a Curious Trail"), *The Saturday Evening Post*, July 23, 1910; *The Storyteller*, September 1910

"The Secret Garden," *The Saturday Evening Post*, September 3, 1910; *The Storyteller*, October 1910

"The Queer Feet," *The Saturday Evening Post*, October 1, 1910; *The Storyteller*, November 1910

"The Hammer of God" (as "The Bolt from the Blue"), *The Saturday Evening Post*, November 5, 1910; *The Storyteller*, December 1910

"The Wrong Shape," *The Saturday Evening Post*, December 10, 1910; *The Storyteller*, January 1911

"The Sign of the Broken Sword," *The Saturday Evening Post*, January 7, 1911; *The Storyteller*, February 1911

"The Invisible Man," *The Saturday Evening Post*, January 28, 1911; *Cassell's Magazine*, February 1911

"The Eye of Apollo," *The Saturday Evening Post*, February 25, 1911; *Cassell's Magazine*, March 1911

"The Honour of Israel Gow" (as "The Strange Justice"), *The Saturday Evening Post*, March 25, 1911; *Cassell's Magazine*, April 1911

"The Sins of Prince Saradine," *The Saturday Evening Post*, April 22, 1911; *Cassell's Magazine*, May 1911

"The Flying Stars," *The Saturday Evening Post*, May 20, 1911; *Cassell's Magazine*, June 1911

"The Three Tools of Death," *The Saturday Evening Post*, June 24, 1911; *Cassell's Magazine*, July 1911

The Innocence of Father Brown, published by Cassell, July 1911

"The Absence of Mr. Glass," *McClure's Magazine*, November 1912; *The Pall Mall Magazine*, March 1913

"The Purple Wig," *The Pall Mall Magazine*, May 1913

"The Head of Caesar," *The Pall Mall Magazine*, June 1913
"The Strange Crime of John Boulnois," *McClure's Magazine*, February 1913; *The Pall Mall Magazine*, July 1913
"The Paradise of Thieves," *McClure's Magazine*, March 1913; *The Pall Mall Magazine*, August 1913
"The Man in the Passage," *McClure's Magazine*, April 1913; *The Pall Mall Magazine*, September 1913
"The Mistake of the Machine," *The Pall Mall Magazine*, October 1913
"The Perishing of the Pendragons," *The Pall Mall Magazine*, June 1914
"The Salad of Colonel Cray," *The Pall Mall Magazine*, July 1914
"The Duel of Dr Hirsch," *The Pall Mall Magazine*, August 1914
"The God of the Gongs," *The Pall Mall Magazine*, September 1914
"The Fairy Tale of Father Brown," no magazine publication, unknown date
The Wisdom of Father Brown, published by Cassell, October 1914
"The Oracle of the Dog," *Nash's Magazine*, December 1923
"The Dagger with Wings," *Nash's Magazine*, February 1924
"The Miracle of Moon Crescent," *Nash's Magazine*, May 1924
"The Mirror of the Magistrate," *Cassell's Magazine*, April 1925
"The Man with Two Beards," *Cassell's Magazine*, May 1925
"The Curse of the Golden Cross," *Nash's Magazine*, May 1925
"The Chief Mourner of Marne," *Harper's Magazine*, May 1925; *Cassell's Magazine*, July 1925
"The Doom of the Darnaways," *Nash's Magazine*, June 1925
"The Arrow of Heaven," *Nash's Magazine*, July 1925
"The Song of the Flying Fish," *Cassell's Magazine*, August 1925
"The Worst Crime in the World," *Cassell's Magazine*, November 1925
"The Actor and the Alibi," *Cassell's Magazine*, March 1926
"The Ghost of Gideon Wise," *Cassell's Magazine*, April 1926
The Incredulity of Father Brown, published by Cassell, June 1926
"The Vanishing of Vaudrey," *Harper's Magazine*, October 1925; *The Storyteller*, January 1927
"The Red Moon of Meru," *The Storyteller*, April 1927
The Secret of Father Brown, published by Cassell, September 1927
"The Green Man," *Ladies' Home Journal*, November 1930
"The Point of a Pin," *The Saturday Evening Post*, September 17, 1932; *The Storyteller*, October 1932; *Liberty*, August 26, 1933
"The Blast of the Book" (as "The Five Fugitives"), *The Storyteller*, October 1933
"The Scandal of Father Brown," *The Storyteller*, November 1933
"The Quick One," *The Storyteller*, February 1934
"The Pursuit of Mr. Blue," *The Storyteller*, June 1934

"The Crime of the Communist," *Collier's Weekly*, July 14, 1934; *The Storyteller*, September 1934
"The Insoluble Problem," *The Storyteller*, March 1935
The Scandal of Father Brown, published by Cassell, March 1935
"The Vampire of the Village," *Strand Magazine*, August 1936

B: *Episodes with Josef Meinrad as Pater Brown, 1966–1972*

"Der Fehler der Maschine"[1]	January 1966	"The Error of the Machine"
"Der Admiral im Tümpel"	February 23, 1966	"The Admiral in the Swamp"
"Der Mann mit dem Zylinder"	March 16, 1966	"The Man with the Top Hat"
"Das unlösbare Problem"	no date	"The Unsolvable Problem"
"Der Kopf Caesars"	May 13, 1966	"The Head of Caesar"
"Das Lied an die fliegenden Fische"	June 10, 1966	"The Song to the Flying Fish"
"Das Auge des Apoli"	July 22, 1966	"The Eye of Apollo"
"Die drei Sternschnuppen"	January 12, 1968	"The Three Flying Stars"
"Das Alibi einer Schaupielerin"	January 26, 1968	"The Alibi of the Actress"
"Ein Glas Whisky"	February 9, 1968	"A Glass of Whiskey"
"Salat für den Oberst"	February 16, 1968	"Salad for the Colonel"
"Die Sünden des Prinzen Saradin"	February 23, 1968	"The Sins of Prince Saradine"
"Das Paradies der Diebe"	March 1, 1968	"The Paradise of Thieves"
"Die Spitze einer Nadel"	June 4, 1969	"The Tip of a Needle"
"Der Unsichtbare"	June 11, 1969	"The Invisible"
"Die Form stimmt nicht"	June 18, 1969	"The Wrong Shape"
"Der Fluch des Buches"	June 25, 1969	"The Curse of the Book"
"Wer war der Täter?"	July 2, 1969	"Who Was the Culprit?"
"Hölle, Hölle, Hölle"	July 9, 1969	"Hell, Hell, Hell"
"Das blaue Kreuz"	October 15, 1970	"The Blue Cross"
"Das Duell"	October 22, 1970	"The Duel"
"Der rote Mond von Meru"	October 29, 1970	"The Red Moon of Meru"
"Der himmlische Pfeil"	November 5, 1970	"The Arrow of Heaven"
"Die Erbschaft des Robert Musgrave"	November 12, 1970	"The Inheritance of Robert Musgrave"

"Der Vamp von Protters Pond"	November 26, 1970	"The Vamp of Protters Pond"
"Skandal um Gloria"	December 3, 1970	"Scandal about Gloria"
"Das Attentat"	December 17, 1970	"The Assassination"
"Der richterliche Spiegel"	June 9, 1972	"The Judge's Mirror"
"Der Club der sieben Fischer"	June 16, 1972	"The Club of the Seven Men"
"Vaudreys Verschwinden"	June 30, 1972	"Vaudrey's Disappearance"
"Der Fluch aus dem Hause Pendragon"	July 10, 1972	"The Pendragon Curse"
"Der Mann in der Passage"	July 17, 1972	"The Man in the Passage"
"Die purpurfarbene Perücke"	July 31, 1972	"The Purple Wig"
"Wer bedroht Sir Claude?"	August 14, 1972	"Who Threatens Sir Claude?"
"Das Rätsel Michael" "Mondschein"	September 11, 1972	"The Riddle of Michael Moonshine"
"Der geflügelte Dolch"	October 2, 1972	"The Winged Dagger"
"Der Hammer Gottes"	October 16, 1972	"The Hammer of God"
"Das Hundeorakel"	November 6, 1972	"The Oracle of the Dog"
"Treffpunkt Tigerkäfig"	December 4, 1972	"Meeting at the Tiger Cage"

C: *Episodes with Renato Rascel as Padre Brown, 1970–1971*

"La croce azzurra"	December 29, 1970	"The Blue Cross"
"Il duello del dottor Hirsch"	January 5, 1971	"Dr. Hirsch's Duel"
"La forma sbagiata"	January 12, 1971	"The Wrong Shape"
"Le colpe del principe Saradine"	January 19, 1971	"The Faults of Prince Saradine"
"I tre strumenti di morte"	January 26, 1971	"The Three Instruments of Death"
"Il re dei ladri"	February 2, 1971	"The King of Thieves"

D: *Episodes with Kenneth More as Father Brown, 1974*

"The Hammer of God," September 26, 1974
"The Oracle of the Dog," October 3, 1974
"The Curse of the Golden Cross," October 10, 1974
"The Eye of Apollo," October 17, 1974

"The Three Tools of Death," October 24, 1974
"The Mirror of the Magistrate," October 31, 1974
"The Dagger with Wings," November 7, 1974
"The Actor and the Alibi,"[2] November 14, 1974
"The Quick One," November 21, 1974
"The Man with Two Beards," November 28, 1974
"The Head of Caesar," December 5, 1974
"The Arrow of Heaven," December 12, 1974
"The Secret Garden," December 19, 1974

E: *Episodes with Andrew Sachs as Father Brown, 1984–1986*

"The Blue Cross," December 2, 1984
"The Queer Feet," December 9, 1984
"The Eye of Apollo," December 16, 1984
"The Invisible Man," January 6, 1985
"The Honour of Israel Gow," January 13, 1985
"The Hammer of God," January 20, 1985
"The Sins of Prince Saradine," January 27, 1985
"The Perishing of the Pendragons," October 5, 1986
"The Arrow of Heaven," October 12 ,1986
"The Mistake of the Machine," October 19, 1986
"The Curse of the Golden Cross," October 26, 1986
"The Actor and Alibi," November 2, 1986
"The Absence of Mr. Glass," July 14, 2008
"The Secret Garden,"May 11, 2011[3]

F: *Episodes with Ottfried Fischer as Pfarrer Braun, 2003–2014*

"Der siebte Tempel"	April 17, 2003	"The Seventh Temple"
"Das Skelett in den Dünen"	April 25, 2003	"The Skeleton in the Dunes"
"Ein verhexter Fall"[4]	April 15, 2004	"A Bewitched Case"
"Der Fluch der Pröpstin"	April 22, 2004	"The Curse of the Provost"
"Bruder Mord"	March 31, 2005	"Brother Murder"
"Adel vernichtet"	April 14, 2005	"Nobility Destroys"
"Der unsichtbare Beweis"	September 14, 2006	"The Invisible Proof"
"Drei Särge und ein Baby"	September 21, 2006	"Three Coffins and a Baby"

"Kein Sterbenswörtchen"	September 28, 2006	"Not a Single Word"
"Ein Zeichen Gottes"	March 29, 2007	"A Sign of God"
"Das Erbe von Junkersdorf"	April 5, 2007	"The Legacy of Junkers-dorf"
"Braun unter Verdacht"	April 12, 2007	"Brown Under Suspicion"
"Die Gärten des Rabbiners"	April 3, 2008	"The Gardens of the Rabbi"
"Heiliger Birnbaum"	April 10, 2008	"Holy Pear Tree"
"Im Namen von Rose"	April 9, 2009	"In the Name of Rose"
"Glück auf! Der Mörder kommt!"	April 16, 2009	"Good Luck! The Murderer Is Coming"
"Schwein gehabt!"	April 1, 2010	"You Were Lucky!"
"Kur mit Schatten"	April 8, 2010	"Infidelity at the Health Spa"
"Grimms Mördchen"	October 21, 2010	"Grimm's Little Murder"
"Altes Geld, junges Blut"	February 17, 2011	"Old Money, Young Blood"
"Ausgegeigt!"	May 10, 2012	"Played Out!"
"Brauns Heimkehr"	March 20, 2014	"Brown Returns Home"

G: Episodes with Mark Williams as Father Brown, 2013–2023

Season 1 (2013)

1.1 "The Hammer of God"
1.2 "The Flying Stars"
1.3 "The Wrong Shape"
1.4 "The Man in the Tree"
1.5 "The Eye of Apollo"
1.6 "The Bride of Christ"
1.7 "The Devil's Dust"
1.8 "The Face of Death"
1.9 "The Mayor and the Magician"
1.10 "The Blue Cross"

Season 2 (2014)

2.1 "The Ghost in the Machine"
2.2 "The Maddest of All"
2.3 "The Pride of the Prydes"

2.4 "The Shadow of the Scaffold"
2.5 "The Mysteries of the Rosary"
2.6 "The Daughters of Jerusalem"
2.7 "The Three Tools of Death"
2.8 "The Prize of Colonel Gerard"
2.9 "The Grim Reaper"
2.10 "The Laws of Motion"

Season 3 (2015)

3.1 "The Man in the Shadows"
3.2 "The Curse of Amenhotep"
3.3 "The Invisible Man"
3.4 "The Sign of the Broken Sword"
3.5 "The Last Man"
3.6 "The Upcott Fraternity"
3.7 "The Kembleford Boggart"
3.8 "The Lair of the Libertines"
3.9 "The Truth in the Wine"
3.10 "The Judgment of Man"
3.11 "The Time Machine"
3.12 "The Standing Stones"
3.13 "The Paradise of Thieves"
3.14 "The Deadly Seal"
3.15 "The Owl of Minerva"

Season 4 (2016)

4.1 "The Mask of the Demon"
4.2 "The Brewer's Daughter"
4.3 "The Hangman's Demise"
4.4 "The Crackpot of the Empire"
4.5 "The Daughter of Autolycus"
4.6 "The Rod of Asclepius"
4.7 "The Missing Man"
4.8 "The Resurrectionists"
4.9 "The Sins of the Father"
4.10 "The Wrath of Baron Samdi"

Season 5 (2016–17)

5.1 "The Star of Jacob"
5.2 "The Labyrinth of the Minotaur"

5.3. "The Eve of St. John"
5.4 "The Chedworth Cyclone"
5.5. "The Hand of Lucia"
5.6 "The Eagle and the Daw"
5.7 "The Smallest of Things"
5.8 "The Crimson Feather"
5.9 "The Lepidopterist's Companion"
5.10 "The Alchemist's Secret"
5.11 "The Sins of Others"
5.12 "The Theatre of the Invisible"
5.13 "The Tanganyika Green"
5.14 "The Fire in the Sky"
5.15 "The Penitent Man"

Season 6 (2018)

6.1 "The Tree of Truth"
6.2 "The Jackdaw's Revenge"
6.3 "The Kembleford Dragon"
6.4 "The Angel of Mercy"
6.5 "The Face of the Enemy"
6.6 "The Devil You Know"
6.7 "The Dance of Death"
6.8 "The Cat of Mastigatus"
6.9 "The Flower of the Fairway"
6.10 "The Two Deaths of Hercule Flambeau"

Season 7 (2019)

7.1 "The Great Train Robbery"
7.2 "The Passing Bell"
7.3 "The Whistle in the Dark"
7.4 "The Demise of the Debutante"
7.5 "The Darkest Noon"
7.6 "The Sacrifice of Tantalus"
7.7 "The House of God"
7.8 "The Blood of the Anarchists"
7.9 "The Skylark Scandal"
7.10 "The Honourable Thief"

Season 8 (2020)

8.1 "The Celestial Choir"
8.2 "The Queen Bee"

8.3 "The Scales of Justice"
8.4 "The Wisdom of the Fool"
8.5 "The Folly of Jephthah"
8.6 "The Numbers of the Beast"
8.7 "The Canal Corrupted"
8.8 "The Curse of the Aesthetic"
8.9 "The Fall of the House of St. Gardner"
8.10 "The Tower of Lost Souls"

Season 9 (2022)

9.1 "The Menace of Mephistopheles"
9.2 "The Viper's Tongue"
9.3 "The Requiem for the Dead"
9.4 "The Children of Kalon"
9.5 "The Final Devotion"
9.6 "The New Order"
9.7 "The Island of Dreams"
9.8 "The Wayward Girls"
9.9 "The Enigma of Antigonish"
9.10 "The Red Death"

Season 10 (2023)

10.1 "The Winds of Change"
10.2 "The Company of Men"
10.3 "The Gardeners of Eden"
10.4 "The Beast of Wedlock"
10.5 "The Hidden Man"
10.6 "The Royal Visit"
10.7 "The Show Must Go On"
10.8 "The Sands of Time"
10.9 "The Wheels of Wrath"
10.10 "The Serpent Within"

Chapter Notes

Preface

1. *New York Times*, January 24, 1915, BR27.

2. G.K. Chesterton, *What I Saw in America* (New York: Dodd, Mead, 1922), 59. https://www.gutenberg.org/files.

3. G.K. Chesterton, "The Crime of the Communist," *The Complete Father Brown Stories* (Ware, Hertfordshire: Wordsworth Editions, 2006), 720. Hereafter, GKC, *Complete Father Brown Stories*.

4. Michael Warren Davis, "What Has the BBC Done to Father Brown," *Catholic Herald*, January 18, 2018.

Chapter 1

1. GKC, "The Pursuit of Mr. Blue," *The Complete Father Brown Stories*, 693, 699.

2. "Delivering Quality First: Final Conclusions," May 8, 11, 14, 2012, https://www.bbc.co.uk/bbctrust, accessed January 29, 2021. In the United States, daytime dramas are usually referred to as "soap operas" that adapt and grow to accommodate new storylines with a cast of original actors and newcomers. The longest running is *General Hospital*, which has broadcast since 1963. In the UK, daytime drama is funded out of the primetime budget. Neil McCaw, *Adapting Detective Fiction: Crime, Englishness and the TV Detectives* (London: Continuum, 2011), 2.

3. *Development of a BBC Diversity Strategy. Summary of Responses to Public and Staff Consultations*, 31 January 2011. According to the 2021 census of England and Wales, Christianity has since become a minority religion, having decreased from 59 percent of self-described Christians in 2011 to 46 percent in 2021. Richard Allen Greene, "England and Wales Are No Longer Majority Christian, Census Data Show," CNN, November 29, 2022, www.cnn.com/2022/11/29/uk, accessed December 1, 2022.

4. "The Before Times," *New York Times* (hereafter *NYT*), September 10, 2022.

5. McCaw, 129.

6. "The Mystery of Father Brown: Ann Widdecombe Investigates," BBC Radio 4, May 10, 2011.

7. Richard Wolff, *The Church on TV: Portrayals of Priests, Pastors and Nuns on American Television Series* (New York: Continuum International, 2010), 45.

8. Rachel Flowerday, "Father Brown— The 'Making of' Blog," accessed July 4, 2017.

9. Sean Salai, "G.K. Chesterton's 'Way of Wonder': Q&A with Author Dale Ahlquist," *America: The Jesuit Review*, May 11, 2016, https://www.americamagazine.org, accessed February 21, 2020.

10. "Who Is G.K. Chesterton?" https://www.chesterton.org/category/discover-chesterton/, accessed May 20, 2019.

11. Ronald Knox, *Literary Distractions* (New York: Sheed & Ward, 1958), 193.

12. G.K. Chesterton, "How to Write a Detective Story," *The Chesterton Review*, vol. X, no. 2 (May 1984), 111–118.

13. Father Brown was not the first clerical detective. In 1903, Silas Hocking wrote a series a mystery stories about Latimer Field, an Anglican curate. John Tibbetts, *The Dark Side of G.K. Chesterton* (Jefferson, NC: McFarland, 2021), 45. G.K Chesterton, *Autobiography* (London: Hutchinson, 1936), 323. Hereafter GKC, *Autobiography*.

14. Kathleen Mawhinney, "The

Priesthood of Father Brown," April 30, 2020, https://puddleglumsprogress.com, accessed January 11, 2022.

15. GKC, "The Blue Cross," *Complete Father Brown Stories*, 17–32.

16. Martin Gardner, ed., *The Annotated Innocence of Father Brown* (Oxford: Oxford University Press, 1987), 15 n.

17. Ronald Knox, "G.K. Chesterton: The Man and His Work," in D. Conlon, ed. *G.K. Chesterton: A Half Century of Views* (Oxford: Oxford University Press, 1987), 134–135.

18. Joseph Bottum, "God and the Detectives," *Books and Culture*, September/October 2011, n.p.

19. J.D. Douglas, "G.K. Chesterton, the Eccentric Prince of Paradox," *Christianity Today*, August 1, 2001, https://www.christianitytoday.com, accessed January 17, 2020.

20. *Ibid.*

21. GKC, *Autobiography*, 323.

22. *Yorkshire Post* (Leeds, England), June 15, 1936.

23. GKC, *Autobiography*, Chapter VII, "The Crime of Orthodoxy."

24. John O'Connor, *Father Brown on Chesterton* (London: Frederick Muller, 1937), 1.

25. *Ibid.*

26. GKC, *Autobiography*, 326.

27. O'Connor, *Father Brown on Chesterton*, 6.

28. Episode 5.8, "The Crimson Feather."

29. GKC, *Autobiography*, 328.

30. Maisie Ward, *Gilbert Keith Chesterton* (New York: Sheed & Ward, 1943), 218. Agatha Christie obliquely referred to the Father Brown tales in *The Murder at the Vicarage*. As in Chesterton's chapter XVI of "The Invisible Man," Christie has one character allude to another as "someone whose presence would be so natural that you wouldn't think of mentioning it," like a postman or servant. The vicar observes, "You've been reading G.K. Chesterton." In the next chapter, when the vicar offers an opinion, he is scolded by the inspector. "[Y]ou're a clergyman. You don't know half of what goes on."

31. Gardner, 15 n.

32. John C. Tibbetts, "G.K. Chesterton," in *Mystery and Suspense Writers*, vol. 1, ed. Robin W. Winks (New York: Charles Scribner's Sons, 1998), 186.

33. "Queer trade" in this sense means a strange occupation.

34. GKC, *Autobiography*, 322, 323.

35. Yet, in "The Dagger with Wings," Chesterton described Father Brown as having "large grey eyes ... which were the one notable thing in his face." A Norfolk native might commonly be called a "Norfolk dumpling," and the shallow crowned hat with broad brim was the style typical of Edwardian clergymen. GKC, "The Blue Cross," *Complete Father Brown Stories*, 18.

36. Knox, *Literary Distractions*, 171.

37. GKC, "The Green Man," *Complete Father Brown Stories*, 680.

38. O'Connor, *Father Brown on Chesterton*, 9.

39. O'Connor, *Father Brown on Chesterton*, 40. In a Chesterton story, Father Brown says something eerily similar. To the colonel's observation that he would like to see what's inside the priest's head, Father Brown replies, "If you want the inside of my head, you can have it.... What it's worth you can say afterwards." GKC, "The Flying Stars," *Complete Father Brown Stories*, 73.

40. Ward, *Gilbert Keith Chesterton*, 253.

41. Dermot Quinn, "The Meaning of Father Brown," *The Chesterton Review*, vol. XXXVII, nos. 3 & 4 (Fall/Winter 2001,) 409.

42. William David Spencer, *Mysterium and Mystery: The Clerical Crime Novel* (Carbondale: Southern Illinois University Press, 1989), 80.

43. Daniel Frampton, *The 'Old Western Men': A Religious Mode of Response to the Conditions of 'Secular' Modernity, 1900–1970*, PhD dissertation, University of East Anglia, September 2017, 219.

44. Horton Davies, *Worship and Theology in England: The Ecumenical Century, 1900–1965* (Princeton: Princeton University Press, 1965) 257, 258, 261. For more on Chesterton's conversion, see G.K. Chesterton, *The Catholic Church and Conversion* (New York: Macmillan, 1926).

45. P.D. James, "Introduction," *The Essential Tales of Father Brown* (New York: Modern Library, 2005), in *The Chesterton Review* vol. 39, nos. 1 & 2 (Spring/Summer 2013), 219.

46. Ian Ker, *G.K. Chesterton: A Biography* (Oxford: Oxford University Press, 2011), 472.

47. GKC, "The Green Man," *Complete Father Brown Stories*, 686.

48. Gardner, 237.
49. *The Leeds Mercury* (Leeds, England), November 10, 1931.
50. GKC, "The Queer Feet," *Complete Father Brown Stories*, 49.
51. GKC, "The Eye of Apollo," *Complete Father Brown Stories*, 147.
52. G.K. Chesterton, "A Piece of Chalk," https://www.chesterton.org/a-piece-of-chalk/, accessed February 13, 2018. The essay was first published in the *Daily News*, November 4, 1905. In his novel *The Club of Queer Trades*, which preceded the Father Brown stories, Chesterton had the detective investigate an assault brought by a Major Brown.
53. GKC, "The Arrow of Heaven," *Complete Father Brown Stories*, 364.
54. Chesterton, "Chalk."
55. G.K. Chesterton, *What I Saw in America* (New York: Dodd, Mead, 1922), 65.
56. GKC, "The Sins of Prince Saradine," 117, "The Invisible Man," 76, "The Sign of the Broken Sword," 160, "The Head of Caesar," 252, "The God of the Gongs," 292, "The Fairy-Tale of Father Brown," 329, "The Flying Stars," 65, "The Curse of the Golden Cross," 416 in *Complete Father Brown Stories*.
57. G.K. Chesterton, "The Toy Theatre," www.online-literature.com/chesterton/-tremendous-trifles/23/, accessed March 15, 2018.
58. G.K. Chesterton, *Generally Speaking* (Leipzig: Bernhard Tauchnitz, 1929), 14, http://www.gkc.org.uk/gkc/books/Generally_Speaking_scan.pdf.
59. GKC, "The Eye of Apollo," *Complete Father Brown Stories*, 156.
60. Gertrude M. White, "Mirror and Microcosm: Chesterton's Father Brown Stories," *The Chesterton Review*, vol. X, no. 2 (May 1984), 187.
61. GKC, "The Secret of Flambeau," *Complete Father Brown Stories*, 624.
62. G.K. Chesterton, *Orthodoxy*, https://www.gutenberg.org.
63. Gareth Leyshon, *Catholic Statistics—2011 Update Priests and Population in England and Wales, 1841–2011*, October 2012, http://www.drgareth.info/-CathStat-2012.pdf, accessed February 14, 2018.*Catholic Emancipation 1829–1929* (Freeport, NY: Books for Libraries Press, 1929), 260.

64. Alec Stephen Corio, *Historical Perceptions of Roman Catholicism and National Identity, 1869–1919*, Thesis for Doctor of Philosophy, Open University, 2013, 265–266, 332–335.
65. Davies, 26.
66. GKC, "The Three Tools of Death," *Complete Father Brown Stories*, 183, 184. GKC, "The Divine Detective," http://www.online-literature.com/chesterton, accessed March 3, 2018.
67. GKC, "The Hammer of God," *Complete Father Brown Stories*, 145.
68. GKC, "The Secret of Father Brown," *Complete Father Brown Stories*, 496–497.
69. Many cozy mysteries currently on the market rely on this premise. A local baker, librarian, knitter, or pet shop owner *must* uncover the murderer because the police are too busy, too lazy, uninterested, or uninformed about local affairs to be competent.
70. Chesterton, *Autobiography*, 320–321.
71. Mitzi Brunsdale, *Icons of Mystery and Crime Detection: From Sleuths to Superheroes*, vol. 1 (Santa Barbara: Greenwood, 2010), 83, quoting H.R.F. Keating, "G.K. Chesterton," in *St. James Guide to Crime & Mystery Writers*, ed. Jay P. Pederson (Detroit: St. James Press, 1996), 183.
72. Brunsdale, 89. The other three were Edgar Allen Poe's *Tales* (1845), Conan Doyle's *Adventures of Sherlock Holmes* (1892), and Melville D. Post's *Uncle Abner* (1918).
73. GKC, "The Miracle of Moon Crescent," *Complete Father Brown Stories*, 400.
74. Quoted in Celia Fremlin, "The Christie Everybody Knew," *Agatha Christie: First Lady of Crime*, ed. H.R.F. Keating (New York: Holt, Rinehart, Winston, 1977), 115. LeRoy Lad Panek, *An Introduction to the Detective Story* (Bowling Green, OH: Bowling Green State University Popular Press, 1987), 78.
75. Douglas G. Greene, "A Mastery of Miracles: G.K. Chesterton and John Dickson Carr," *The Chesterton Review*, Vol. X, No. 3 (August 1984), 314.
76. *Western Mail* (Cardiff, Wales), June 17, 1926. It must be noted also that Chesterton suffered a near-fatal physical collapse in fall 1914, leaving him semi-comatose until early April 1915.
77. "Errors about Detective Stories,"

The Chesterton Review, vol. XXXVII, nos. 1 & 2 (Spring/Summer 2011), 15–18.

78. Quinn, 412.

79. GKC, "The Resurrection of Father Brown," *Complete Father Brown Stories*, 354.

80. Dudley Barker, *G.K. Chesterton: A Biography* (New York: Stein & Day, 1973), 196–197.

81. White, 196. For more on Chesterton's interest in science fiction, see John Tibbetts, *The Dark Side of G.K. Chesterton: Gargoyles and Grotesques* (Jefferson, NC: McFarland, 2021).

82. Martin Gardner, ed., *The Annotated Innocence of Father Brown* (Oxford: Oxford University Press, 1987), 5.

83. Ian Ker, *G.K. Chesterton: A Biography* (Oxford: Oxford University Press, 2011), 82–83.

84. G.K. Chesterton, "Errors about Detective Stories," *The Chesterton Review*, vol. XXXVII, nos. 1 & 2 (Spring/Summer 2011), 15–16.

85. Anthony Grist, "Father Brown at the Movies," *The Chesterton Review*, vol. X, no. 4 (November 1984), 479.

Chapter 2

1. Anthony Grist, "Kenneth More as Father Brown," *The Chesterton Review*, vol. X, no. 2 (May 1984), 178.

2. GKC, "Errors about Detective Stories," *The Chesterton Review*, vol. XXXVII, nos. 1 & 2 (Spring/Summer 2011), 16. Original from the *Illustrated London News*, August 28, 1920.

3. *New York Clipper*, September 11, 1929, 29.

4. *Duluth Herald* (Duluth, Minnesota), March 11, 1921.

5. *Yorkshire Post* (Leeds, England), June 15, 1936.

6. Ward, *Gilbert Keith Chesterton*, 597.

7. *The Interlaken Review* (Interlaken, NY), March 25, 1932, 2; *Yorkshire Post* (Leeds, England), June 15, 1936.

8. *GKC Autobiography*, Chapter 16.

9. *NYT*, July 1, 1934; *Los Angeles Times* (hereafter *LAT*), September 17, 1934, 13.

10. *NYT*, July 1, 1934; *LAT*, September 17, 1934, 13.

11. *LAT*, August 30, 1934, 18; September 17, 1934; and May 13 and 29, 1940;

NYT, October 1, 1934, 14; *LAT*, October 4, 1934, 13.

12. *LAT*, October 10, 1934, 11.

13. Ward, *Gilbert Keith Chesterton*, 549.

14. Victor Berch, Karl Schadow, and Steve Lewis, "Murder Clinic: Radio's Golden Age of Detection," https://mysteryfile.com/M_Clinic.html, accessed March 2, 2022.

15. GKC, "The Invisible Man," *Complete Father Brown Stories*, 81.

16. "The Business of Broadcasting," *Broadcasting*, December 4, 1944, 36; "The Mystified Mind," https://www.oldtimeradiodownloads.com/crime/the-adventures-of-father-brown; "Father Brown," http://www.greatdetectives.net, accessed February 5, 2021.

17. Dialogue from *Father Brown, Detective* starring Alec Guinness.

18. *LAT*, July 16, 1952.

19. G.K. Chesterton, "About the Films," *As I Was Saying: A Book of Essays* (London: Methuen, 1936).

20. *Variety*, December 31, 1954, and October 13, 1954.

21. *NYT*, November 7, 1954.

22. Grist, "Father Brown at the Movies," *The Chesterton Review*, vol. X, no. 4 (November 1984) 477–478.

23. Mark Williams would later have a similar experience in Cartagena, Spain, when a little girl approached and threw her arms around his legs, crying, "Father Brown!" https://www.bbc.co.uk/mediacentre, accessed June 5, 2020.

24. Alec Guinness, *Blessings in Disguise* (New York: Alfred A. Knopf, 1986), 36.

25. GKC, "The Arrow of Heaven," *Complete Father Brown Stories*, 358–377.

26. Michael Pitts, *Famous Movie Detectives III* (Lanham, MD: Scarecrow Press, 2004), 65; "Das Schwarze Schaf (1960)," http://schlombies-filmbesprechungen.blogspot.com, accessed November 19, 2019.

27. https://www.youtube.com, accessed March 25, 2022.

28. https://www.youtube.com, accessed April 9, 2022.

29. "Die besten Kriminalfälle des Pater Brown," http://sofahelden.com/index, accessed April 17, 2018.

30. *Die Abenteuer des Kardinal Braun*, 1967, a dubbed German version of the Italian, can be found at https://www.dailymotion.com, accessed February 5, 2021.

31. GKC, "The Quick One," *Complete Father Brown Stories*, 654.

32. "Josef Meinrad," https://en.wiki pedia.org, accessed October 5, 2021.

33. https://www.youtube.com, accessed March 15, 2022.

34. Milly Buonanno, *Italian TV Drama and Beyond: Stories from the Soil, Stories from the Sea* (Bristol: Intellect, 2012), 113.

35. Kenneth More, *More or Less* (London: Hodder and Stoughton, 1978), 223.

36. Grist, "Kenneth More as Father Brown," *Chesterton Review*, vol. X, no. 2 (May 1984), 178, 181.

37. Hazel Holt, "A Plodding Father Brown," *The Stage and Television Today*, October 3, 1974, 17.

38. *NYT*, November 2, 1982, and June 1, 2014.

39. Hugh Leonard, "The Curmudgeon," *Sunday Independent* (Dublin, Ireland), January 23, 2005.

40. More, 9.

41. "Father Brown: Collected Cases by G.K. Chesterton," https://soundcloud.com/penguin-books, accessed February 3, 2022.

42. *LAT*, April 23, 1979; *NYT*, April 23, 1979.

43. *The Guardian* (London), December 2, 2016.

44. "Il delitto del Signore di Marne di Vittorio De Sisti: la serie tv deimenticata di Padre Brown," http://www.frontedelblog.it, accessed May 6, 2018, Google Translate.

45. *Pfarrer Braun* no. 1, https://www.youtube.com, accessed March 27, 2022.

46. "Pfarrer Braun," https://www.daserste.de/unterhaltung/film.html, accessed July 18, 2018.

47. http://thwordinc.blogspot.com.html, accessed February 24, 2018. http://www.ewtn.com/series/2009/theater.htm, accessed April 21, 2018. The latter site has since been removed.

48. *LAT*, April 4, 2013.

49. GKC, "The Invisible Man," *Complete Father Brown Stories*, 76–89.

50. GKC, "The Curse of the Golden Cross," *Complete Father Brown Stories*, 416–436.

51. Siobhan Newman, Review of "Father Brown at the Theatre Royal Windsor," March 29, 2017, http://www.theatreroyalwindsor.co.uk, accessed February 5, 2018.

52. "Father Brown—the Murderer in the Mirror," July 3, 2021, https://www.anvilarts.org.uk, accessed February 12, 2022.

53. John O'Connor, "Father Brown on Chesterton," *Times Literary Supplement* (London), October 1, 1908.

54. *LAT*, April 23, 1979.

55. "Mark Williams on Father Brown Coming Back to Our Screens and Making the Permanent Move to Sussex," January 19, 2017, https://www.sussexlife.co.uk, accessed February 16, 2019.

56. Episode 3.15, "The Owl of Minerva."

Chapter 3

1. Mark Williams quoted in *The Southland Times* (Invercargill, New Zealand), October 23, 2017, 16.

2. Sinclair McKay, "Bring Back Father Brown," *The Spectator* (London), December 19, 2009, 26.

3. *NYT*, April 23, 1979.

4. Martin Marty, *The Improper Opinion: Mass Media and the Christian Faith* (Philadelphia: Westminster Press, 1961), 29.

5. Ceri Meyrick, "How I Accidentally Produced Father Brown," May 30, 2013, http://www.writersguild.org.uk, accessed June 4, 2017.

6. Rachel Flowerday, "Father Brown—the 'Making of' Blog," http://rachelflowerday.com, accessed July 4, 2017.

7. Tahsin Guner and Rachel Flowerday, "Developing Father Brown for BBC One," January 14, 2013, http://www.bbc.co.uk/blogs/writersroom, accessed February 12, 2018.

8. *Ibid.*

9. Michael Newton, "Father Brown: The Empathetic Detective," *The Guardian* (London), January 18, 2013, https://www.theguardian.com/books, accessed July 21, 2017.

10. Knox, *Literary Distractions*, 177.

11. Flowerday, "Father Brown—the 'Making of' Blog," accessed July 4, 2017.

12. Richard Wolff, *The Church on TV: Portrayals of Priests, Pastors and Nuns on American Television Series* (New York: Continuum International, 2010), 7.

13. "Father Brown Is Back in Town," https://issuu.com/cotswoldhomes

magazine, August 14, 2013, 11, accessed February 25, 2018.

14. Rachel Flowerday, "Father Brown—the 'Making of' Blog," accessed July 4, 2017.

15. Behind the Scenes of Episode 8.6, "The Number of the Beast," January 13, 2020, https://www.bbc.co.uk/programmes, accessed August 15, 2020, and November 17, 2020.

16. Olly Grant, "Clued-Up Confessor on the Box," January 11, 2013, https://www.churchtimes.co.uk/articles, accessed May 20, 2020.

17. Ibid. "Father Brown Is Back in Town," Cotswolds Homes, August 14, 2013, 11, accessed February 25, 2018. "Father Brown: Saving Souls, Solving Crimes," https://vimeo.com, accessed January 29, 2015.

18. Kate O'Hare, "Taking Tea with 'Father Brown' Star Mark Williams," August 3, 2020, https://www.patheos.com/blogs/, accessed August 5, 2020.

19. Jeremy Peters, "TV Murders: Filming of Father Brown at Former Cotswolds Hospital," http://www.property.nhs.uk, accessed July 21, 2021. https://www.bbc.co.uk/mediacentre, accessed July 6, 2021.

20. Tahsin Guner and Rachel Flowerday, "Developing Father Brown for BBC One," January 14, 2013, accessed February 12, 2018. Daniel Chipperfield, "BBC One Drama Father Brown Returns Next Month After Filming in Gloucester," November 16, 2017, https://www.gloucestershirelive.co.uk, accessed February 24, 2018.

21. Grant, "Clued-Up Confessor on the Box."

22. The Southland Times (Invercargill, New Zealand), October 23, 2017, 16.

23. "Mark Williams on Father Brown Coming Back to Our Screens and Making the Permanent Move to Sussex," January 19, 2017, https://www.sussexlife.co.uk, accessed February 16, 2019. "Welcome Back, Father Brown," http://www.worcesternews.co.uk, January 11, 2014, accessed May 24, 2017.

24. "With God on His Side," Sunday Star-Times (Wellington, New Zealand), January 10, 2016, E.26.

25. Grant, "Clued-Up Confessor on the Box."

26. Louise Gannon, "The Fast Show's Mark Williams Insists He Is NOT a Comedian," Event Magazine, January 6, 2018.

27. Grant, "Clued-Up Confessor on the Box."

28. "Mark Williams—Things You Didn't Know about the 'Harry Potter' Star," June 9, 2021, https://www.whattowatch.com/, accessed January 11, 2022.

29. Behind the scenes of Episode 8.5, "The Folly of Jephtha," January 10, 2020, https://www.bbc.co.uk, accessed August 15, 2020, and November 15, 2020. The Roman Catholic Church's Second Vatican Council (Vatican II) met in Rome in the autumns of 1962 through 1965. It had been called by Pope John XXIII, and its purpose was to update the church, a cause that had its own supporters and opponents.

30. "Father Brown: Saving Souls, Solving Crimes"; Grant, "Clued-Up Confessor on the Box."

31. Ibid.

32. "Emer Kenny (Bunty)," December 11, 2019, www.bbc.com/mediacentre, accessed July 6, 2021.

33. "Father Brown: Saving Souls, Solving Crimes."

34. Behind the Scenes, Season 8, episode 3, "The Scales of Justice," January 8, 2020, https://www.bbc.co.uk, accessed August 15, 2020. GKC, "The Blue Cross," Complete Father Brown Stories, 18.

35. "With God on His Side," Sunday Star-Times (Wellington, New Zealand), January 10, 2016, E.26.

36. Kenneth More, More or Less (London: Hodder and Stoughton, 1978), 9.

37. Vivien Mason, "Filming for Latest Cotswold-Based BBC TV Series, Father Brown, Comes to an End," August 6, 2015, http://www.cotswoldjournal.co.uk, accessed March 31, 2018. "Mark Williams—Things You Didn't Know about the 'Harry Potter' Star," June 9, 2021, accessed January 11, 2022.

38. Claire Webb, "Father Brown's Mark Williams on Following in Benedict Cumberbatch's Footsteps," The Chesterton Review, vol. 39, nos. 1 & 2 (Spring 2013), 234–235.

39. Roz Laws, "Birmingham-Made Drama Father Brown Needs Primetime Spot, Says Star Mark Williams," December 30, 2013, http://www.birminghammail.co.uk, accessed November 6, 2018.

40. Melenie Parkes, "Father Brown's Mark Williams: 'I Have to Work Hard at Not Making Him a Cliché,'" May 6, 2020, https://www.stuff.co.nz/entertainment/tv-radio/tv-guide, accessed May 8, 2020.

41. Claire Webb, "Father Brown's Mark Williams on Following in Benedict Cumberbatch's Footsteps," *The Chesterton Review*, vol. 39, nos. 1 & 2 (Spring 2013) 234-235.

42. "Father Brown: Saving Souls, Solving Crimes."

43. Sarah Thomas, "Mark Williams on Why 'Nosey' Father Brown Has Proved to Be a Popular, If Unlikely, Sleuth," April 4, 2016, https://www.smh.com.au/entertainment, accessed May 11, 2018.

44. Roz Laws, "Birmingham-Made Drama Father Brown."

45. "With God on His Side," *Sunday Star-Times* (Wellington, New Zealand), January 10, 2016, E.26.

46. Louise Gannon, "The Fast Show's Mark Williams Insists He Is NOT a Comedian," *Event Magazine*, January 6, 2018.

47. "Jesuits Help Father Brown Get It Right," January 2015, https://www.indcatholicnews.com, accessed January 25, 2019.

48. Grant, "Clued-Up Confessor on the Box."

49. Gardner, 149–150 n 10; GKC, "The Quick One," *Complete Father Brown Stories*, 646, "The Dagger with Wings," 443.

50. Wolff, 25.

51. "With God on His Side," *Sunday Star-Times* (Wellington, New Zealand), January 10, 2016, E.26.

52. Neil McCaw, *Adapting Detective Fiction: Crime, Englishness and the TV Detectives* (London: Continuum International, 2011), 130.

53. Alexander Manshel, Laura B. McGrath, J.D. Porter, "The Rise of Must-Read TV: How Your Netflix Habit Is Changing Contemporary Fiction," *The Atlantic*, July 16, 2021.

54. Rachel Flowerday, "Father Brown—the 'Making of' Blog."

55. Episode 4.4, "The Crackpot of the Empire." Pamela Milne likewise observed that the two characters interact as though they had long been married in "The BBC's Father Brown Series: Moving Beyond Chesterton," December 20, 2020, https://milnesmusings.wordpress.com, accessed March 15, 2021.

56. Kevin O'Brien, "Trading on Chesterton Without a Trace of Chesterton," July 8, 2012, accessed February 24, 2018. The site has since been removed.

57. Episode 1.9, "The Mayor and the Magician."

58. "Father Brown: Saving Souls, Solving Crimes."

59. Behind the scenes of Episode 1, "The Celestial Choir," January 6, 2020, https://www.bbc.co.uk/programmes, accessed August 16, 2020.

60. Episode 2.2, "The Maddest of All," and episode 1.9, "The Mayor and the Magician."

61. Episode 2.6, "The Daughters of Jerusalem."

62. Episode 5.11, "The Sins of Others."

63. In Chesterton's story "The Worst Crime in the World," readers are informed that Father Brown does have a sister.

64. Milne, "The BBC's Father Brown Series."

65. GKC, "The Mirror of the Magistrate," *Complete Father Brown Stories*, 500.

66. Episodes 7.9, "The Skylark Scandal," episode 7.8, "The Blood of the Anarchists," episode 8.10, "The Tower of Lost Souls."

67. GKC, "The Secret Garden," *Complete Father Brown Stories*, 43, 48.

68. "Father Brown Is Back in Town," *Cotswolds Homes*, August 14, 2013, 10, https://issuu.com/cotswoldhomesmagazine, accessed February 25, 2018.

69. "Jack Deam (Inspector Mallory)," https://www.bbc.co.uk/mediacentre, accessed September 11, 2020.

70. Episode 7.2, "The Passing Bell."

71. Episode 4.6, "The Rod of Asclepius."

72. "In this exclusive behind the scenes interview John Burton shows what a real 'Goodfellow' he is, by revealing what it's like working on Father Brown," January 9, 2017, https://www.facebook.com/BBCFatherBrown, accessed March 31, 2019.

73. "Who Is Father Brown's Emer Kenny?" *Radio Times*, December 9, 2019, https://www.radiotimes.com, accessed January 10, 2020.

74. Episode 8.2, "The Queen Bee." "Emer Kenny (Bunty)," December 11, 2019, www.bbc.com/mediacentre, accessed July 6, 2021.

75. GKC, "The Wrong Shape," *Complete Father Brown Stories*, 112.

76. Clifford J. Stumme, *Detective Fiction Reinvention and Didacticism in G.K. Chesterton's Father Brown*, Master Thesis, Liberty University, Lynchburg, Virginia, 2014, 51, 52.

77. Stumme, 58.

78. Tahsin Guner and Rachel Flowerday, "Developing Father Brown for BBC One," accessed February 12, 2018.

79. Roz Laws, "Birmingham-Made Drama."

80. "Jack Deam (Inspector Mallory)," https://www.bbc.co.uk/mediacentre, accessed September 11, 2020.

81. "Father Brown: Saving Souls, Solving Crimes."

82. "Mark Williams on Father Brown Coming Back to Our Screens and Making the Permanent Move to Sussex," January 19, 2017, https://www.sussexlife.co.uk, accessed February 16, 2019.

83. Claire Webb, "Father Brown's Mark Williams on Following in Benedict Cumberbatch's Footsteps," *The Chesterton Review*, vol. 39, nos. 1 & 2 (Spring 2013), 234–235.

84. Daniel Chipperfield, "BBC One Drama Father Brown Returns Next Month After Filming in Gloucester," November 16, 2017, https://www.gloucestershirelive.co.uk, accessed February 24, 2018.

85. "Harry Potter Star Mark Williams to Star in BBC Drama 'Father Brown,'" June 22, 2012, https://www.entertainmentwise.com, accessed May 24, 2017.

86. Wolff, 209.

87. Dale Ahlquist, *G.K. Chesterton: The Apostle of Common Sense* (San Francisco: Ignatius Press, 2003), 166.

Chapter 4

1. Episode 3.1, "The Man in the Shadows."

2. GKC, "The Flying Stars," *Complete Father Brown Stories*, 68.

3. "Regulating Sex and Sexuality: The 20th Century," https://www.parliament.uk, accessed March 3, 2019.

4. "Sudeley Castle," https://sudeleycastle.co.uk/history, accessed January 5, 2018.

5. "When the BBC's Father Brown Visited Princethorpe," May 13, 2020, https://connect.princethorpe.co.uk, accessed May 21, 2021.

6. *World War II: Day by Day* (London: Dorling Kindersley, 2004), 196.

7. *Ibid.*, 319.

8. Arnstein, 348.

9. Luke 23: 42–43.

10. "Welcome Back, Father Brown," January 11, 2014, http://www.worcesternews.co.uk, accessed February 10, 2017.

11. Tom Eames, "Mark Williams's 'Father Brown' Renewed for Second Series by BBC One," January 23, 2013, https://www.digitalspy.com, accessed January 26, 2020.

12. "Hit TV Show Makes a Return," June 20, 2013, http://www.cotswoldjournal.co.uk, accessed June 18, 2019.

13. "Father Brown S2 (BBCOne)," January 18, 2014, https://takingtheshortview.wordpress.com/, accessed June 18, 2019.

14. Christopher Stevens, "Father Brown's Biggest Mystery Why Is He Stuck on Daytime TV?" *Daily Mail* (London), January 15, 2014, http://www.dailymail.co.uk, accessed January 5, 2018.

15. "Jude Tindall," https://www.bbc.co.uk/writersroom/resources, accessed February 26, 2021.

16. Steven Greydanus, "BBC's Amiable 'Father Brown' Doesn't Keep Faith with Chesterton," September 19, 2014, https://cruxnow.com, accessed February 20, 2017.

17. *Ibid.*

18. Stevens, "Father Brown's Biggest Mystery."

19. "Father Brown S2 (BBCOne)," accessed March 7, 2020.

20. Grant, "Clued-Up Confessor on the Box."

21. "Crime Solving Priest Is Back; Mark Williams Returns for Second Series of Father Brown," *Daily Post* (Conwy, Wales), January 4, 2014, 3.

22. "The WI Inspiring Women," https://www.thewi.org.uk, accessed August 15, 2022.

23. Lynette Hunter, *G.K. Chesterton: Explorations in Allegory* (New York: St. Martin's Press, 1979), 144.

24. "With God on His Side," *Sunday Star-Times* (Wellington, New Zealand), January 10, 2016, E.26.

25. GKC, "The Salad of Colonel Cray," *Complete Father Brown Stories*, 305.

26. "The BBC Took Over Shelsley Walsh Hill Climb Near Worcester for Three Days to Film an Episode of the TV Detective Series Father Brown," *Gloucestershire Echo* (Gloucestershire, England), August 30, 2013.

27. "Jesuits Help Father Brown Get It Right," January 6, 2015, https://www.indcatholicnews.com, January 25, 2019.

28. Ephraim Hardcastle, "The BBC's Father Brown, [...]," *Daily Mail* (London), February 20, 2019, 19. Diane Snyder, "'Sister Boniface': Crime-Solving Nun Gets the Spotlight in 'Father Brown' Spinoff," February 6, 2022, https://www.tvinsider.com, accessed April 1, 2022.

29. "Actor Mark Williams' Verdict on Sunday Night Slot Shift for BBC Drama Series Father Brown," February 8, 2015, https://www.sundaypost.com, accessed March 9, 2018.

30. Bill Young, "On the Set with 'Father Brown' in the Cotswolds," July 18, 2014, http://tellyspotting.kera.org, accessed April 9, 2018.

31. "You Ask Us: What's the Story with TV Theme Tunes?" *Radio Times*, February 5, 2019.

32. Walter L. Arnstein, *Britain Yesterday and Today: 1830 to the Present*, 6th ed. (Lexington, MA: D.C. Heath, 1992), 342. For more on the 3rd Army Division, see https://dbpedia.org/page/3rd_(United_Kingdom)_Division.

33. Gardner, 237, and 52 n 8.

34. Aditya Iyer, "UK Election 2017: 'Bloody Foreigners' and Other Aspects of Britain's History of Immigration Controls Against Indian Migrants," June 8, 2017, https://www.firstpost.com/, accessed May 16, 2018.

35. *The Southland Times* (Invercargill, New Zealand), October 23, 2017, 16.

36. "On Lying," https://www.newadvent.org, accessed June 24, 2020.

37. Emma Simon, "Diamond Jubilee: How Much Was £1 Worth in 1952?" *The Telegraph*, June 3, 2012, www.telegraph.co.uk, accessed March 19, 2022.

38. "Filming for BBC1 Daytime Period Drama Father Brown Will Take Place in Tewkesbury Later This Month," *Gloucestershire Citizen* (Gloucestershire, England), August 6, 2014.

39. For more on the symbolism of owls, see https://neologikonblog.wordpress.

com/tag/what-is-the-owl-of-minerva, accessed July 31, 2022.

40. "With God on His Side," *Sunday Star-Times* (Wellington, New Zealand), January 10, 2016, E.26. Sarah Thomas, "Mark Williams on Why 'Nosey' Father Brown Has Proved to Be a Popular, If Unlikely, Sleuth," April 4, 2016, https://www.smh.com.au/entertainment, accessed May 11, 2018.

41. Tim Lambert, "A History of Capital Punishment in the UK," March 14, 2021, https://localhistories.org; Marek Pruszewicz, "When Murderers Were Hanged Quickly," August 7, 2014, https://www.bbc.com, accessed March 18, 2022.

42. https://catholicstraightanswers.com, August 7, 2014, accessed July 24, 2022.

43. "The Coroner, Father Brown and Doctors Recommissioned for BBC One Daytime," n.d., https://www.bbc.co.uk/mediacentre/, accessed July 21, 2021.

44. Sarah Thomas, "Mark Williams on Why 'Nosey' Father Brown Has Proved to be a popular, If Unlikely, Sleuth," April 4, 2016, https://www.smh.com.au/entertainment, accessed May 11, 2018.

45. "Woyzeck," https://www.imdb.com, accessed June 27, 2022.

46. The line is almost a direct quote from Chesterton's story "The Blue Cross"—"The most incredible thing about miracles is that they happen."

47. Ryan Merrifield, "BBC Announces Air Date for Father Brown Christmas Special Shot in Blockley Over the Summer in 22C Heat," *Wilts & Gloucestershire Standard* (Cirencester, England), December 2, 2016, accessed January 5, 2018. Vivien Mason, "Blockley Carpeted in Snow for Father Brown Scene as Cotswolds Bakes in 22 Degree Heat," *Cotswold Journal* (Evesham, England), May 10, 2016, accessed January 5, 2018.

48. "Let It Snow," December 23, 2016, https://www.bbc.co.uk/programmes, accessed January 26, 2019.

49. "The Tales of a Crime-Solving Roman Catholic Priest," n.d., https://www.bbcstudios.com, accessed May 11, 2018.

50. Gill Sutherland, "On the Set of Father Brown," *Stratford Herald*, June 9, 2016, www.stratford-herald.com, accessed August 14, 2018.

51. Martin Kemp Interview, January 4, 2017, https://www.bbc.co.uk/programmes, accessed January 26, 2019.

52. John Dickson Carr, "The Locked Room Lecture," http://www.thelocked room.com, accessed March 2, 2022.

53. GKC, "The Hammer of God," *Complete Father Brown Stories*, 145.

54. GKC, "The Toy Theatre," *Tremendous Trifles*, https://www.gutenberg.org, accessed March 15, 2018.

55. https://en.wikitionary.org, accessed January 31, 2022.

56. David Chipperfield, "BBC One Drama Father Brown Returns Next Month After Filming in Gloucester," November 16, 2017, https://www.gloucestershirelive.co.uk, accessed February 24, 2018.

57. Kim Horton, "BBC Series Father Brown Is Being Filmed in the City," June 14, 2017, https://www.gloucestershirelive.co.uk, accessed February 24, 2018.

58. Louise Gannon, "The Fast Show's Mark Williams Insists NOT a Comedian," *Event Magazine*, January 6, 2018.

59. *Ibid.*

60. Jean Sergent, "Murder Has Never Been More Delightful Than on Father Brown," July 4, 2018, https://thespinoff.co.nz, accessed February 16, 2019.

61. *World War II: Day by Day*, 141.

62. Christopher Stevens, "Blissful Crime Caper That Proves Daytime TV Can Be Super-Duper," *Daily Mail* (London), January 7, 2019, https://www.dailymail.co.uk, accessed February 16, 2019.

63. GKC obituary, *Yorkshire Post*, June 15, 1936.

64. Grant Smithies, "English Actor Mark Williams on Life After Harry Potter and the Fast Show," January 6, 2016, https://www.stuff.co.nz, accessed August 20, 2019.

65. Kerry Harvey, "Mark Williams on Father Brown and Our Fascination with the 1950s," October 24, 2017, https://www.stuff.co.nz, accessed October 10, 2019.

66. BBC One, "Father Brown," https://www.bbc.co.uk/programmes, accessed January 26, 2019.

67. Ceri Peach, "The Caribbean in Europe: Contrasting Patterns of Migration and Settlement in Britain, France and the Netherlands," October 1991, https://warwick.ac.uk, accessed October 15, 2020.

68. "Peter Bullock," December 11, 2019, https://www.bbc.co.uk/mediacentre, accessed July 6, 2020.

69. Brittany Bennett, "Mark Williams Discusses 'Father Brown' Series," May 12, 2020, https://www.mugglenet.com/, accessed March 12, 2021.

70. Melenie Parkes, "Father Brown's Mark Williams: 'I Have to Work Hard at Not Making Him a Cliché,'" May 6, 2020, https://www.stuff.co.nz, accessed May 9, 2021.

71. "Claire Collins (Costume Designer)," December 11, 2019, https://www.bbc.com/mediacentre, accessed July 6, 2020.

72. Behind the scenes of Episode 1, "The Celestial Choir," January 6, 2020, https://www.bbc.co.uk/programmes, accessed August 16, 2020.

73. "Peter Bullock," December 11, 2019, https://www.bbc.co.uk/mediacentre, accessed July 6, 2020.

74. Behind the scenes of Episode 1, "The Celestial Choir," January 6, 2020, https://www.bbc.co.uk/programmes, accessed August 16, 2020.

75. Peter Hart, "The White Feather Campaign," 2010, http://www.inquiriesjournal.com, accessed March 29, 2021.

76. Behind the Scenes of Episode 2, "The Queen Bee," January 7, 2020, https://www.bbc.co.uk/programmes, accessed August 16, 2020.

77. Behind the Scenes of Episode 3, "The Scales of Justice," January 8, 2020, https://www.bbc.co.uk/programmes, accessed August 16, 2020.

78. For more on sexual harassment, see Reva Siegel, "A Short History of Sexual Harassment," https://law.yale.edu, accessed October 24, 2021.

79. Behind the Scenes of Episode 4, "The Wisdom of the Fool," January 9, 2020, https://www.bbc.co.uk/programmes, accessed August 15, 2020.

80. Behind the Scenes of Episode 6, "The Number of the Beast," January 13, 2020, https://www.bbc.co.uk/programmes, accessed August 15, 2020, November 17, 2020.

81. *Illustrated London News*, January 14, 1911.

82. Behind the Scenes of Episode 7, "The River Corrupted," January 14, 2020, https://www.bbc.co.uk/programmes, accessed August 15, 2020.

83. "The Blackpool Tower Heritage," https://www.theblackpooltower.com, accessed April 23, 2021.

84. https://www.nairaland.com, accessed January 15, 2022.

85. Behind the Scenes of Episode 8, "The Curse of Aesthetic," January 15, 2020, https://www.bbc.co.uk/programmes, accessed August 16, 2020.

86. For more on convent girls, see *There's Something about a Convent Girl*, edited by Rosemary Bennett for true stories, some by famous authors, about being raised by nuns.

87. Behind the Scenes of Episode 9, "The Fall of the House of St Gardner," January 16, 2020, https://www.bbc.co.uk/programmes, accessed August 18, 2020.

88. GKC, "The Hammer of God," *Complete Father Brown Stories*, 144.

89. Arnstein, 318.

90. Behind the Scenes of Episode 10, "The Tower of Lost Souls," January 17, 2020, https://www.bbc.co.uk/programmes, accessed August 20, 2020.

91. "BBC Daytime's Father Brown Returns to Filming for the Ninth Series," June 4, 2021, https://www.bbc.com/mediacentre, accessed November 11, 2021.

92. "Father Figure; Mark Williams Is Back as the Beloved Detective Cleric," *Sun* (London) January 1, 2022, 8.

93. *Ibid. Cluedo* is the original British version of the mystery game *Clue*.

94. "Versatile Actor Cannot Wait to Play Festive Part; Talented Star of TV and Film Mark Williams Shares Details of His Varied Career and His Latest Role—Aiming to Jolly Audiences Up," *Shropshire Star* (Shropshire, England), December 4, 2021, 22.

95. Naomi Gordon, "Father Brown Stars Reflect on Show's Endurance Ahead of 100th Episode," *Radio Times*, January 13, 2022, https://www.radiotimes.com, accessed January 14, 2022.

96. Abbie Bernstein, "Sister Boniface Mysteries: Actress Lorna Watson and Executive Producer Will Trotter on New Britbox Series," February 9, 2022, https://www.assignmentx.com, accessed March 9, 2022.

97. Peter White, "ITV Adapting Val McDermid's Cold Case Thriller 'Karen Pirie' from 'Harlots' Writer Emer Kenny & 'Bodyguard' Producer World," February 4, 2020, https://deadline.com, accessed April 5, 2022.

98. "Voragine, Golden Legend, c. 1483," https://bridwell.omeka.net/, accessed March 18, 2022.

99. "Knobbly Knees Contests: The Weirdest Beauty Contents [*sic*] in England from the Past," https://www.bygonely.com, accessed May 21, 2022.

100. Heather Shore, "Revisiting Borstal: Youth, Crime and Penalty, c. 1902–1982," December 5, 2018, https://www.leedsbeckett.ac.uk, accessed March 13, 2022.

101. "How Much Will You Have to Pay," May 30, 2022, https://www.carbuyer.co.uk, accessed June 6, 2022.

102. "Apricot Kernels Pose Risk of Cyanide Poisoning," https://www.efsa.europa.eu, accessed May 23, 2021.

103. GKC, "The Dagger with Wings," *Complete Father Brown Stories*, 448.

104. "Anthony Eden," https://www.britannica.com/biography/, accessed March 14, 2022; Arnstein, 386.

105. Arnstein, 394; "Mau Mau Uprising: Bloody History of Kenya Conflict," April 7, 2011, https://www.bbc.com/news, accessed March 15, 2022.

106. Rupert Neate, "Super-Rich Jet Off to Disaster Bunkers Amid Coronavirus Outbreak," *The Guardian* (London), March 11, 2020, https://www.theguardian.com/, accessed March 12, 2022.

107. https://www.phrases.org.uk/bulletin_board/26/messages/91.html, accessed March 14, 2022.

108. Roger Mosey, "BBC Should Cut Daytime Drama Like Father Brown, Says Ex-Editorial Director," January 26, 2022, https://www.radiotimes.com/tv/drama, accessed January 31, 2022. "Nadine Dorries: BBC Licence Fee Announcement Will Be the Last," January 16, 2022, https://www.bbc.com/news/entertainment-arts-60014514, accessed December 8, 2022.

109. Naomi Gordon, "Father Brown's Mark Williams Reveals What Storylines He Wants Next," *Radio Times*, January 14, 2022, https://www.radiotimes.com/tv, accessed January 31, 2022.

110. Matt Browning, "Father Brown Star Addresses Major Shake-Up Ahead of New Series," *The Express* (London), December 13, 2022, www.express.co.uk, accessed December 14, 2022.

111. Sukaina Benzakour, "Tom Chambers Has Revealed He 'Begged' BBC Bosses to Return to Father Brown Eight Years After Sudden Exit," *The Sun* (London), December 10, 2022, www.thesun.co.uk/tv/20658130, accessed December 13, 2022.

Chapter 5

1. GKC, "The Arrow of Heaven," *Complete Father Brown Stories*, 358.

2. Alexander Manshel, Laura B. McGrath, and J.D. Porter, "The Rise of Must-Read TV: How Your Netflix Habit Is Changing Contemporary Fiction," *The Atlantic*, July 16, 2021.

3. Ryan Lizardi, "The Nostalgic Revolution Will Be Televised," in Lavigne, 40.

4. McCaw, 1.

5. David Bianculli, "A Modern 'Sherlock' Is More Than Elementary," *NPR*, October 21, 2010, https://www.npr.org, accessed February 25, 2022.

6. GKC, "Errors about Detective Stories," *The Chesterton Review*, Vol. XXXVII, nos. 1 & 2 (Spring/Summer 2011), 16.

7. Milne, "The BBC's Father Brown Series: Moving Beyond Chesterton."

8. Deborah Cartmell, "100+ Years of Adaptation, or, Adaptation as the Art Form of Democracy," in Deborah Cartmell, ed., *A Companion to Literature, Film, and Adaptation* (Chichester: Wiley Blackwell, 2012), 3.

9. This is not to suggest that anyone else who worked on the series, from gaffers to set designers to the directors and producers, did not in some crucial way contribute to its success.

10. "Interview with Mark Williams (Father Brown)," December 11, 2019, https://tvarchive2020.bradfordzone.co.uk, accessed January 11, 2022; Kerry Harvey, "Mark Williams on Father Brown and Our Fascination with the 1950s."

11. "Interview with Mark Williams (Father Brown)."

12. Maggie Brown, "BBC1's Mid-Afternoon Audience Share Rises by 10 Percentage Points on Same Period Last Year, in First Two Weeks of Schedule Without Kids' Shows," *The Guardian* (London), January 25, 2013, http://www.guardian.co.uk, accessed April 1, 2019; "Widespread Snow January 2013," https://www.

metoffice.gov.uk/weather, accessed February 11, 2022.

13. "United States TV Audience Demand for Father Brown," https://tv.parrotanalytics.com/, accessed February 22, 2022.

14. *Ibid.*, accessed September 29, 2022.

15. McCaw, quoting Sue Parrill, *Jane Austen on Film and Television: A Critical Study of the Adaptations* (Jefferson, NC: McFarland, 2002), 2.

16. Damian Lanigan, "Imperial Nostalgia Invades American Television," *The New Republic*, April 21, 2015.

17. "'Father Brown' Has Been Picked Up by '232 Countries' Around the World," https://britishperioddramas.com, August 8, 2018, accessed February 25, 2019; With the introduction of BritBox, a streaming collection of British television, viewers can subscribe and watch *Father Brown* (and hundreds of other British series and films) whenever they wish.

18. "Father Brown," n.d., https://www.bbcstudios.com/case-studies/father-brown, accessed December 1, 2021.

19. "BBC Releases Special Images to Celebrate 100 Episodes of Father Brown," January 14, 2022, https://www.bbc.com/mediacentre, accessed February 10, 2022.

20. The obvious conclusion is that a wise producer might take this information and monitor the availability of the actors who had left the series and request their return.

21. McCaw, 7, quoting George Bluestone, *Novels into Films: The Metamorphosis of Fiction into Cinema* (Berkeley: University of California Press, 1966), viii, 18, 64.

22. McCaw, 7.

23. G.K. Chesterton, Introduction to "The Old Curiosity Shop," *Appreciations and Criticisms of the Works of Charles Dickens*, http://www.online-literature.com.

24. GKC, "The Blue Cross," *Complete Father Brown Stories*, 20.

25. Hannah Long, "Father Brown—Style and Sunny Skies, But No Substance," April 17, 2013, http://longish95.blogspot.com, accessed May 21, 2018.

26. David Parkinson, "Father Brown: Review," *Radio Times*, n.d., https://www.radiotimes.com, accessed March 21, 2019.

27. TM, "Father Brown," September 10, 2012, https://www.timeout.com, accessed January 21, 2022.

28. Kevin O'Brien, "Trading on Chesterton without a Trace of Chesterton," July 8, 2012, http://staustinreview.org/, accessed February 24, 2018. "The Real Father Brown," March 2014, http://thwordinc.blogspot.com, accessed February 24, 2018. The latter webpage has since been removed.

29. Kent Conrad, "Father Brown Season One DVD Review: Uninspired Priest Detective series," October 13, 2014, http://cinemasentries.com, accessed January 5, 2018.

30. G.K. Chesterton, Introduction to "The Old Curiosity Shop,'" *Appreciations and Criticisms of the Works of Charles Dickens* (London: J.M. Dent & Sons, 1911), https://www.gutenberg.org, accessed August 14, 2021.

31. Postman, 122.

32. Episode 1.1, "The Hammer of God"

33. David Vineyard, "A British TV Series Review, Father Brown 2013–2015," March 15, 2015, https://mysteryfile.com, accessed February 10, 2021.

34. Patrick Ohl, "The Sound and the Fury," September 6, 2013, http://at-scene-of-crime.blogspot.com, accessed June 4, 2018.

35. Tony Evans, "Definitely *Not* Chesterton's Father Brown!" *The Chesterton Review*, vol. XXXX, nos. 3 & 4 (Fall/Winter 2014), 554.

36. Manshel, "The Rise of Must-Read TV," *The Atlantic*, July 16, 2021.

37. "Ojciec Mateusz," https://en.wikipedia.org/wiki/Ojciec_Mateusz#Awards, accessed April 2, 2022.

A Final Word

1. Episode 7.8, "Blood of the Anarchists."

2. Andrew Crome, "'Wonderful,' 'Hot,' 'Good' Priests: Clergy on Contemporary British TV and New Visibility of Religion," PhD Thesis, Manchester Metropolitan University, January 10, 2020.

3. Susan Schwartz, who is Jewish, email to the author, September 30, 2020.

4. Wolff, 209–10.

5. Milne, "The BBC's Father Brown Series: Moving Beyond Chesterton."

6. Bottum, n.p.

7. John Peterson, "Introduction," *The Collected Works of G.K. Chesterton, XIII. The Father Brown Stories: Part 2* (San Francisco: Ignatius Press, 2006) 15; W.W. Robson, "Father Brown and Others," *G.K. Chesterton; A Centenary Appraisal*, ed. John Sullivan (London: Paul Elek, 1974) 59; W.H. Auden, "The Guilty Vicarage," *Harper's Magazine*, May 1948, 411.

8. G.K. Chesterton, *What I Saw in America* (New York: Dodd, Mead, 1922), 258.

9. Marty, 116.

10. Ruth Deller, "Faith in View: Religion and Spirituality in Factual British Television 2000–2009," PhD dissertation, 2008, 117, http://shura.shu.ac.uk, accessed January 4, 2022.

11. Neil Postman, *Amusing Ourselves to Death: Public Discourse in the Age of Show Business* (New York: Viking, 1985), 87.

12. Marty, 108.

13. Newman, 106.

Appendices

1. Many of Meinrad's episodes, like this one, can be found on YouTube: https://www.youtube.com/watch?v=-W_fj-Y3a0g, accessed April 2, 2022.

2. Several of Kenneth More's Father Brown episodes can be found on YouTube: https://www.youtube.com/watch?v=PJxtdyrz_E0, accessed April 8, 2022.

3. "Father Brown Stories," https://www.bbc.co.uk/sounds/brand, accessed September 28, 2021.

4. Ottfried Fischer's Father Brown episode, like this one can be found at https://www.youtube.com, accessed March 29, 2022.

Bibliography

Primary Sources

Ahlquist, Dale. "The Art of Murder: G. K. Chesterton and the Detective Story." Anya Morlan and Walter Raubicheck, eds., *Christianity and the Detective Story.* Newcastle upon Tyne: Cambridge Scholars, 2013.

_____. *G.K. Chesterton: The Apostle of Common Sense.* San Francisco: Ignatius Press, 2003.

Arnstein, Walter L. *Britain Yesterday and Today: 1830 to the Present*, 6th ed. Lexington, MA: D.C. Heath, 1992.

The Athenaeum no. 4375, September 2, 1911, 265.

Auden, W.H. "The Guilty Vicarage." *Harper's Magazine*, May 1948, 406–412.

Barker, Dudley. *G.K. Chesterton.* New York: Stein and Day, 1973.

Beaumont, Matthew, and Matthew Ingleby, eds. *G.K. Chesterton, London and Modernity.* London: Bloomsbury Academic, 2013.

Beck, Amanda Martinez. "A Priest for All Seasons, Murder, Mystery, and Contentment in *Father Brown* and *Grantchester.*" *Special Summer Edition: Some Summertime Issue of Christ and Pop Culture Magazine*, October 30, 2017.

Beck, George A. *The English Catholics, 1850–1950.* London: Burns Oates, 1950.

Belmonte, Kevin. *Defiant Joy: The Remarkable Life & Impact of G.K. Chesterton.* Nashville: Thomas Nelson, 2011.

Binyon, T.J. *'Murder Will Out': The Detective in Fiction.* Oxford: Oxford University Press, 1989.

Blackwell, Laird D. *The Metaphysical Mysteries of G.K. Chesterton: A Critical Study of the Father Brown Stories and*

Other Detective Fiction. Jefferson, NC: McFarland, 2018.

Block, Mathew. "Chesterton on the Small Screen." *The Chesterton Review*, vol. 39 nos. 1 & 2 (Spring/Summer 2013), 235–236.

Bluem, A. William. *Religious Television Programs: A Study of Relevance.* New York: Hastings House, 1969.

Bluestone, George. *Novels into Films: The Metamorphosis of Fiction into Cinema.* Berkeley: University of California Press, 1966.

Bottum, Joseph. "God and the Detectives." *Books and Culture*, September/October 2011, n.p.

Boyd, Ian. *The Novels of G.K. Chesterton: A Study in Art and Propaganda.* London: Paul Elek, 1975.

_____. "Parables of Father Brown." *The Chesterton Review*, vol. XXXVII, nos. 3 & 4 (Fall/Winter 2011), 421–427.

Brunsdale, Mitzi M. *Icons of Mystery and Crime Detection: From Sleuths to Superheroes*, vol. 1. Santa Barbara: Greenwood, 2010.

Buonanno, Milly. *Italian TV Drama and Beyond: Stories from the Soil, Stories from the Sea.* Bristol: Intellect, 2012.

Burgess, Anthony. "On the Hopelessness of Turning Good Books into Films." *New York Times,* April 20, 1975, sec. 2, 1.

Cardwell, Sarah. *Adaptation Revisited: Television and the Classic Novel.* Manchester: Manchester University Press, 2002.

Cartmell, Deborah, ed. *A Companion to Literature, Film, and Adaptation.* Chichester: Wiley Blackwell, 2012.

Catholic Emancipation 1829–1929. Freeport, NY: Books for Libraries Press, 1929.

Cherno, Melvin. "Father Brown and the

Historian." *The Chesterton Review*, vol. X, no. 2 (May 1984), 159–164.

Chesterton, G.K. "About the Films." *As I Was Saying: A Book of Essays*. London: Methuen, 1936.

_____. *The Complete Father Brown Stories*. Ware, Hertfordshire: Wordsworth Editions, 2006.

_____. "A Defense of Detective Stories." https://www.chesterton.org/a-defence-of-detective-stories/, accessed February 13, 2018.

_____. "The Divine Detective." http://www.online-literature.com/chesterton/2603/, accessed March 3, 2018.

_____. "Errors about Detective Stories." *The Chesterton Review*, vol. XXXVII, nos. 1 & 2 (Spring/Summer 2011). 15–18.

_____. *G.K. Chesterton Autobiography*. London: Hutchinson, 1936; 1969 edition, copyright Dorothy Edith Collins.

_____. *Generally Speaking*. Leipzig: Bernhard Tauchnitz, 1929.

_____. "How to Write a Detective Story." *The Chesterton Review*, vol. X, no. 2 (May 1984), 111–118.

_____. "The Ideal Detective Story." *The Chesterton Review*, vol. XXXVII, nos. 1 & 2 (Spring/Summer 2011), 9–12.

_____. *A Miscellany of Men*. New York: Dodd, Mead, 1912.

_____. "A Piece of Chalk." https://www.gutenberg.org., accessed February 13, 2018.

_____. *The Spice of Life and other Essays*. Ed. Dorothy Collins. Beaconsfield: Darwen Finalyson, 1964.

_____. "The Toy Theatre." https://www.gutenberg.org, accessed March 15, 2018.

_____. *What I Saw in America*. New York: Dodd, Mead, 1922.

Clark, Stephen R.L. *G.K. Chesterton: Thinking Backward, Looking Forward*. Philadelphia: Templeton Foundation Press, 2006.

Cock, Douglas. No title. *The Chesterton Review*, vol. XX, no. 2, 3 (May, August 1994), 412–414.

Conlon, D., ed. *G.K. Chesterton: A Half Century of Views*. Oxford: Oxford University Press, 1987.

Corio, Alec Stephen. *Historical Perceptions of Roman Catholicism and National Identity, 1869–1919*. Thesis for Doctor of Philosophy, Open University, 2013.

Dale, Alzina Stone. *The Outline of Sanity: A Biography of G. K. Chesterton*. Grand Rapids: William B. Eerdmans, 1982.

Davies, Horton. *Worship and Theology in England: The Ecumenical Century, 1900–1965*. Princeton: Princeton University Press, 1965.

Dervaes, Claudine, and John Hunter. *The UK to USA Dictionary: British English vs. American English*. Inverness, FL: Solitaire Publishing, 2012.

Edwards, Owen Dudley. "The Immortality of Father Brown." *The Chesterton Review*, vol. XV, no. 3 (August 1989), 295–319.

Evans, Tony. "Definitely *Not* Chesterton's Father Brown!" *The Chesterton Review*, vol. XXXX, nos. 3 & 4 (Fall/Winter 2014), 554–556.

Farmer, Ann. "Who Killed Father Brown?" *The Chesterton Review*, vol. 39, nos. 1 & 2 (Spring/Summer 2013,) 77–87.

Ffinch, Michael. *G.K. Chesterton*. New York: Harper & Row, 1986.

Frampton, Daniel. *The 'Old Western Men': A Religious Mode of Response to the Conditions of 'Secular' Modernity, 1900–1970*. PhD dissertation, University of East Anglia, September 2017.

Gardner, Martin, ed. *The Annotated Innocence of Father Brown*. Oxford: Oxford University Press, 1987.

Green, Douglas G. "A Mastery of Miracles: G. K. Chesterton and John Dickson Carr." *The Chesterton Review*, vol. X, no. 3 (August 1984), 307–15.

Griggs, Yvonne. *Adaptable TV: Rewiring the Text*. London: Palgrave Macmillan, 2018.

Grist, Anthony. "Father Brown and Kenneth More." *The Chesterton Review*, vol. IX, no. 1 (February 1983), 85–87.

_____. "Father Brown at the Movies." *The Chesterton Review*, vol. X, no. 4 (November 1984), 477–479.

_____. "Kenneth More as Father Brown." *The Chesterton Review*, vol. X, no. 2 (May 1984), 177–182.

Guinness, Alec. *Blessings in Disguise*. New York: Alfred A. Knopf, 1986.

Holt, Hazel. "A Plodding Father Brown." *The Stage and Television Today*, October 3, 1974, 17.

Hornsby-Smith, Michael. *Roman Catholic Beliefs in England*. Cambridge: Cambridge University Press, 1991.

_____, ed. *Catholics in England 1950–2000*. London: Cassell, 1999.

Hunter, Allan. *Alec Guinness on Screen*. Edinburgh: Polygon Books, 1982.

Hunter, Lynette. *G.K. Chesterton: Explorations in Allegory*. New York: St. Martin's Press, 1979.

James, P. D. "Introduction." *The Essential Tales of Father Brown* (New York: Modern Library, 2005) in *The Chesterton Review*, vol. 39, nos. 1 & 2 (Spring/Summer 2013), 216–221.

Ker, Ian. *G.K. Chesterton: A Biography*. Oxford: Oxford University Press, 2011.

Knox, Ronald A. *Literary Distractions*. New York: Sheed & Ward, 1958.

Kroetsch, Judy A. "Father Brown and Miss Marple: Similar Yet Unlike." *The Chesterton Review*, vol. XII, no. 3 (August 1986), 345–351.

Lanigan, Damian. "Imperial Nostalgia Invades American Television." *The New Republic*, April 21, 2015.

Lavigne, Carlen, ed. *Remake Television: Reboot, Re-Use, Recycle*. Lanham, MD: Lexington Books, 2014.

Lehman, David. *The Perfect Murder: A Study in Detection*. Ann Arbor: University of Michigan Press, 2000.

Leonard, Hugh. "The Curmudgeon." *Sunday Independent*, January 23, 2005.

Levay, Matthew. "Remaining a Mystery: Gertrude Stein, Crime Fiction and Popular Modernism." *Journal of Modern Literature*, vol. 36, no. 4, Summer 2013, 1–22.

Malone, Peter. *Screen Priests: The Depiction of Catholic Priests in Cinema from 1900–2018*. Hindmarsh, South Australia: ATF Press Publishing, 2019.

Manshel, Alexander, Laura B. McGrath, and J.D. Porter. "The Rise of Must-Read TV: How Your Netflix Habit Is Changing Contemporary Fiction." *The Atlantic*, July 16, 2021.

Marty, Martin E. *The Improper Opinion: Mass Media and the Christian Faith*. Philadelphia: The Westminster Press, 1961.

McCaw, Neil. *Adapting Detective Fiction: Crime, Englishness and the TV Detectives*. London: Continuum International, 2011.

McKay, Sinclair. "Bring Back Father Brown." *The Spectator*, December 14, 2009, 26.

More, Kenneth. *More or Less*. London: Hodder and Stoughton, 1978.

Murray, Henry. "Gilbert-Conan-Chesterton-Doyle." *The Bookman*, vol. 40, no. 240 (September 1911), 257–258.

Newman, Jay. *Religion vs. Television: Competitors in Cultural Context*. Westport, CT: Praeger, 1996.

O'Connor, John. *Father Brown on Chesterton*. London: Frederick Muller, 1937. October 25, 2009, Project Gutenberg Canada ebook #407, http://www.gkc.org.uk/gkc/Father_Brown_on_Chesterton.pdf, accessed November 22, 2017.

_____. "Recollections of G.K. Chesterton." *Mark Twain Quarterly*, vol. 1, no. 3 (Spring 1937), 6, 24.

Panek, LeRoy Lad. *An Introduction to the Detective Story*. Bowling Green, OH: Bowling Green State University Popular Press, 1987.

Paul, Robert S. *Whatever Happened to Sherlock Holmes*. Carbondale: Southern Illinois University Press, 1991.

Peterson, John, "Father Brown and the Ten Commandments." *Gilbert!* vol. 1, issue 7 (March/April 1998), 18–19.

_____. "Introduction." G.K. Chesterton, *The Collected Works of G. K. Chesterton, XII. The Father Brown Stories: Part 1*. San Francisco: Ignatius Press, 2005.

_____. "Introduction." G.K. Chesterton, *The Collected Works of G. K. Chesterton, XIII. The Father Brown Stories: Part 2*. San Francisco: Ignatius Press, 2006.

_____. *The Return of Father Brown: 44 New Mystery Stories Featuring G.K. Chesterton's Incomparable Priest-Detective*. Wheaton, IL: American Chesterton Society, 2015.

Pitts, Michael. *Famous Movie Detectives III*. Lanham, MD: Scarecrow Press, 2004.

Price, R.G.G. "A Check-Up on Chesterton's Detective." *G.K. Chesterton: A Half Century of Views*, ed. D.J. Conlon. Oxford: Oxford University Press, 1987.

Quinn, Dermot. "The Meaning of Father Brown." *The Chesterton Review*, vol. XXXVII, nos. 3 & 4 (Fall/Winter 2001), 409–418.

Raubicheck, Walter. "Father Brown and the 'Performance' of Crime." *The Chesterton Review*, vol. XIX, no. 1 (February 1993), 39–45.

Read, Piers Paul. *Alec Guinness: The Authorised Biography.* New York: Simon & Schuster, 2003.

Robson, W.W. "Father Brown and Others." *G.K. Chesterton; A Centenary Appraisal,* John Sullivan, ed. London: Paul Elek, 1974, 58–72.

Robson, W.W. "G.K. Chesterton's 'Father Brown' Stories." *The Southern Review,* Autumn 1969, 611–29.

Routley, Erik. *The Puritan Pleasures of the Detective Story.* London: Victor Gollancz, 1972.

Rzepka, Charles J. *Detective Fiction.* Cambridge: Polity Press, 2005.

Schenkel, Elmar. "Visions from the Verge: Terror and Play in G.K. Chesterton's Imagination." *G. K. Chesterton,* ed. Harold Bloom. New York: Chelsea House, 2006.

Schur, Norman W. *British English A to Zed.* New York: Harper Perennial, 1987.

Snyder, Mary H. *Analyzing Literature-to-Film Adaptations: A Novelist's Exploration and Guide.* New York: Continuum, 2011.

Spencer, William David. *Mysterium and Mystery: The Clerical Crime Novel.* Carbondale: Southern Illinois University Press, 1989.

Standford, Peter. *Cardinal Hume and the Changing Face of English Catholicism.* New York: Geoffrey Chapman, 1993.

Stumme, Clifford James. *Detective Fiction Reinvention and Didacticism in G.K. Chesterton's Father Brown.* Master Thesis, Liberty University, Lynchburg, Virginia, 2014.

Taylor, Bryony. *More TV Vicar? Christians on the Telly: The Good, the Bad and the Quirky.* London: Darton, Longman & Todd, 2015.

Terrace, Vincent. *Radio Programs, 1924–1984.* Jefferson, NC: McFarland, 2010.

Tibbetts, John C. *The Dark Side of G.K. Chesterton: Gargoyles and Grotesques.* Jefferson, NC: McFarland, 2021.

_____. "G.K. Chesterton." *Mystery and Suspense Writers,* vol. 1, ed. Robin W. Winks. New York: Charles Scribner's Sons, 1998, 181–194.

Turley, K.V. "The Actor, the Author, and the Real 'Father Brown.'" *The Chesterton Review,* vol. XXXXI, nos. 3 & 4 (Fall/Winter 2015), 611–615.

Ward, Maisie. *Gilbert Keith Chesterton.* New York: Sheed & Ward, 1943.

Webb, Claire. "Father Brown's Mark Williams." *The Chesterton Review,* vol. 39 nos. 1 & 2 (Spring/Summer 2013), 234–235.

White, Gertrude M. "Mirror and Microcosm: Chesterton's Father Brown Stories." *The Chesterton Review,* vol. X, no. 2 (May 1984), 183–197.

Wilson, A.N. *God's Funeral: The Decline of Faith in Western Civilization.* New York: W.W. Norton, 1999.

"With God on His Side." *Sunday Star-Times* (Wellington, New Zealand), January 10, 2016, E.26.

Wolff, Richard. *The Church on TV: Portrayals of Priests, Pastors and Nuns on American Television Series.* New York: Continuum International, 2010.

World War II: Day by Day. London: Dorling Kindersley, 2004.

Wynne-Jones, Jonathan. "Britain Has Become a 'Catholic Country.'" *The Telegraph* (London), December 26, 2007.

Secondary Sources

Aird, Catherine. "The Devout: Vicars, Curates and Relentlessly Inquisitive Clerics." *Murder Ink,* ed. Dilys Winn. New York: Workman, 1984.

Alton, David. "Chesterton and Ann Widdecombe, the Mystery of Father Brown on the BBC." *The Chesterton Review,* vol. 39, no. 1 & 2 (Spring/Summer 2013).

"Brown Studies." *The Bookman,* vol. 47, no. 279 (December 1914), 106.

Burns, Timothy. "The Rationalism of Father Brown." *Perspectives on Political Science,* vol. 34, no. 1 (Winter 2005).

Carney, James. "Supernatural Intuitions and Classic Detective Fiction: A Cognitivist Appraisal." *Style,* vol. 48, no. 2 (Summer 2014), 203.

Carroll, James. *The Truth at the Heart of the Lie.* New York: Random House, 2021.

Eberwein, Jane Donahue. "The Priest and the Poets." *The Chesterton Review,* vol. X, no. 2 (May 1984), 165–176.

Griffiths, Richard. "The Strange Case of the Simple Little Priest." *The Chesterton Review,* vol. 39, nos. 1 & 2 (Spring/Summer 2013), 233–234.

Heady, Chene. "Autobiography as Mystery:

Father Brown and the Case of G. K. Chesterton." *Renascence*, vol. 69, no. 1 (Winter 2017), 49–65.

Houswitschka, C. "Paradox and Orthodoxy in Father Brown's Conduct of Investigation." International Symposion [*sic*] on Gilbert Keith Chesterton, *Inklings*; Leipzig, Germany, May 1996, 125–154.

Kabatchnik, Amnon. *Blood on the Stage, 1925–1950*. Lanham, MD: Scarecrow Press, 2009.

Knille, Robert, ed. *As I Was Saying: A Chesterton Reader*. Grand Rapids: William B. Eerdmans, 1985.

Morlan, Anya, and Walter Raubichick, eds. *Christianity and the Detective Story*. Newcastle upon Tyne: Cambridge Scholars, 2013.

Nietzsche, Friedrich Wilhelm. *Basic Writings of Nietzsche*. Walter Kaufmann, trans. New York: Random House, 2000.

O'Connor, John. *Father Brown Reforms the Liturgy: Being the Tract: Why Revive the Liturgy, and How?* Hugh Somerville Knapman, ed. Waterloo, Ontario: Arouca Press, 2021.

Postman, Neil. *Amusing Ourselves to Death: Public Discourse in the Age of Show Business*. New York: Viking, 1985.

Reinsdorf, Walter. "The Perception of Father Brown." *The Chesterton Review*, vol. X, no. 3 (August 1984), 265–274.

Ryken, Leland. *J.I. Packer: An Evangelical Life*. Wheaton, IL: Crossway, 2015.

Schultze, Quentin J. *Television: Manna from Hollywood?* Grand Rapids: Zondervan, 1986.

Wilson, A.N. *Our Times: The Age of Elizabeth II*. New York: Farrar, Straus and Giroux, 2008.

Internet Sources

Achouche, Mehdi. "TV Remakes, Revivals, Updates, and Continuations: Making Sense of the Reboot on Television." January 2017, https://representations.univ-grenoble-alpes.fr.pdf, accessed February 19, 2022.

"Actor Mark Williams' Verdict on Sunday Night Slot Fhift for BBC Drama Series Father Brown." February 8, 2015, https://www.sundaypost.com.

"Apricot Kernels Pose Risk of Cyanide Poisoning." https://www.efsa.europa.eu.

"BBC Releases Special Images to Celebrate 100 Episodes of Father Brown." January 14, 2022, https://www.bbc.com/mediacentre.

Bennett, Brittany. "Mark Williams Discusses 'Father Brown' Series." May 12, 2020, https://www.mugglenet.com.

Berch, Victor, Karl Schadow, and Steve Lewis. "Murder Clinic: Radio's Golden Age of Detection." https://mysteryfile.com/M_Clinic.html.

Bernstein, Abbie. "Sister Boniface Mysteries: Actress Lorna Watson and Executive Producer Will Trotter on New Britbox Series." February 9, 2022, https://www.assignmentx.com.

Bianculli, David. "A Modern 'Sherlock' Is More Than Elementary." *NPR*, October 21, 2010, https://www.npr.org.

"The Blackpool Tower Heritage." https://www.theblackpooltower.com.

Boslaugh, Sarah. "Kenneth More's 'Father Brown' Gives Us a Reassuring Voice of Reason and Moderation." May 1, 2014, http://www.popmatters.com/review/181215.

Brown, Maggie. "BBC1's Mid-Afternoon Audience Share Rises by 10 Percentage Points on Same Period Last Year, in First Two Weeks of Schedule Without Kids' Shows." *The Guardian* (London), January 25, 2013. http://www.guardian.co.uk.

Carr, John Dickson. The Locked Room Lecture. http://www.thelockedroom.com.

Chipperfield, Daniel. "BBC One Drama Father Brown Returns Next Month After Filming in Gloucester." November 16, 2017, https://www.gloucestershirelive.co.uk.

Conrad, Kent. "Father Brown Season One DVD Review: Uninspired Priest Detective Series." October 13, 2014, http://cinemasentries.com.

"The Coroner, Father Brown and Doctors Recommissioned for BBC One Daytime." n.d., https://www.bbc.co.uk/mediacentre.

"Das Schwarze Schaf." http://schlombies-filmbesprechungen.blogspot.com.

"Delivering Quality First: Final Conclusions." May 2012, https://www.bbc.co.uk/bbctrust.

Deller, Ruth. "Faith in View: Religion and

Spirituality in Factual British Television 2000–2009." PhD dissertation, 2008, http://shura.shu.ac.uk.

"Die besten Kriminalfälle des Pater Brown." http://sofahelden.com/index.

Douglas, J. D. "G.K. Chesterton, the Eccentric Prince of Paradox." *Christianity Today*, August 1, 2001, https://www.christianitytoday.com.

Eames, Tom. "Mark Williams's 'Father Brown' renewed for second series by BBC One." January 23, 2013, https://www.digitalspy.com.

"Father Brown." http://www.great detectives.net.

"Father Brown: Collected Cases by G.K. Chesterton." https://soundcloud.com/penguin-books.

"'Father Brown' Has Been Picked Up by '232 Countries' Around the World." August 8, 2018, https://british perioddramas.com.

"Father Brown Is Back in Town." August 14, 2013, https://issuu.com/cotswoldhomesmagazine.

"Father Brown: Saving Souls, Solving Crimes." https://vimeo.com.

"Father Brown S2 (BBCOne)." January 18, 2014, https://takingtheshortview.wordpress.com.

"Father Brown—the Murderer in the Mirror." July 3, 2021, https://www.anvilarts.org.uk.

Flowerday, Rachel. "Father Brown—the 'Making of' Blog." http://rachel flowerday.com.

Gordon, Naomi. "Father Brown Stars Reflect on Show's Endurance Ahead of 100th Episode." *Radio Times*, January 13, 2022, https://www.radiotimes.com.

Grant, Olly. "Clued-Up Confessor on the Box." *Church Times*, January 11, 2013, https://www.churchtimes.co.uk/articles.

Greydanus, Steven. "BBC's Amiable 'Father Brown' Doesn't Keep Faith with Chesterton." September 19, 2014, https://cruxnow.com.

Guner, Tahsin, and Rachel Flowerday. "Developing Father Brown for BBC One." January 14, 2013, http://www.bbc.co.uk/blogs/writersroom.

"Harry Potter Star Mark Williams to Star in BBC Drama 'Father Brown.'" June 22, 2012, https://www.entertainmentwise.com.

Hart, Peter. "The White Feather Campaign." 2010, http://www.inquiries journal.com.

Harvey, Kerry. "Mark Williams on Father Brown and Our Fascination with the 1950s." October 24, 2017, https://www.stuff.co.nz.

Horton, Kim. "BBC Series Father Brown Is Being Filmed in the City." June 14, 2017, https://www.gloucestershirelive.co.uk.

"How Much Will You Have to Pay." May 30, 2022, https://www.carbuyer.co.uk.

https://catholicstraightanswers.com. August 7, 2014.

"Il delitto del Signore di Marne di Vittorio De Sisti: la serie tv deimenticata di Padre Brown." July 6, 2017, http://www.frontedelblog.it.

"In This Exclusive Behind the Scenes Interview John Burton Shows What a Real 'Goodfellow' He Is, by Revealing What It's Like Working on Father Brown." January 9, 2017, https://www.facebook.com/BBCFatherBrown.

"Interview with Mark Williams (Father Brown)." December 11, 2019, https://tvarchive2020.bradfordzone.co.uk.

Iyer, Aditya. "UK Election 2017: 'Bloody Foreigners' and Other Aspects of Britain's History of Immigration Controls Against Indian Migrants." June 8, 2017, https://www.firstpost.com.

"Jesuits Help Father Brown Get It Right." January 6, 2015, https://www.indcatholicnews.com.

"Jude Tindall." https://www.bbc.co.uk/writersroom/resources.

"Knobbly Knees Contests: The Weirdest Beauty Contents [sic] in England from the Past." https://www.bygonely.com.

Lambert, Tim. "A History of Capital Punishment in the UK." March 14, 2021, https://localhistories.org.

Laws, Roz. "Birmingham-Made Drama Father Brown Need Primetime Spot, Says Star Mark Williams." December 30, 2013, http://www.birminghammail.co.uk.

"Let It Snow." December 23, 2016, https://www.bbc.co.uk/programmes.

Leyshon, Gareth. *Catholic Statisitcs—2011 Update. Priests and Population in England and Wales, 1841–2011.* October 2012, http://www.drgareth.info/-CathStat-2012.pdf.

Long, Hannah. "Father Brown—Style and

Sunny Skies, But No Substance." April 17, 2013, http://longish95.blogspot.com.

"Mark Williams on Father Brown Coming Back to Our Screens and Making the Permanent Move to Sussex." January 19, 2017, https://www.sussexlife.co.uk.

"Mark Williams—Things You Didn't Know about the 'Harry Potter' Star." June 9, 2021, https://www.whattowatch.com.

Martin Kemp Interview. January 4, 2017, https://www.bbc.co.uk/programmes.

Mason, Vivien. "Filming for Latest Cotswold-Based BBC TV series, Father Brown, Comes to an End." August 6, 2015, http://www.cotswoldjournal.co.uk.

"Mau Mau Uprising: Bloody History of Kenya Conflict." April 7, 2011, https://www.bbc.com/news.

Mawhinney, Kathleen. "The Priesthood of Father Brown." April 30, 2020, https://puddleglumsprogress.com.

Meyrick, Ceri. "How I Accidentally Produced Father Brown." May 30, 2013, http://www.writersguild.org.uk.

Milne, Pamela. "The BBC's Father Brown Series: Moving Beyond Chesterton." December 20, 2020, https://milnesmusings.wordpress.com.

"The Mystified Mind." https://www.oldtimeradiodownloads.com/crime/the-adventures-of-father-brown.

Neate, Rupert. "Super-Rich Jet Off to Disaster Bunkers Amid Coronavirus Outbreak." *The Guardian* (London), March 11, 2020, https://www.theguardian.com.

Newman, Siobhan. Review of "Father Brown at the Theatre Royal Windsor." March 29, 2017, http://www.theatreroyalwindsor.co.uk.

Newton, Michael. "Father Brown: The Empathetic Detective." *The Guardian* (London), January 18, 2013. https://www.theguardian.com/books

O'Brien, Kevin. "Trading on Chesterton without a Trace of Chesterton." July 8, 2012, http://staustinreview.org.

O'Hare, Kate. "Taking Tea with 'Father Brown' Star Mark Williams." August 3, 2020, https://www.patheos.com/blogs.

Ohl, Patrick. "The Sound and the Fury." September 6, 2013, http://at-scene-of-crime.blogspot.com.

"On Lying." https://www.newadvent.org.

Parkes, Melenie. "Father Brown's Mark Williams: 'I Have to Work Hard at Not Making Him a Cliché.'" May 6, 2020, https://www.stuff.co.nz.

Parkinson, David. "Father Brown: Review." *Radio Times*, n.d., https://www.radiotimes.com.

Peach, Ceri. "The Caribbean in Europe: Contrasting Patterns of Migration and Settlement in Britain, France and the Netherlands." October 1991, https://warwick.ac.uk.

"Peter Bullock." December 11, 2019, https://www.bbc.co.uk/mediacentre.

Peters, Jeremy. "TV Murders: Filming of Father Brown at Former Cotswolds Hospital." http://www.property.nhs.uk.

"Pfarrer Braun." https://www.daserste.de/unterhaltung/film.html.

Pruszewicz, Marek. "When Murderers Were Hanged Quickly." August 7, 2014, https://www.bbc.com.

"The Real Father Brown." March 2014, http://thwordinc.blogspot.com.

"Regulating Sex and Sexuality: The 20th Century." https://www.parliament.uk.

Salai, Sean. "G.K. Chesterton's 'Way of Wonder': Q&A with Author Dale Ahlquist." May 11, 2016, https://www.americamagazine.org.

Sergent, Jean. "Murder Has Never Been More Delightful Than on Father Brown." July 4, 2018, https://thespinoff.co.nz.

Shore, Heather. "Revisiting Borstal: Youth, Crime and Penalty, c. 1902–1982." December 5, 2018, https://www.leedsbeckett.ac.uk.

Smithies, Grant. "English Actor Mark Williams on Life After Harry Potter and the Fast Show." January 6, 2016, https://www.stuff.co.nz.

Snyder, Diane. "'Sister Boniface': Crime-Solving Nun Gets the Spotlight in 'Father Brown' Spinoff." February 6, 2022, https://www.tvinsider.com.

Stevens, Christopher. "Blissful Crime Caper That Proves Daytime TV Can Be Super-Duper." *Daily Mail* (London), January 7, 2019, https://www.dailymail.co.uk.

Stevens, Christopher. "Father Brown's Biggest Mystery Why Is He Stuck on Daytime TV?" *Daily Mail* (London), January 15, 2014, http://www.dailymail.co.uk.

"Sudeley Castle." https://sudeleycastle.co.uk/history.

Sutherland, Gill. "On the Set of Father Brown." June 9, 2016, www.stratford-herald.com.

"The Tales of a Crime-Solving Roman Catholic Priest." n.d. https://www.bbcstudios.com/case-studies/father-brown.

Thomas, Sarah. "Mark Williams on Why 'Nosey' Father Brown Has Proved to Be a Popular, If Unlikely, Sleuth." April 4, 2016, https://www.smh.com.au/entertainment.

TM. "Father Brown." September 10, 2012, https://www.timeout.com.

"United States TV Audience Demand for Father Brown." https://tv.parrot analytics.com.

Vineyard, David. "A British TV Series Review, Father Brown 2013–2015." March 15, 2015, https://mysteryfile.com.

"Voragine, Golden Legend, c. 1483." https://bridwell.omeka.net.

"Welcome Back, Father Brown." January 11, 2014, http://www.worcesternews.co.uk.

"When The BBC's Father Brown Visited Princethorpe." May 13, 2020, https://connect.princethorpe.co.uk.

White, Peter. "ITV Adapting Val McDermid's Cold Case Thriller 'Karen Pirie' from 'Harlots' Writer Emer Kenny & 'Bodyguard' Producer World." February 4, 2020, https://deadline.com.

"Who is Father Brown's Emer Kenny?" *Radio Times*, December 9, 2019. https://www.radiotimes.com.

"Who Is G.K. Chesterton?" https://www.chesterton.org/category/discover-chesterton.

"The WI Inspiring Women." https://www.thewi.org.uk.

"Widespread Snow January 2013." https://www.metoffice.gov.uk.

Young, Bill. "On the Set with 'Father Brown' in the Cotswolds." July 18, 2014, http://tellyspotting.kera.org.

Index